THE CROWN AND THE CROSS

Books by Theodore Maynard:

QUEEN ELIZABETH
THE STORY OF AMERICAN CATHOLICISM
TOO SMALL A WORLD: THE LIFE OF FRANCESCA CABRINI
COLLECTED POEMS
RICHEST OF THE POOR: THE LIFE OF ST. FRANCIS OF ASSISI
HENRY VIII
HUMANIST AS HERO: THE LIFE OF SIR THOMAS MORE
THE CROWN AND THE CROSS

THOMAS CROMWELL by Holbein

The Crown and the Cross

A BIOGRAPHY

OF THOMAS CROMWELL

BY THEODORE MAYNARD

McGRAW-HILL BOOK COMPANY, INC.

NEW YORK   TORONTO   LONDON

THE CROWN AND THE CROSS

Published by the McGraw-Hill Book Company, Inc.

Printed in the United States of America

TO
RIDGELY TORRENCE

CONTENTS

Chapter One

THE START

ONE OF the generally accepted truisms of biography is that a biographer should have either wholehearted admiration or wholehearted hatred of his subject. If this be true, I am unlucky to have chosen Thomas Cromwell, for it is not in my nature to hate anyone heartily, and the admiration I must give Cromwell's abilities is often qualified by disgust at the use to which those abilities were put. I cannot even feel compassion for the eventual fate of a man who felt no compassion for others; his cold-bloodedness is more appalling than the fierce animosity of the king he served. When Cromwell struck people down, it was never in personal vindictiveness; on the contrary he rather liked some of them. In their case he was doing a job dispassionately, just as he did every other sort of job he was called upon to perform. His innocent air makes him all the more sinister.

The early sixteenth-century world that saw the advent of Thomas Cromwell as an obscure adventurer extended, in his personal experience of it, no farther than Italy and, in the foreign diplomacy of his last years, no farther than Bavaria. But it was a new world, of new vistas—some of them dangerous—and geographically it had expanded to include the Spanish conquests in America, of Mexico in 1519, at which time we first begin to hear of Cromwell, and of Peru, in 1531, just after he had come to political power in England. It was, in short, the world of the Renaissance, and Cromwell

I

was the very embodiment of certain Renaissance political ideas.

Catholicism was still the binding tie among the nations, though one that was soon to be loosened. The spiritual authority of the Papacy went unchallenged as yet, but it was also a temporal power, one which, while hardly strong enough to stand alone, could be, and was, used as a makeweight in the rivalries about to be intensified. In these, England, under its supremely great statesman, Cardinal Wolsey, nearly always backed the Papacy, to which the Tudor dynasty was so deeply indebted. Henry VII, the first Tudor, had brought order and stability to the country after the savage Wars of the Roses, and this fact gave his son, Henry VIII, proud and handsome and gifted, a strong position which he made all the stronger by his personal popularity.

France, which seemed so far away across the choppy Channel, still provided England with a foothold in Calais, and the English kings continued to assert their claim to the French throne. It was, at the beginning of Henry's reign, ruled by the Valois Louis XII. Spain was almost fanatically Catholic in tradition and atmosphere, all the more so after its successful struggle with the Moors, and the memory of Isabella the Catholic lingered around her widower, the able if unpleasant Ferdinand. The central part of Europe was known as the Roman Empire, and at its helm was the fabulous and fantastic figure of Maximilian. The office of Emperor was obtained by election, so that any king of Christendom could theoretically aspire to it, but it had long since become in fact a Hapsburg preserve. On the other hand, the Emperor's claim to suzerainty over Christendom was fictitious and unenforceable.

Royal marriages were of course one of the main instruments in diplomacy, and princesses were educated to marry for the sake of consolidating a political alliance. Spain had sent Katherine of Aragon to England to marry the young heir, Prince Arthur, a sickly boy of fifteen. He died four and a half months later, and immediately the haggling began between the Kings of England and Aragon as to the payment of her dowry and her marriage to the new heir, the future Henry VIII. Eight years later Henry VIII arranged the marriage of his sister Mary, over her protests, to the aging King Louis XII of France. It was Henry's way of taking revenge against his father-in-law Ferdinand who had so cynically befooled him. A few weeks of marriage were enough to bring the prematurely aged Louis to

2

his grave. Though he had been married three times, his successor was his nephew Francis I.

Francis at first won brilliant military successes in Italy. But when the youthful Charles V succeeded his grandfather Maximilian as Emperor, the situation drastically changed. For Charles, upon the death of his other grandfather Ferdinand in 1516, had inherited the kingdoms of Spain. And when in 1519 he became Emperor, his possessions so completely encircled France as to involve that country in a life-and-death struggle with the Empire. The circumstance provided Cardinal Wolsey with ample scope for the exercise of his virtuosity in foreign affairs. Though his aims were largely chimerical, he was enabled to play off the two formidable antagonists against one another. Until his fall ten years later the Cardinal was the dominating political figure in Europe.

Several factors contributed to his fall, but of these the main one was his failure to obtain for his King an annulment of his marriage to Queen Katherine. He did all that was humanly possible to bring this about, but Anne Boleyn, selected since 1527 to supplant Katherine, would never believe that he did enough; and she, with the support of the nobles led by her uncle the Duke of Norfolk, contrived to ruin the man whom she looked upon as her enemy. With the death of Cardinal Wolsey at the end of 1530, the way was open for Cromwell. It was not he who had implanted in Henry's conscience the doubt—sincere and yet open to question because of its coincidence with his convenience—of the validity of his marriage to his brother's widow, nor did he even need to stress what went with it, a desire for the male heir which Katherine had been unable to bear. But it was Cromwell who exploited these ideas, as it was he who triumphed where Wolsey had failed, effecting at the same time a number of most sweeping changes that had originally not been so much as thought of.

About these more will be said in a moment. At this stage it is perhaps enough to remark that the Devil has a kind of providence of his own, though this we must believe is permitted only because it will serve some purpose of God's providence still hidden from us. Immense as were Cromwell's abilities, nowhere except in England, and at the particular moment when he appears in history, could those abilities have been fully exercised. Nor was it possible for Cromwell himself to have imagined how a set of unforeseen chances would make possible his astonishing career. He, even more than Luther, was responsible for the success of the Protestant Reformation, for had it not been for Henry VIII's breach with Rome, the Lutheran heresy would have been confined to the Baltic countries —however loud the repercussions were elsewhere—and probably would have eventually been subdued.

The occasion of Luther's quarrel with the Papacy did not touch England at all. But what did affect all Christendom was the notorious fact that a profligate pope was succeeded by men who, though sufficiently respectable, were more worldly than they should have been. The same was true of the higher clergy in all countries; their wealth was a scandal and their rapacity a constant irritant. Blind to the need for a drastic renovation of discipline and morals, and often resisting reform, they unwittingly helped to raise a storm that eventuated in a rejection of Catholic doctrine and of what can be the only secure basis for that doctrine—the authority of the Holy See. The result was the emergence of various sects whose sole bond of union was their opposition to the Church and a disastrous division of Christendom into two camps. It was a lesion of the soul.

This was not of course the only factor involved. Indeed, all the factors never have been, and in all likelihood never will be, assessed with perfect accuracy. One of these factors was an increasing national consciousness, something that tended to grow with the fancied discovery of a need for a national religion. Inevitably this made for an enormous augmentation of the authority of the prince as the visible embodiment of the nation.

Nowhere was this more strongly felt than in insular England. Yet England was more free of heresy than perhaps any other part of Europe. However, religion was practiced, only too often, in a formal, perfunctory, and somnolent fashion. No animosity could be found against the Pope, to whom England's King had always shown himself a firm friend, but some ill will existed against the local clergy. This was not because the clergy were corrupt—for though individuals may have been, as a group they were better than the clergy of several other lands—but because they were, some of them, mere functionaries, and as such too insistent upon the privileges and profits of their order.

The wealth of the English clergy—that is, the wealth of those who held well-endowed benefices—was considered excessive and was a constant temptation to the devising of schemes of spoliation. At the same time there was slight complaint of the wealth of the monasteries. Most of these monasteries were far from being inordinately rich, and even those that were rich received grateful recognition from the people at large because of the social benefits they offered to the localities in which they were established. There was a loud outcry when Cardinal Wolsey suppressed a few of them, even though their revenues were applied to praiseworthy purposes.

As we shall see, it was Wolsey's suppressions, carried out under his agent Cromwell, that gave Cromwell his idea of seizing all the monasteries, *i.e.*, estates for the enrichment of the Crown. But when that process began, the land hunger which had been so keen in England for fifty years or more led the powerfully placed to give their backing to what was being done, a backing for which they demanded and received their reward. The ultimate outcome was that the whole face of England and—because of the position that England came to occupy—of much of Europe was changed, not only religiously but socially and economically. This, while going a good deal beyond what had been originally intended, was the work of Thomas Cromwell. The diseases from which we now suffer—secularism, nationalism, capitalism, and industrialism—were by-products, inevitable by-products, of what he accomplished. Only a man like Cromwell—with his intelligence, assiduity, merciless lack of scruple, and coldly inhuman competence—could have carried out what he did.

There must be something (could it only be discovered) to account for Cromwell's strange lack of humanity, a quality he usually managed to conceal under affability of manner and the charm that constantly surprised people who, at first glance, took him to be merely a dull, industrious fellow. They saw a heavy-set figure, waddling in its walk, and a big pasty face in which were set sharp little eyes. Then as soon as Cromwell began to talk, his face lit up and became wonderfully mobile. From his thin pursed lips, above which was a great expanse to where the bulbous nose bloomed, flowed a wit that he never indulged in in his businesslike letters. Yet his lips hardly moved, though the eyes seemed to be set on swivels, from the way they were cast this way and that in sly sidelong glances. In his moments of relaxation Cromwell exercised great fascination—a fearful fascination as soon as one remembered what it was not possible to forget for long, the power he possessed or the ruthlessness with which he exercised it. Nobody liked him, and many were seeking a chance of ruining him. But everybody feared him, except for a few men like Eustache Chapuys, the Imperial Ambassador, who, because of enjoying diplomatic immunity, were safe and so could relish his engaging companionship with an easy mind. These few, while under no illusions regarding his rascality, seem to have discerned not only his engaging traits but some good in him. Nevertheless, his good impulses, when they occurred, were kept under control and were never allowed to interfere with his policy or his personal profit. He had about as much heart as an adding machine and the same degree of infallible efficiency.

When he enters history, at first inconspicuously, he was nearing forty and so was past the age when a man has any further great development. Even after that time, had it not been for an altogether unlooked-for set of circumstances, he would have continued in Cardinal Wolsey's service, with a law practice and a shearman's business on the side—adding to his income by moneylending and minor extortions until the day came when he would have overreached himself and paid the penalty on the gallows. History would hardly have heard of him.

His parentage and upbringing do not seem to account for what he came to be. Yet his character must have been developed by a formative history about which we have very slight information. Walter Cromwell, our Cromwell's father, was of fairly prosperous stock in Nottinghamshire but had migrated about 1461 to Wimbledon, then a village not far from London, where he followed a number of trades.[1] He kept a tavern, for which he brewed his own ale (as did most tavern keepers in those days), but he was also a blacksmith, a fuller, and a sheep raiser, to the extent of keeping a flock of thirty on Putney Common—too many for one man fairly to main-

[1] Professor Merriman seems to suggest (Vol. I, pp. 3 ff.) that the Ralph, Lord Cromwell, whom Thorold Rogers in his *History of Agriculture and Prices* describes as one of the richest men of the fifteenth century, was his grandfather. But though Thomas did in fact have a Ralph as his grandfather, it could not have been this Ralph, who was the fourth baron of his line. Otherwise there could not have been the constant reproach that Thomas Cromwell came from base blood.

6

tain there, so his neighbors considered. From him his son inherited his versatility.

Walter Cromwell's reputation was far from good. He was repeatedly fined for unprovoked assaults on other people and nearly fifty times for selling beer that did not come up to standard. Yet that beer was evidently strong enough for him to get drunk upon it frequently, which probably accounts for his quarrelsome disposition. In spite of this he had some standing in his small community, for we learn that he was on several occasions called to serve on juries and even of his being given a magistracy. His dishonesties were on a small scale until toward the end of his life when, in 1514, as a result of being convicted of fraud against the lord of the manor, the beadle was ordered to seize everything that he possessed in copyhold, after which Walter Cromwell disappears from sight.

Walter's elder brother John was more respectable; he was for a time cook to Archbishop Warham. John Cromwell's connection with the Archbishop may account for the fact that his son Robert took holy orders and was appointed Vicar of Battersea; and this fact in its turn may account for the introduction of Robert's cousin Thomas to the notice of another archbishop, the Cardinal of York, were there need to explain it on this ground. In short, the Cromwells were of lowly origin, though of a lowliness that has often been exaggerated.

Thomas Cromwell was born about 1485—certainly not later— and must have had a tolerably good education, though nobody knows where. Whatever formal instruction he received one must suppose to have been supplemented by his own efforts. His mind was of the clear, precise, and powerful sort that mastered instantly what it needed to know and retained it for ever. Foxe the Martyrologist tells us that as a young man Cromwell memorized the whole of the Erasmus translation of the New Testament. The statement would have to be regarded as incredible were it not that in those days, when printed books were still few, people trained their memories as we never do. Of one thing we can be sure: he never attended a university, though this would not have been beyond the reach of families of even more humble circumstances than the Cromwells. He might have gone to either Oxford or Cambridge had he not been obliged to get out of England in a hurry. He had made it too unsafe for himself there. We hear of a quarrel with his father, also of his being imprisoned for a while.

Just what Thomas Cromwell had done to compel this flight abroad does not appear; it must, however, have been rather more than the youthful wildness which, in later life, he confided to Archbishop Cranmer of Canterbury. His conduct abroad—first in Italy and then in the Low Countries, where he worked as a clerk at Antwerp under the name of Smith—was harmless enough, to judge from the gossip that Matteo Bandello, the Italian novelist, and Reginald Pole, Cardinal and cousin to the King, collected. We hear of him at the battle of Garigliano, serving with the French. As this battle was fought at the end of December, 1503, he would have been about eighteen at the time, if the conjectural date of his birth is correct. We must dismiss as impossible the suggestion several times advanced—as recently as 1893 by Cardinal Gasquet—that he took part in the Sack of Rome. Though Cromwell described himself to Cranmer as having been a "ruffian," he was never that sort of a ruffian. Moreover, he was in England in 1527.

His temperament was not military, and he soon found employment better suited to his talents. In the Frescobaldi banking house at Florence he acquired that exact knowledge of finance afterward to be so useful to him. It was in Italy that his intelligence and character were formed. There is a proverb that an Italianate Englishman is a devil incarnate; and if Cromwell did not indulge in the ordinary modes of deviltry—for these are not often conducive to worldly advancement—as an Italianate Englishman he picked up what was worse than even the licentious paganism of the more corrupt variety of Italian humanism when he came across a book that was being circulated in manuscript.[2] That book was Machiavelli's *The Prince*. It gave the young Englishman a political philosophy and obliterated for him, in the practice of politics, distinctions between right and wrong. It also revealed to him that the cruder methods of dishonesty

[2] It is, however, possible that Cromwell did not come across the book then, though it is also quite possible that he might have encountered Machiavelli in person during his time in Florence. As we shall see, Cromwell was acquainted with this work at least as early as 1527, though the book was not printed until several years later. Manuscript copies of such things were often circulated long before the printed version, and there was a large Italian colony in London.

are seldom the most remunerative and that an appearance of rectitude should be aimed at. Whatever Cromwell's life may have been
in his youth, he soon coolly decided that from henceforth it should
have a façade of perfect propriety. It was this that made him so
different from most of the other adventurers of whom Europe was
full. Though, like theirs, his early life—so we must suspect from
many of the hints and half tones from which we are obliged to
reconstruct it—was not only shadowy but shady, he soon made it
one of outward decorum. If he was a bad man, he was able to pass
as a good one; his "respectability" was impeccable. He was also
different from other adventurers in that he had exceptional ability
and an exceptional opportunity for exercising it.

By about 1514 whatever circumstances had made unsafe his
presence in England had disappeared. He could return home confident that his early misbehavior was forgotten or would be overlooked. In England he could put to use what he had learned in
Florence and Antwerp, those great commercial and financial centers,
of foreign markets and the intricacies of moneylending. He established himself in business; he married; and he became a solicitor.

Just how he obtained his legal qualifications is a mystery; all that
we know is that his name appears in 1524 as a member of Gray's
Inn and that in certain departments of his calling—especially those
relating to conveyancing—he proved himself an expert. He appears
also to have married soon after his return, his wife being an Elizabeth
Wykys, whose father had been a shearman but whose grandfather
was of good enough family to have been a gentleman usher to King
Henry VII. It must be surmised from what we know of Cromwell's
calculating make-up that he married his wife in order to obtain the
necessary capital for the shearman's business he set up.

That is almost all that we know of Elizabeth Cromwell, except
that she bore her husband two daughters named Anne and Grace
and a son named Gregory. It would appear from the revision of
Cromwell's will made in 1529 that she had died in 1528 and that
her daughters soon followed her to the grave. The chief fact about
Gregory, who survived his father, is that he was stupid almost to
the point of idiocy, which nevertheless did not prevent his marrying
the sister of Jane Seymour.

In his shearman's business Cromwell was in a fortunate position
for exploiting the trade in wool, almost the only commodity raised

in England that had a large foreign market. And as a solicitor he had opportunities for cautious moneylending and perhaps even more dubious activities in which a knowledge of the law was very useful. Whatever he undertook was always performed with the utmost dispatch and proficiency. But though his eye was peeled for the main chance, he could have had no idea as to what chance was going to come his way.

All through his life Cromwell showed himself ready to take advantage of making money by little odd jobs, and an account of one of these jobs, assigned by the relater, John Foxe, to the year 1510, is worth being drawn upon, even if it is open to some suspicion. Foxe is notoriously not the most reliable of historians, but in this instance, as what he relates is somewhat to the discredit of his hero, he had at least no ulterior motive for telling the story, except perhaps that of casting ridicule on Pope Julius II. It seems that young Cromwell was engaged as an agent by the town of Boston to go with a Geoffrey Chambers and another man to Rome to obtain a renewal of some special "pardon" or indulgence the town had been given.[3] Foxe of course makes a great play as to how "the Pope's merchandise is always dear ware" and indicates that Boston, knowing this, provided its emissaries with ample funds. For acting as he did, Cromwell is given some exculpation, as he was not as yet "grounded in the judgment of religion." Yet, according to Foxe's own tale, what turned the trick was not the payment of money (of which we hear nothing further); it was rather that Cromwell and his two English companions waylaid the Pope and caught his attention with a "three-man song." This gave Cromwell his chance to present Julius, "whose holy tooth greatly delighted to find new fangled strange delicates and dainty dishes" with some English jelly, sure that His Holiness would relish this in his "jolly junkets." Julius liked the jelly so much that, as soon as he had tasted it, he stamped both the pardons for which his renewal was asked. The story is fantastic and is obviously told to raise a laugh. One finds it hard to believe that the great warrior Pope could be won over in such a way. It would be less difficult to believe that Cromwell forged the documents he sent to Boston.

This much, however, may be admitted: if that was the worst thing

[3] A Geoffrey Chambers was subsequently employed as one of Cromwell's agents, in all probability the same man.

that could be related of the papal regime as Cromwell saw it in Italy, there would hardly have been any need of any Reformation. Alexander VI, the most scandalous of the popes, had died only ten years before Cromwell went there, and what the young Englishman heard of him could not have increased his respect for the Holy See. He was before long to find that the English clergy were weak. Therefore the political system of thought he worked out was perfectly fitted to deal with them.

Yet there is no reason to suppose that Cromwell at this time or for some years afterward had developed the total indifference to religion characterizing his later life. This indifference, when it came about, I take to have been calculated. Cromwell's whole aim from 1529 on was a political one, and with it religion was never allowed to interfere, however much, according to the Machiavellian maxims, religion could be made to subserve political ends. While I must regard him as merely playing a part when he kept up the external forms of religion, during the years when he was the Vicar-General of the royal Head of the Church in England, I do not believe that he lied, even then, to his own soul, as King Henry constantly lied. I credit Cromwell with a cynic's honesty and of never deluding himself on this or any other point.

Moreover, though his Catholic piety was no doubt perfunctory and intermittent until his final decision to discard it, it welled up in him from time to time. Even if we regard his invocations of the Blessed Trinity in his letters as no more than formal, as was his signature, "heartily your friend," to letters that were often like a dagger to those who received them, at least his will of 1529 manifests a genuine Catholic faith in its careful allocation of sums to the five orders of friars and to other religious bodies. These were stipends for Masses for the repose of his own soul, those of his wife and parents, and for the faithful departed in general. Similarly he made charitable requests to the poor of his parish, asking in return for their prayers. It is true that he had already (in 1527) expounded his Machiavellianism to the greatly shocked Reginald Pole, but as yet the maxims probably were, with him, no more than speculative, as he had been given no chance to carry them into practice. Only later, by application, did they come to constitute the very fabric of his mind. In his case, as in that of other men, there was a slow, gradual process before the final stage was reached.

11

This will of Cromwell's shows that he was already a man of considerable means, as would be also indicated by his having been thought eligible to be a member of Parliament, to which only well-established men were elected. On the strength of this he ventures to describe himself as a "gentleman," a term then of strict social significance, and, as such, one he could hardly apply to himself. We find him comfortably established near Fenchurch until, after 1524, he moved into still more commodious quarters at the gate of the Austin Friars, with whose Prior (afterward the head of the English province of his order), George Browne, he formed a close friendship. It was one that was to take Dr. Browne into strange paths later and eventually to the Archbishopric of Dublin. At that time this eventuality was hardly less imaginable than Cromwell's own dazzling rise. Cromwell probably soon discovered that his landlord was very ready to accommodate himself to his times. It may even be that he learned facts about him that proved useful to bring pressure upon him when the right moment arrived. But all that we positively know is that Cromwell was in a steady and unspectacular way advancing, adding to his fortune year by year but exhibiting no vaunting ambition. It was an unpredictable accident that sent him suddenly soaring.

His chance came with his employment by Cardinal Wolsey; or rather that employment gave him the chance he was quick to seize after Wolsey's fall, though even then Cromwell could not have guessed where it would lead. This opportunity occurred as a direct result of his election to Parliament in 1523, and more particularly because of a famous speech he delivered there. Though there are indications that Wolsey had used his services now and then as a solicitor in private practice, until this time Cromwell seems to have had no closer connection with the Cardinal than that.[4] The reason I offer is that had Cromwell obtained his seat as one of "Wolsey's men"—that is, by Wolsey's nomination—he would never have opposed the project of the French war as he did. Though no positive evidence exists that the speech was actually delivered, it may be taken for granted that it was, and it probably was heard by the Cardinal and the King himself, as both personages used to go to

[4] *The Dictionary of National Biography* says that Wolsey employed him as early as 1514 as collector of his revenues. But there is no evidence for this statement, and it is inherently unlikely.

the House of Commons when matters of importance were under discussion. It well may be that Wolsey then and there decided that he should have a man of such marked ability in his service; perhaps he also wished by employing him to silence so acute a critic.

The Cardinal, it may be remarked, had a dislike for Parliament, never possessing Cromwell's ability for managing it. He had therefore summoned no Parliament between 1515 and 1523, in which latter year he was compelled to do so in order to obtain the necessary subsidy for the continuation of the war with France. As to this Parliament, we have the first of Cromwell's extant letters—one written on August 15, 1523—to John Cheke, at that time a merchant tailor in London but on a visit abroad. Nor does Cromwell's respect for the gathering in which he had sat for the first time seem very high, for he says he has "endured" a session of sixteen whole weeks and that "in conclusion we have done as our predecessors have been wont to do, that is to say, as well as we might and left where we began." He adds, however, "We have in our Parliament granted unto the King's Highness a right large subsidy, the like whereof was never granted in this realm." As Cromwell makes no reference to the part he played, it would seem desirable to indicate what this was and to quote some passages of a speech which occupies pages 30 to 44 of the first volume of Professor Merriman's study.[5]

The opposition to the subsidy—the unheard of amount of £800,000 was demanded—was general in the House of Commons. It was argued that such a sum could not be raised, and Cromwell himself estimated the entire coin and bullion in the realm as not much over £1,000,000, with perhaps three times more for the valuation of all estates. Sitting under their new Speaker, Sir Thomas More, the members made their protest and then sent a delegation to Wolsey. He, according to More's son-in-law and biographer, William Roper, "curishly answered that he would rather have his tongue plucked from his head with a pair of pincers than move the King to any less sum." Further, he let it be known that he proposed

---

[5] In *Letters and Papers of Henry VIII* it receives only a brief summary. In quoting from this and from Cromwell's letters, I shall spare the reader the reproduction of Cromwell's spelling, which was more than usually odd, even for that age. (It became better in his later years.) But at this time "Where icaenst the turkye, or barbarowse" has to be painfully translated as "War against the Turk and Barbary."

going in person to the Commons, of course in the expectation of overawing them; whereupon, after a long debate, More said, "Masters, forasmuch as my Lord Cardinal lately, ye well wot, laid to our charges the lightness of our tongues . . . it shall not be to my mind amiss with all his pomp to receive him, with his maces, his pillars, his poleaxes, his crosses, his hat, and Great Seal too; to the intent that, if he find fault with us hereafter, we may be the bolder from ourselves to lay the blame on those that his Grace bringeth with him."

When Cardinal Wolsey arrived, demanding what he called "some reasonable answer," all the members maintained what he told them was "without doubt a marvellous obstinate silence." Even when individual members were directed to say something, they would make no reply. Nor would the Speaker do so, except to fall on his knees and plead "the ancient liberty of the House." It was probably during the debate that preceded this visit that Cromwell delivered his speech. In it he gathered up all the arguments that were being used in the country against the continuation of a war that proved to have no result except to impoverish England and leave a few hundred French peasants with their barns and haystacks burned.

Cromwell took care to insert some flattering passages about the King, who, whether or not he was present, would be sure to hear about Cromwell's speech afterward. But this was only the coating of the bitter pill of an attack on the war policy. Nevertheless he artfully seemed to admit the force of the war policy before bringing forward his strong case against it. "All," he said, "have clearly perceived as well by the mouth and report of my Lord Legate's good Grace as by the recapitulation of the right worshipful and best assured and discreet Speaker, in so much that we have been advertised of the indentures already passed between our said most noble Sovereign and the Emperor's Majesty, containing not only the number of horsemen and footmen esteemed sufficient for the said enterprise, but also the day prefixed for the arrival beyond the sea of the said army." [6] A little later he notes that King Henry has

[6] More as a private person was in favor of peace, but in his official capacity as Speaker, in which he was the connecting link between the Council and the Commons, he was obliged to present the government's case. He had, as we have seen, upheld the liberty of the House against the Cardinal; yet it was largely due to his efforts that a somewhat scaled down subsidy was eventually voted.

undertaken to go to France "in his own noble person," and he expresses the hopes of all those present "that this so glorious, so profitable and so wishful an enterprise might prosperously be achieved, and our Sovereign with assured honor to return again." He goes on to speak of the justice of the English cause—the withholding by France of the dowry of the Queen Dowager (Henry's sister Mary), the wrongs done to the King's subjects, and the general perfidy of the French nation.

It was at this point in the speech that Cromwell cleverly began to undermine everything. He is dismayed that "our most gracious Sovereign, more dearer to his subjects that hath any manner zeal to our commonwealth than his own proper life," intends to take command of the invading army.[7] This Cromwell prays God he may never live to see; the King's person is too precious to risk in the hazards of war. He appeals to the King "that he will for our sakes and specially for the tender and fatherly love he beareth to his most dear and only daughter, upon whose weal and circumspect bestowing (next his noble person) dependeth all our wealth . . . to refrain his high magnanimous courage." Then he comes to the very practical consideration of the immense difficulty it would be to provision an army of 30,000 foot and 10,000 horse in a hostile country where lines of communications would always be in danger of being cut. Moreover, the support of the army would drain England not only of all its gold but of corn and cattle and wearing apparel. He declares that "if we should take this way or ever did our enemy any hurt that were worthy to be regarded we should be brought into that case that we should never be able to him nor none other, nor to help our Prince, nor this his noble realm." In short, the unanswerable argument against conducting large-scale military operations in France is that it would be the economic ruin of England.

Cromwell reminded his audience that no strongholds could be left untaken behind the army in its advance and that "the most sage and politic King Henry VII of gracious memory" had soon discovered this in the course of his one brief military adventure abroad. He suggested therefore that no more be attempted than the siege

[7] Henry in fact changed his mind about this and entrusted the command to his brother-in-law, the Duke of Suffolk. Henry was a famous rider in the tilting yard, but he was most careful never to expose himself in battle.

of Boulogne, for in the war of 1513 only Tournai and Thérouanne were taken. But Tournai had not been permanently held, and Thérouanne had been leveled at the demand of the Emperor Maximilian, who had brought a contingent to Henry. The cost unto "our most dread sovereign lord" had been more than the winning of twenty such "ungracious dogholes" could be worth to him. Cromwell was able to see nothing but danger on every side, for though he acknowledged the King's "high courage of marvellous wisdom and well tried experience in all martial conduct" and the invincibility of England, under existing conditions a war carried deep into France would prove prohibitively costly.

He forbore from pointing out—perhaps not to hurt the patriotic feelings of those listening to him but probably also because his case was strong enough without this—that since the time of Henry V the art of war had so changed as to make English armies incapable of meeting the French in a pitched battle. What the French were capable of doing had been proved in 1515 by their extraordinary feat of crossing the Alps at a place considered impassable and then overwhelming the famous Swiss infantry at Marignano. Englishmen were still thinking in terms of Cressy and Agincourt, where the impact of fully armored knights followed up the demoralization wrought by the longbow. But the bow, though still useful, could never again be decisive—not in the face of artillery or the new military formations which Englishmen scorned to use. The situation was such that the French would be under no necessity to give actual battle; all they would have to do was what they had done the previous year, when the Earl of Surrey (soon to succeed his father as Duke of Norfolk) had led an army into France, only to have the enemy retire slowly so as to make the invaders exhaust themselves. This meant the ravaging of a small district but, for France, nothing worse.

Cromwell may have shrewdly guessed that Charles V, the successor to his grandfather Maximilian as Emperor, would turn out to be an unreliable ally, but it was of course impolitic to say so. Though he showed that he had no hope of preventing the renewal of the war, as this had already been decided upon by the King and the Cardinal, it was open to him to say only what was calculated to discourage Parliament from throwing good money after bad. So as an alternative policy he suggested the conquest of Scotland, remarking that though there was a proverb that there was nothing to win in Scotland but strokes, there was another proverb which ran, "Who that intendeth France to win, with Scotland let him begin." It was not that he seriously advocated an attack on Scotland —for when he came into power he left Scotland severely alone— but the hint was thrown out as a sop to the bellicose appetite of his fellow countrymen. His argument was that of a practical businessman: England could not afford another war in France; if it did fight, it might find itself obliged, as previously, "to coin leather again." Cromwell's tone throughout was deferential to his audience, who had vouchsafed "to hear so patiently my ignorance," and he humbly besought "the tender benignity of my most dear and most redoubted Sovereign." All the same he had scored point after point against the war policy.

Many other people in England held the same common-sense view of the matter. Archbishop Warham was one of these, and he told Wolsey quite bluntly that, even if the King were able to conquer France, it would impoverish England, as France would cost more to keep than to win. He reminded the Cardinal that after all his wars and outlay of money the King "hath not one foot of land more in France than his most noble father had, who lacked no riches or wisdom to win the kingdom of France, if he had thought it expedient." Unfortunately there was too much hatred of the traditional enemy for common sense to prevail. All that was accomplished was that the subsidy was slightly reduced and its collection distributed over four years. The campaign of 1523 followed the same futile lines as that of 1522. The earlier year Surrey had ravaged and burned, winning nothing except the accusation of the French commander that he waged "foul warfare." Now Suffolk, who wished to be humane, found that only plunder could hold his army together and so burned and ravaged in his turn. As Wolsey dared not summon Parliament again, when the subsidy was close to being exhausted, he fell back on the expedient of what was called an Amicable Loan—barefaced extortion. Suffolk and Kent were on the verge of insurrection, and a common councilor of London told the Cardinal, "An it please your Grace, although King Richard did evil, yet in his time were many good acts made, not by him only but by the consent of the body of the whole realm, which is Parliament." King Henry, on the other hand . . . !

Nothing had been gained by the expeditions to France. Even after the battle of Pavia in 1525, when Francis was captured along with his entire army and Henry fell on his knees sobbing with joy at the thought that now he and the Emperor could divide France between them, Charles refused to act, and England was so impoverished it could not attack France alone. Cromwell had been amply justified, and though by that time he had begun to acquire an unsavory reputation for some of his deeds in the service of Cardinal Wolsey, he had also established for himself a reputation for political sagacity.

To understand properly Cromwell's connection with Wolsey, it should be said that his master had been Chancellor since 1515, holding also the Archbishopric of York, as well as several other sees and the rich abbacy of St. Albans as its titular head. Then by bringing pressure upon Pope Leo X at a crucial moment in 1518, he was created Papal Legate, a position previously asked for but refused. His ambition did not stop even at this point. In 1524, shortly after Cromwell entered his service, he was made Legate for life (something unheard of) and, pluralist though he was, proposed to reform the Church in England. He had even thought himself equal to reforming the Church Universal and had aimed at the Papacy in 1521 and 1523, on the deaths of Leo and Adrian VI, only to be tricked each time by the Emperor, who failed to give the support he had promised.

In England, however, Wolsey obtained a free hand, and some of the reforms he wished to effect were sound, though he always found himself too busy to carry them very far. A main factor in his scheme of reform—and it was with this that Thomas Cromwell was engaged as an agent—was the raising of standards of clerical education by founding at Oxford a college on a scale of unprecedented magnificence and rich endowments, with another college at Ipswich, Wolsey's birthplace, which should serve as a kind of nursery for Oxford. His motives were good, though mingled with them was a thirst for personal glory. The establishment of these colleges was the dearest desire of his heart, meaning more to him even than his bishoprics, his chancellorship, and his office of Legate, all thought of by him as necessary to the furthering of his schemes of reform.

To build and endow in the way that he had in mind, money

18

was essential—money in very large quantities. There was only one source from which this money could be drawn—from the Church itself. Part of his plan—a part never carried out—was the creation of nineteen new bishoprics; and for these also money would have had to come from ecclesiastical endowments. What Wolsey intended was a process of apportioning old revenues to his new purposes. In practice this meant the suppression of a number of the smaller monasteries or of those that might be considered as no longer serving any very useful purpose. The monks and nuns of these houses would be placed in other monasteries of their orders, and part of the income they had had was to be applied to the founding of his colleges. The Pope's permission for this had to be obtained and was reluctantly given, and suitable agents had to be secured. Among these were several priests, the chief of whom was the ruthless and unscrupulous Dr. John Allen, whom Wolsey was to appoint in 1528 Archbishop of Dublin and Chancellor of Ireland. The chief man of business used in the suppression of the thirty or so monasteries was the clever and assiduous Thomas Cromwell.

Wolsey's suppression of these monasteries was unpopular in itself and still more unpopular because of the methods by which it was carried out. The proceedings were highhanded, and threats were used against many religious houses as a means of forcing them to make adequate contributions to the Cardinal's project. Moreover, when an abbacy or even lesser offices fell vacant, Wolsey had a way of demanding that the election of the new superiors be what was called "promitted"—that is, left to him—whereupon the office was virtually put up to auction. It was well understood that the best way of currying favor with the reforming Cardinal was to offer a big bribe. And though he was scrupulous about not using these contributions except for the purpose intended, his agents were not at all troubled in conscience about extracting smaller bribes for themselves.

In fairness to Wolsey it must be said that there were precedents for monastic suppressions. It was by this method that Bishop Waynflete had founded Magdalen College at Oxford in 1459 and that the saintly John Fisher, the Bishop of Rochester, had suppressed two run-down religious houses to apply their endowments to St. John's College at Cambridge. Nor were these the only instances that might be cited; the criticism Wolsey received was on the ground of the unexampled extent of his suppressions and the roughshod way he went about them. Also of course there was objection to the extortionate methods he used, and the corruption of the men he employed.

Further resentment was aroused because Wolsey had represented to the Pope that some of the houses he wiped out of existence contained members of evil life. At the time of his fall one of the charges brought against him was that he vilified these monasteries and had, in fact, given the English clergy a bad name in Rome. There is no doubt that had Wolsey continued in office a good many other monasteries would have been swallowed up, for at his fall the building of his colleges was still uncompleted and nothing had been done about the erection of the new bishoprics. Yet Wolsey, however lukewarm may have been his admiration for monks, had no intention of doing more than prune some twigs from the monastic institution. It was never in his mind to do anything even faintly approaching what was afterward carried out by Cromwell.

It must be admitted that there were—or appeared to be—good reasons for the adjustment proposed. Slackness had overtaken some communities since the Black Death, when, with half or more of the members of a religious house swept away, it had been impossible to maintain strict discipline. But discipline once relaxed is exceedingly difficult to restore, and, though very rarely could worse be said of a monastery than that it was perfunctory in the performance of its duties, conditions at least called for reform. Other religious establishments were burdened with debts or were being mismanaged: what was done in their case could be regarded as putting them into the hands of a receiver. On the other hand, communities in which the numbers had dwindled often had larger endowments than they needed. Reorganization in such cases seemed reasonable enough.

Another argument was that in many houses the number of monks or nuns was insufficient for the solemn chanting of the Divine Office in choir, an obligation to which every order of that time was committed. It could be maintained that twelve religious were the minimum needed for this and that, rather than have a slovenly performance by a few feeble voices, those voices should augment the resonant choir of a great abbey, where the liturgy was carried out with exact observance of the rubrics and discipline strictly enforced. This was the argument specifically accepted as valid by the retroactive bull issued by Clement VII on November 14, 1528.

It is, however, certain that Wolsey's representations to the Holy See were often, to say the least, disingenuous. And there exists a bull drawn up in England and presented to Clement for signature, though never executed, which shows that the King and the Cardinal-Legate had in mind powers so wide as to have put all the monasteries of England at their mercy. The document reads in part: "Our beloved son in Christ, Henry now King of England, may take possession of all moveables and immoveables and rights of all and every monastery or other religious place founded by him and his predecessors, which for any reason or by any means is left or deserted, by virtue of his own authority, and without leave, asking, or consent of anyone, and dispose of them in the same way as of other royal property at his own pleasure." Had such powers been granted—and the effrontery of asking for them is amazing—there can be no doubt that something very like the suppression of the smaller monasteries in 1536 would have occurred long before the breach with the Holy See. For though the unsigned bull contained —it had to contain for form's sake—some restrictions, these on one pretext or another could have been nullified.

The amplitude of this bull's provisions was Cromwellian and may have actually originated with Cromwell. However this may be, it is certainly true that it was in Wolsey's service that Cromwell learned the technique he was later to use in suppressing monasteries or of allowing them to purchase their right to continue by paying extortionate sums into the royal treasury and suitable bribes to Cromwell himself. That he was already hated for what he was doing comes out in a letter written to him by his friend Stephen Vaughan on October 30, 1529, though Vaughan tells him that the odium he had incurred was on Wolsey's account rather than for any of his own actions. Another letter from a man who worked with him at Ipswich, Sir Thomas Rush, also warns him of the damaging reports in circulation about him. And in 1527 we hear of a man who had taken refuge from the law in a sanctuary, lying in wait to kill Cromwell.

He was aware of his danger but accepted it for the sake of the profit and influence he had. Many requests made to the Cardinal were sent to "the right worshipful Mr. Cromwell." Such requests to be effective had to be accompanied by a *douceur*. But this fact and that he was commonly called the "Councillor to my Lord Legate" did not increase his popularity. He must have clearly understood that his fortunes had become so closely woven with those of Wolsey that, should the Cardinal ever fall, Thomas Cromwell would almost certainly fall too. If he continued his course, as he did, it must have been because he considered Cardinal Wolsey impregnable.

Chapter Two

THE MODEL

Though Cardinal Wolsey was, in the matter of the suppression of monasteries, the model upon which Thomas Cromwell molded himself and the provider of the school in which he got his training, he was of course far from standing as Cromwell's example in all respects. It has been noted that Cromwell apparently deeply engaged his interest by his masterly speech in the Parliament of 1523 when he opposed the Cardinal's policy of war with France. Yet Cromwell believed in an alliance with the Emperor, as a businessman aware that only from the Emperor's dominions could essential imports be obtained and that much the best market for English exports was also in those dominions. Broadly speaking, however, the Wolseian method was that of playing off the King of France and the Emperor against each other, something he did with a dazzling virtuosity. While Cromwell may have learned a good deal from him about foreign affairs as an acute observer at close quarters, these were not matters in which he was allowed directly to participate. But he studied the Cardinal's technique and his character, and he studied the character of King Henry as mirrored in the Cardinal's mind. Above all he studied the ecclesiastical situation in England and meditated the possible application to this of his own political philosophy.

It could not have been lost upon Cromwell that Cardinal Wolsey was hardly a model of clerical propriety and for that reason, if for no other, was damaging the Church. The splendor in which the Cardinal lived—a splendor that equaled the King's—was proof enough, were other proof lacking, that the Church was rich. Yet Cromwell was discovering in his dealings with monks that the Church, while seemingly powerful, was actually weak. It was a fact he stored up for future reference.

For that matter the Cardinal himself was weak, except for the authority conferred on him by the King. Even his authority as Papal Legate could be exercised only at the King's pleasure. There was no man in England more hated than he, both by the bishops who suffered from his tyranny and by the nobility who were outraged by his studied insolence. As for the mass of the common people (who hardly counted), they hated the Cardinal for his suppression of monasteries and found a new reason for hatred when the divorce proceedings against Queen Katherine began, of which they believed him to be the initiator.

The Cardinal nevertheless considered himself, almost up to the moment of his fall, indispensable and therefore secure. But he was giving or had given his enemies many handles against him which they would not be slow to use when the time came. Wolsey's "uncanonical wife," Miss Larke, herself a daughter of a cleric attached to St. Stephen's, Westminster, had, it is true, by now been married off, taken by a man who was practically forced into the marriage but consoled by the substantial dowry given. But though she was no longer in evidence, her children were, a daughter and the son, passing under the name of Thomas Winter, who was already loaded with benefices despite his youth and was soon to be proposed for the wealthy See of Durham. Such things were not forgotten, and Cromwell, as the Cardinal's man of business, could not have been unaware that of the annual twenty-seven hundred pounds sterling the boy received from his various ecclesiastical endowments, he was allowed to retain less than a tenth and that his father pocketed the balance.[1]

Moreover the Cardinal, that reformer of the Church, gave a bad example with his pluralities and his nonresidence. He had never seen his cathedral at York, though he had been its archbishop since 1515; nor was he ever to see it. He held the revenues of Bath and of

[1] But even that was ample provision. It was worth at least six thousand pounds sterling in modern values.

24

Durham, retaining the latter until Fox of Winchester died, when he took that see in exchange for Durham. And perhaps because the holding of an abbacy *in commendam* was much less common in England than in Scotland—and was to become in France—it was regarded as scandalous. Because of these factors, what might have passed with other men as of relatively slight consequence was, in the case of the Cardinal, looked upon as peculiarly offensive and greatly hampered the reforms he proposed to effect in the Church.

Cromwell returned to England just in time to witness one of the most striking proofs that anticlerical feeling was, at any rate in London, growing extremely bitter. Some wise ecclesiastics saw the danger and tried to warn their brethren. Thus when in 1511 a synod against the Lollards—a small heretical sect still existing underground —was held in London, John Colet, the Dean of St. Paul's, instead of lashing out against them in the sermon he preached, denounced the shortcomings of the clergy—their worldliness, their laziness, their hunting and hawking, and their frequenting of taverns. Colet well understood that the real root of anticlericalism was here and that, if only priests would live up to their calling, heresy would soon disappear. For the Lollards were, for the most part, muddleheaded people whose heresy was hardly more than accidental: their protest was directed against the very things the highly orthodox Colet denounced.

Then in 1514 the storm broke, a storm that revealed how heartily the clergy in England were coming to be detested but which had nothing whatever to do with the doctrines of the Church, which were everywhere taken for granted, or with the Pope's jurisdiction, also taken for granted, little as was the enthusiasm it aroused. A man named Richard Hunne had refused the demand of his parish priest for his mortuary rights after the burial of Hunne's infant son —in this case it was merely the winding sheet—and when this demand was pressed, as was technically correct, he retaliated by taking action against the priest in the secular courts under the Statute of Praemunire.[2]

[2] As we shall hear much of this law, a word of explanation may be desirable. It forbade any exercise of foreign authority in England and was aimed at the Papacy. But it meant, in effect, that Papal authority was void only when it contravened the civil law; in its own sphere the jurisdiction of the Holy See was unquestioned.

25

In doing so Hunne overreached himself; this was not a matter that fell within Praemunire, which was directed only against the exercise of papal authority in contravention of English laws. He had long been suspected of heresy, and a search of his house yielded the authorities sufficient proof so that he was arrested and lodged in the Lollard's Tower to await trial. There one morning his body was found hanged by a silken girdle. And the vast majority of Londoners, who had been eagerly looking for something to bring against the ecclesiastical authorities, were firmly convinced that Hunne had been murdered by Dr. Horsey, the Chancellor of the London diocese, assisted by the bell ringer of the prison and the summoner. The summoner indeed, under torture—"by pain and durance" as it was called—made some sort of a confession, and Bishop Fitzjames had to protest to the King that, in the inflamed condition of London, those accused, even were they "as innocent as Abel," would be found guilty.

The upshot was that Henry ordered all the circumstances of the case inquired into by a commission sitting in Baynard's Castle. And anyone who reads Sir Thomas More's account of the examination of the witnesses who offered to prove murder can hardly fail to see, as against all London of 1514, that the charge of murder was fantastic. The generally held opinion of historians today is that Hunne committed suicide in despair.[3] Dr. Horsey, as a result of the inquiry, was allowed to plead not guilty in one of the King's courts of law, and his plea was accepted.

The importance of the matter, however, is not the solution of the mystery of Hunne's death but what it brought to light of the prevalent opinion in London. Though Horsey had, in fact, been acquitted, it was generally believed that he had been pardoned of murder. The real cause of irritation was of course the exaction of mortuary dues—one of many such clerical exactions—and murder was thrown in merely for good measure.

The Horsey case brought up the question whether clerics accused of criminal offenses should be tried before ecclesiastical or secular courts. Dr. Henry Standish, the Guardian of the Grey Friars, maintained before Convocation, the legislative assembly of the Church,

[3] Arthur Ogle in his recently published *The Tragedy of the Lollard's Tower* takes a different view, but one that I find unconvincing in the face of More's judgment.

that no wrong was done the Church in having those in holy orders summoned for misdemeanors before one of the King's courts of law. When Convocation threatened to punish him, he appealed to the King, and Henry heard his case before his bench of bishops and the assembled judiciary. Standish stood his ground, though assailed by Archbishop Warham, Bishop Fox of Winchester, and by Wolsey himself, with Dr. Veysey, later Bishop of Bath, upholding him. The opinion handed down by Fineux, the Chief Justice, was that, as ecclesiastical courts were not empowered to pass sentence on a felon, all clerical felonies fell within the competence of the secular courts. This decision was seized on by the King, who declared, "We are, by the sufferance of God, King of England, and the Kings of England in times past never had any superior but God. Know, therefore, that we will maintain the rights of the Crown in this matter like our progenitors; and as to your decrees, we are satisfied that you of the spirituality act expressly against the words of several of them, as has been shown to you by some of our spiritual Council. You interpret your decrees at your pleasure; but as for me, I will never consent to your desire, any more than my progenitors have done."

The words were magnificently spoken but open to some historical question. Moreover the general Council of the Church had declared on May 5, 1514, that laymen had no jurisdiction over the clergy. Perhaps it was with this case in mind that More wrote in his *Utopia* that his Utopians "think it not lawful to touch with man's hand, be he never so vicious, who after so singular a sort was dedicate and consecrate to God, as a holy offering." Yet the King's words were not intended to assert anything like the supremacy over the Church that Henry afterward claimed. What they do show, however, is that Henry VIII was resolved against any such submission to the Church as Henry II made after the murder of Becket. Times had changed; a new era was about to dawn. Had the clergy recognized this fact they might have been able to stave off approaching calamities. Instead, they continued stubbornly to assert the privileges of their order. The most they could obtain in this instance was that Dr. Horsey be tried before a secular court with the assurance of acquittal. The main question was left open—dangerously open.

These matters could not have been lost upon the intelligence of Cromwell. Though no word of his is recorded about the Hunne case, he probably saw that the charges against Dr. Horsey were badly grounded; on the other hand, he would have completely agreed with the royal assertion of supremacy and may in his mind have already gone much beyond it. He must have perceived that the clerical body was ill-advised in insisting so strongly on its prerogatives. And he could not have failed to note the fierce anticlerical temper of London.

Yet about this many moderns tend to exaggerate. Anticlericalism certainly flared up in 1514, but it subsided. At a later period Sir Thomas More—than whom one could have no more honest or better informed witness—when replying to an anonymously published book, now known to have been written by the lawyer Christopher St. German, entitled *The Division between the Spirituality and the Temporality*, affirmed, "The division is nothing such as this man makes it, and is grown as it is only since Tyndale's books and Frith's and Friar Barnes' began to be spread abroad." More was in the position to know, and yet one cannot but feel that the books to which he refers—those in which definite heresy was propounded—received acceptance only because there already existed a good deal of irritation against the clergy. At a date which would appear to have been still earlier, when Roper was saying to him that the country "had so Catholic a prince that no heretic durst show his face," More assented but went on to remark glumly, "Yet, son Roper, I pray God that some of us, as high we sit upon the mountains treading heretics under our feet like ants, live not [until] the day that we would gladly be at league and composition with them and to let them have their churches quietly to themselves, so that they would be contented to let us have ours quietly to ourselves." Hearing his father-in-law say this, Roper, who not very long before had himself been dabbling in heretical opinions, was scandalized and protested, "By my troth, sir, it is very desperately spoken!" To cheer him up, More returned, "Well, well, son Roper, it shall not be so, it shall not be so." In his bones, however, More felt that he was all too true a prophet.

Lutheranism had hardly touched England at all, except indirectly. Not only was the King perfectly orthodox but he had his personal quarrel with Luther, having written against the latter's *Babylonian Captivity* his own *Defence of the Seven Sacraments*. It was a fairly able performance and brought from the Pope and his Consistory, when the presentation was made by Dr. Clerk, the English agent in

Rome, all kinds of effusive compliments and—what was more to the point—the title of Defender of the Faith for the King.

Henry was, indeed, in 1521, a bit too papal even for Sir Thomas More, who advised him to tone down a certain passage. The conversation, as recorded by More, was: "When I found the Pope's authority highly advanced and with such strong arguments defended, I said unto his Grace: 'I must put your Highness in remembrance of one thing, and that is this. The Pope, as your Grace knoweth, is a prince as you are, and in league with other Christian princes. It may hereafter so fall out that your Grace and he may vary upon some points of the league, whereupon may grow breach of amity and war between you both. I think it best, therefore, that the place be amended and his authority more slenderly touched.' 'Nay,' quote his Grace, 'that shall it not. We are so much bounden unto the See of Rome that we cannot do too much honor unto it.' "

More did not let the matter drop but reminded Henry of Praemunire, "whereby a good part of the Pope's pastoral cure here was pared away." The King's answer was: "Whatever impediment be to the contrary, we will set forth that authority to the uttermost. For we received from that see our Crown imperial." More confessed that he did not know what that last statement meant. Possibly Henry was referring to the very ample bull issued by Innocent VIII in 1486 in support of the first Tudor's claim to the throne.

If Henry was orthodox, so also was Cromwell at this time, and later anti-Lutheran in his professions. Writing to Cardinal Wolsey on May 17, 1530, he tells him a report had come that Luther had died and added, "I would he had never been born." Yet Cromwell's own career, at its opening, was made possible only because the breach with the Papacy he advocated could never have been ventured upon had not the upheaval in Germany weakened both Pope and Emperor. His private Machiavellianism could never have been more than a speculative fancy, were it not for this.

What is called Machiavellianism was very much in the air even before Machiavelli crystallized it in *The Prince*. It had been practiced freely enough by Ferdinand of Aragon, Caesar Borgia, Charles V, Francis I, and even by Henry himself. What Cromwell added was the practical program of making the monarchy absolute. In England there was more chance of bringing this about than elsewhere because, after the long dynastic struggles, the hopes of the nation centered in the royal house that had brought stability. To the person of the King had come to be attached a peculiar sacredness, and Henry, up to the time of his divorce proceedings against Katherine, enjoyed a popularity probably never approached by any sovereign anywhere. All of this gave Cromwell an unparalleled opportunity. In his mind was a settled conviction that to tolerate the dual control of the monarchy and the Church, which had been taken for granted for centuries—though it had also resulted in centuries of recurring friction—was to tolerate a two-headed monster. Everything was to be brought under the direct domination of the King. Cromwell honestly believed that no other system was workable. He may, in short, be described as the first totalitarian. And it was his function to insinuate his political ideas into the mind of the King at the appropriate moment.

That moment had not yet come. In fact, the explanation of the Wolseian foreign policy, heartily concurred in by Henry, was the support of the Papacy, even under its temporal aspects, throughout all the complicated changes of European diplomacy. Against both the Emperor Charles and Francis I of France, England was secure because of her geographical position. But England was also able (again because of geography) to bring pressure against either, by closing the Strait of Dover to trade with Spain or by invading France through the bridgehead of Calais. It would have been perfectly possible for Henry to have remained at peace with both, like his wise father, except for the exigencies of papal policy. This necessitated the Pope's throwing his weight now to one side and now to the other but always against the side that was, at the moment, threatening his own sovereignty. And Wolsey, always with an eye on the Papacy for himself, with Henry's backing, supported the Pope in everything. Whatever personal selfishness there was in this, Henry had some right to think of himself as the only true friend of the Pope among the princes of the world. It of course made the King all the more furious when what he considered his just request for a papal pronunciation on his marriage as null and void was not instantly forthcoming. It seemed to him dastardly ingratitude.

The stage was well set for talents such as Cromwell's, especially as they went with a character free of moral prepossessions. Had Cromwell been obliged to act upon a larger stage, in a country always in danger of being invaded, he would hardly have been able to achieve success. But England was small and compact, cut off by the sea, secure. Its main wealth lay in agriculture, trade being for the most part in the hands of the large settlements of foreign merchants in London and the other seaports. Except for wool carried to the Low Countries, little English produce was carried in English bottoms. Similarly most of the imports arrived in Venetian or Genoese ships. Despite a few expeditions of exploration sent out by Henry VII, virtually nothing was done in that direction by his son. The chance for the exploitation of the New World, as of the Indies, was for the time being neglected, to the benefit of the Spanish and the Portuguese.

Another, and a much more important factor, was that under Wolsey, whom Cromwell was serving, a concentration of power was effected such as Europe had never known before. The Cardinal was not merely Chancellor—greatly widening the scope of his authority—he was also Legate, virtually Pope in England so far as the administration of the Church was concerned. The King was content to leave most of the business of government in Wolsey's hands, and though it is true that the state papers show that Henry did concern himself with details, they were only details with which Wolsey allowed him to deal. It was no more than politic to make the King feel that he was, after all, ruling; then, when he had dealt with the bit of business brought to his attention, he could go off and amuse himself.

That had at least been the situation until recently. Cromwell, though he had so far come into but slight personal contact with the King, realized that he was growing cagey and suspicious and required, at times, tactful handling. He must also have realized that, immense as was Henry's authority should he choose to exercise it, he was weak and indolent. Even the obstinacy he frequently showed was a sign of weakness, an unwillingness to admit that he might be mistaken. Here was one who, despite his versatile brilliance, was a self-deceiver. His famous bluffness was largely bluff. Of two French ambassadors, Castillon called him a fool, and Marillac a coward. The judgments were not entirely just, but Henry was at any rate the kind of man who would have been lost without the firm hand of a manager.

Katherine had managed him at first, but her control had been weakened by the perfidy of her father toward her husband and then undermined by Wolsey. No king had ever been so completely controlled as was Henry by his great minister, though there were now signs of restiveness. Cromwell watched all this, making mental notes but not for an instant imagining that it would fall to him to take Wolsey's place. When this did come about, he had on his hands a man aging prematurely, suffering from pain, given to unaccountable outbursts of rage, secretive, sly, and suspicious. It was a very difficult undertaking that awaited Cromwell. But he was being well schooled for it by the practical training he received when in the Cardinal's service, as also by his clear view of what he considered political realities.

The situation was made all the more difficult by the domination Anne Boleyn established over the King during the years when he was trying to nullify his marriage to Katherine. The woman in the case, while ruining Wolsey, also unwittingly gave Cromwell his chance. Anne had her reasons for hating Wolsey. It was he who had broken off the marriage she had hoped to make with Henry Percy, the heir to the earldom of Northumberland. But he had also, so she imagined, been negligent about obtaining Henry's divorce, if he was not surreptitiously working against it. Nevertheless, until his fall she pretended to have a very great affection for the Cardinal and used playfully to upbraid him if he failed to send her presents of the shrimp and carp of which she was especially fond. These presents were also indications of a pretended affection on Wolsey's part. He might call her the Crow of the Night in private, but to her face he poured out a rich stream of flattery. Yet much as he wished to stand well with Anne, now that her hold over the King was so strong, there were some things he would not do, even for her.

An instance of this occurred in 1528, when with the death of the Abbess of Wilton, the election of her successor was—as had become usual under Wolsey—promitted to him. But Anne Boleyn had a candidate and put forward the name of Eleanor Carey, the sister of the man Mary Boleyn (formerly the King's mistress) had married. Under such circumstances it would have been dangerous for Wolsey to have followed a frequent practice with him and have appointed the highest bidder to the office. Yet he learned, upon inquiry, that Eleanor was a woman of loose life and so disregarded Anne's request, which had been made through the King, and appointed Isabel Jordan, until then Prioress of the Abbey, as Abbess.

Anne was very indignant and complained to the King, who wrote to the Cardinal for an explanation. When this had been given, Henry wrote to Anne, "I would not for all the world clog your conscience nor mine to make her [Eleanor] ruler of a house which is of so ungodly demeanor; nor I trust you would not neither for brother nor sister I should distain mine honor or conscience."

Nothing less could be said. Yet the King was distinctly annoyed that Wolsey had acted on his own authority (though he was the Legate!) after the expression of the royal wishes. The Cardinal had to do a little lying and say that he had misunderstood what the King wanted. But though the appointment of Isabel Jordan was allowed to stand, Henry wrote Wolsey one of those personal letters in which he could be really magnificent. While accepting the explanations, he seized the occasion to reprimand the Cardinal about the methods he had been using for the gathering of funds for his college. "There is great murmuring of it," he wrote, "throughout all the realm, both good and bad. They say that not all is ill gotten that is bestowed upon the college, but that the college is the cloak for covering all mischiefs. . . . One more thing I perceive by your letter . . . and that is, that you have received money from the exempts for having their old visitors. Surely this cannot be with a good conscience. For, an they were good, why should you take money? And if they were ill, it were a sinful act. Howbeit your legacy might therein, peradventure, *apud homines* be a cloak, but not *apud Deum*. Wherefore you, thus monished by him who so entirely loveth you, I doubt not will desist, not only from this (if your conscience will bear it) but from all other things which should tangle the same, and in so doing we will sing, *Te laudant angeli atque archangeli, Te laudet omnis spiritus* [angels and archangels praise Thee; all spirits praise Thee]. And thus I make an end of this, though rude, yet loving letter, desiring you benevolently to take it as I do mean it, for I ensure you (and I pray you think it so) that there remaineth at this hour no spark of displeasure towards you in my heart. And thus fare you well, and be no more perplexed. Written with the hand of your loving sovereign and friend, HENRY R."

The King was being extremely forbearing. He could not but uphold Wolsey with regard to Eleanor Carey, though he was annoyed that this put him in danger of being upbraided by the sharp-tongued Anne Boleyn. But a weightier reason for the King's

33

displeasure was that many of the religious houses, because of contributions they had been forced to make at the time of the Amicable Loan, pleaded that they were now unable to contribute to the royal needs.

In his reply the Cardinal thanked the King "for his great zeal that [he] had for the purity and cleanness of my poor conscience, coveting and desiring that nothing should be by me committed or done, by the color of my intended college or otherwise, that should not stand with God's good pleasure and good conscience, or that thereby any just occasion might be given to any person to speak or judge ill of my doings." But while going on to deny he had done anything contrary to the law, he undertakes that henceforth he will accept no contribution "from any religious person, being exempt or not exempt, so that thereby I trust, not by any other thing unlawfully taken, your poor cardinal's conscience shall not be spotted, encumbered, or entangled."

Henry did not allow the matter to rest there. He complained to Wolsey, "These same religious houses would not grant to their Sovereign in his necessity, not by a great deal so much as they have to you for the building of your college. These things bear shrewd appearance, for except they were accustomed to have some benefit, they, and no other I ever heard of, used to show that kindness, *tam enim aliena ab eis ipsa humanitas* [for such would be foreign to human nature]." But while counting upon the Cardinal's good conduct for the future, the King urges him to look more closely into the methods of the agents whom he has commissioned for this "meddling with religious houses."

All this shows that Henry had a clear enough general idea as to what was going on and was aware that many of the contributions made to Wolsey were extorted—as though the Amicable Loan were not highly extortionary—or given for favors received. Though the King probably knew little about details, he at least knew that Wolsey had set up the so-called Legate's Court to enforce his authority, in which, writes Lord Herbert, Henry's seventeenth-century biographer, "all manner of rapines and extortions" were perpetrated. Herbert goes on: "For making enquiry into the life of everybody, no offence escaped censure and punishment, unless privately they gave money; of which they found two commodities: one that it did cost less, the other that it exempted them from shame." Dr. Allen, the judge in this court, soon to be promoted to the Archbishopric of Dublin, was accused by Dr. John London, at that time Warden of New College, Oxford, and later to be one of Cromwell's chief agents in the suppression of monasteries during 1536 to 1540. This accusation brought these matters into the open.

The King knew perfectly well that Allen and Cromwell had an exceedingly bad reputation for rapacity and bribetaking. So notorious was this that William Knight, the King's secretary, wrote to Wolsey in 1527, at the time the Cardinal was at Amiens, warning him not to send Allen, as he had heard was his intention, with a message to the King. "And sir," he said, "in case Mr. Allen be not departed hitherwards on your message, or may be in time revoked, your Grace might use better any about you for your message unto the King than him. I have heard the King and noblemen speak things incredible of the acts of Mr. Allen and Cromwell." In spite of this Allen was made Archbishop of Dublin the following year, and Cromwell not long afterward began his astonishing rise in Henry's service.

Cromwell, like Allen, had great aptitude for work which required ruthlessness and lack of scruples. In Cromwell's case there was also the advantage of a sound knowledge of the laws relating to the transfer of property. The business of the suppression turned out to be a good deal more intricate than Wolsey had imagined, and he did not have time to attend to this himself. Cromwell managed it with the utmost dispatch, thereby making himself invaluable to the Cardinal as he was later to make himself invaluable to the King. It was he who drew up the deeds for the foundation of the colleges at Oxford and Ipswich, and he was appointed in 1527 the receiver-general for Cardinal's College, in which capacity he supervised the workmen engaged in building. In all such undertakings he demonstrated his marvelous efficiency and industry, as may still be seen in the long lists of confiscated or surrendered manors and monasteries, their possession such as plate and vestments, and the accounts of the income to be derived. But as Merriman writes: "The minute Wolsey's back was turned Cromwell and his companion, Dr. Allen, a hard and grasping man, well-trained in business, proceeded to use the power given into their hands to enrich themselves by every possible means, some of which were utterly unjustifiable. The monastery which could pay a large bribe went untouched; of those that were suppressed, probably a certain proportion of the spoils were never employed at Oxford or Ipswich, but went straight into the pockets of the suppressors." Exactly the same thing happened in the later suppressions under Cromwell; he then pilfered from the King, and his agents pilfered from him on a much larger scale than had been possible under the vigilant Wolsey. A certain amount of venality was winked at, and if this subsequently was of an almost heroic sort, the opportunities for it were discovered during the Wolseian suppressions. Cromwell was at least efficient.

Cromwell, reporting to the Cardinal on April 2, 1528, on the progress of his work, wrote, "The building of your noble college most prosperously and magnificently doth arise in such wise that to every man's judgment the like thereof was never seen nor imagined, having consideration to the largeness, beauty, sumptuous, curious and most substantial building of the same. Your chapel within the said college most devoutly and virtuously ordered and the ministers within the same not only diligent in the service of God but also the service daily done within the same, so devout, solemn and full of harmony that in my opinion it hath few peers." He follows this with a request whose significance is not hard to understand: it is that a benefice in the diocese of St. Davids, one in the gift of Wolsey as Chancellor, be bestowed on a Mr. Burton. It may be surmised that Mr. Burton had given Cromwell a bribe with the promise of a further payment should the benefice be bestowed. We have ample documentary proof that this was Cromwell's practice in later life, and though such documentation is meager at this period, we have seen what his reputation was. A report even reached Reginald Pole about 1527 that Cromwell had been arrested and was about to be punished for his misdeeds. He was saved only because Wolsey steadily protected so indispensable a servant.

As Cromwell was doing a special job—one that would eventually come to an end—he retained his private law practice, though he could not have had much time to give to it. But this was something he could always fall back upon. And of course in his profession as a solicitor, he was well placed to make loans at a high rate of interest, using his gains from the monasteries to obtain further gains. He was a man whose substance was steadily increasing, whatever may have been the precariousness of his position.

The shadowy Elizabeth Cromwell having died about 1528—

probably from the sweating sickness so severe that year—and then or shortly afterward her two daughters, Thomas Cromwell packed off his stupid son Gregory to the care of a tutor named John Chekyng at Cambridge. From the correspondence existing it is clear that Gregory's father was somewhat remiss in paying Chekyng's bills, though he was well able to do so. It is also clear that he had little concern for domesticities, as might be expected of one who was more of a machine than a man. Though he tried later, when he was immensely wealthy and had a title of nobility, to arrange a glorious career for his son, we cannot but suspect that in this he was actuated much less by altruism than by self-love. It is vain to look for even a particle of that radiant family affection illuminating Sir Thomas More. Cromwell had no time to spare for such things. On the other hand, he had no time or inclination for loose living. His sole concern at this time was for money, more and more money. Later it was for power as well as money—for power even more than money, though he never ceased to be avid for the latter.

Henry's divorce proceedings—and Cromwell must have caught intimations earlier than most people that unexpected difficulties were being encountered—could not have greatly disturbed Cromwell. Wolsey, though worried by the Queen's stubborn refusal to be "reasonable," confidently counted, like everybody else, upon a decision being given in the King's favor, until the day (July 23, 1529) when Cardinal Campeggio announced, at the very moment when sentence was expected, that the Legatine Court was adjourned until October.

What Cromwell, an imperialist (as were all businessmen), may well have feared more was that Wolsey's policy of a French alliance might, because of its unpopularity, bring the Cardinal down. If that happened, he had reason to fear for his own skin.

Almost everybody on the Council was opposed to the French alliance. Even Henry had believed that his divorce might be more easily obtained if, instead of antagonizing the Emperor further, an alliance against France were offered him. Then it was hoped that he would withdraw his opposition to the divorce of his aunt and thus leave the hands of Clement VII free. Wolsey, however, who hated the Emperor for twice having barred him from the Papacy despite his promise of support, had turned against him and now was steadily backing France. Here this very clever man blundered badly. For

37

by winning Francis as an ally, he gave Henry the courage he might otherwise have lacked to defy the Pope and disregard the opinion of all Europe. This was of course very far from Wolsey's intention, but it was one of the unforseen results of his French policy.

The alliance was to be made firm by marriage. Henry's daughter Mary as an infant had been betrothed to the Dauphin in 1518, and later to her cousin the Emperor, who broke off the engagement to marry the Infanta of Portugal. Now, as Mary was a good deal nearer a marriageable age, a betrothal had to be taken more seriously. Yet all agreed upon in 1527 was that she would marry either Francis or his second son, the Duc d'Orleans. That it was to be a French marriage was enough to make it highly unpopular, so Henry had to let it be known that Mary was still too young to be sent to France. There was no other way of calming public indignation.

Worse was to follow. At the opening of 1528, French and English heralds went to the Emperor at Burgos and formally defied him. Charles, however, refused to accept the English challenge, so that for some time a curious state of affairs existed: nobody—even those at Court—being quite sure whether Henry was at war with Charles or not. What everybody soon discovered was that, if there was to be war, it would hurt England more than either of the other two countries involved. English broadcloth could not be manufactured without oils obtainable only from Spain, and the best market for this material, when it had been manufactured, was in the Low Countries. Accordingly a truce was made in June, which helped to relieve the situation; but it was not until a year later, on August 5, that the peace treaty of Cambrai was finally signed.

This war (such as it was) would never have been thought of if not for the pending divorce suit. It should, however, be noted that the French alliance preceded the opening of the divorce and had no connection with it. That made the blunder all the worse, as it could not be represented as vengeance on the Emperor for the Sack of Rome, or as an attempt to loosen the Emperor's pressure upon the Pope. Yet Wolsey tried to put the alliance to use in the matter of the divorce by going to France, with the idea of sounding Francis as to the possibility of Henry's marrying Renée, the daughter of Louis XII, after the divorce had been obtained. Wolsey was as yet in the dark as to Henry's intention of replacing Katherine with Anne Boleyn. As a sure means of obtaining the divorce, the

English Cardinal hoped to get himself appointed to act for the Pope when he had ignominiously to find a refuge in the Castel San Angelo. When this scheme broke down, he planned to form France and England into a patriarchate, over which he would preside as Archbishop of Rouen. There was even some talk of a new schism. Had any of these schemes proved successful, Wolsey of course would have at once pronounced Henry's marriage to Katherine invalid.

In the end the Cardinal had to fall back upon trying to get the Pope to grant the divorce, with what result we know: it was his failure to do so that brought about his fall and so opened the door for Cromwell. Yet even after his failure, Wolsey, though now out of favor with Henry, did not immediately lose his office, either as Legate or Chancellor. Campeggio remained in England—though Clement had revoked the hearings to Rome—on the chance that the Pope might change his mind and permit the divorce proceedings to continue in October. And when at last Campeggio did leave, there was a wild hope that the customs officials at Dover would find among his baggage the decretal bull, which had been known to exist, empowering either Legate to pass sentence. Had that bull been discovered, Wolsey would have done what was required of him; his position would have been reestablished; and England would not have entered into schism. But Campeggio had destroyed the document, according to his instructions, after reading it to Henry and Wolsey, thereby making it as valueless as a will that had been thrown in the fire. The Pope had issued it only to gain time and had taken pains to see that it could never be used. When that fact was established, the Cardinal of York fell at once.

No time was lost. On October 9, Wolsey was sued under a writ of Praemunire, which must have been prepared in advance. As the safest course to follow, he admitted his guilt and threw himself on the King's mercy. A week later he surrendered the Great Seal of the chancellorship, which was, with universal approval but against his own wishes, conferred on Sir Thomas More.

Henry did not stop there. He had learned a good deal from Wolsey about the confiscation of Church property, so he demanded a complete inventory of everything in the Cardinal's London palace, York House. The scene, at which Cromwell was undoubtedly present—and he in all likelihood was the man who had prepared the inventory—is described by George Cavendish, the Cardinal's gentleman usher: "Then my Lord called his officers before him and took account of all things they had in their charge, and in his gallery were set divers tables, upon which were laid divers and great store of rich stuffs, as whole pieces of silk of all colors, velvets, satins, damask, taffeta, grograin, scarlets and divers rich commodities. Also there were a thousand pieces of fine holland. The hangings of the gallery were cloth of gold and cloth of silver and rich cloth of baudkin of divers colors, which were hung in expectation of the King's coming." In the Council Chamber and the Gilt Chambers were placed two long broad tables covered with plate: "A great part were all of clean gold, and upon every table and cupboard where the plate was set were books reporting every kind of plate and every piece, with the contents and the weight thereof."

But still Henry did not stop at this point. Cavendish tells us, "On one side of the gallery were hung rich suits and copes of his own provision, which were made for the colleges at Oxford and Ipswich; they were the richest that ever I saw in all my life." As these vestments (and presumably a good deal of the plate) belonged to the colleges and not to Wolsey, they should have been inviolate. But no: they and the colleges themselves and their endowments were taken over by the King.

There may be a partial justification for their seizure on the ground that Wolsey by mulcting many religious houses of large contributions had deprived Henry of contributions to his Amicable Loan. But even if this be so, there was no shadow of justification for the seizure by Henry of York House, which did not belong to Wolsey but to his archbishopric. This time the Cardinal, who had meekly yielded everything else, did make a protest when Sir William Shelley arrived to take possession in the name of the King. Even so, Wolsey was careful not to contest the legality of the action but only its justice, whereupon Shelley agreed that there was no great justice in it but that the Cardinal would be well advised not to stand out, as the King could, after all, restore double. Wolsey still protested that what was being done was "only a bare seizure of another's right" and added, very daringly, "I charge your conscience to discharge me, and show his Highness from me, that I must desire his Majesty to remember that there is both heaven and hell." All this must have been a most instructive lesson to Cromwell. A few years later he was acting in precisely the same way.

Everybody expected that Wolsey would be sent to the Tower, for he had been sentenced to perpetual imprisonment. Even Sir William Gascoigne, the Cardinal's treasurer, believed that this was to happen and expressed his regrets, only to be told sharply by Wolsey, "It hath always been your inclination to be light of credit, and much lighter in reporting of lies." There were hundreds of boats and barges on the river, crammed with people hoping to see the hated Cardinal on his way to the Tower, and a howl of rage and disappointment went up when the barge steered upstream to Putney. Wolsey had permission to go with his chaplains and servants (Cromwell among them) to a mansion at Esher belonging to his bishopric of Winchester. He was kept in suspense until early February before receiving pardon from the King, but at least he was already assured that the full penalties were not to be exacted.

Chapter Three

THE SUPPLANTER

THOMAS CROMWELL was Wolsey's supplanter in fact but not by design. He must have been thoroughly scared when his patron fell, for this was something quite likely to touch his own life. Wolsey was indeed going to be let off his prison sentence and even to be allowed to retain his archbishopric; but final decision as to this had not yet been reached. In any event some of the lesser culprits were in serious danger of being sacrificed to the nation's anger. The general expectation was that Cromwell would be hanged.

If he was going to cheat the gallows and still more if he was going to turn the situation to his profit—as we know he did—he had to understand it thoroughly. As the eclipse of the Cardinal, though it seemed to have come on very suddenly, had actually been precipitated by a long series of events, we may be sure that Cromwell had been maturing his own plans.

A few weeks after Wolsey's settlement in Esher, in a great house almost empty of furniture, except for a few pieces loaned by the Bishop of Carlisle, but with enough to eat and drink, Cavendish on All Saints' Day, November 1, saw an extraordinary sight when he went into the great hall.[1] There stood Cromwell praying at a win-

---

[1] George Cavendish, though he held steadily to the Catholic faith and wrote his brilliant little life of Wolsey in the days of Queen Mary, whom he served as Treasurer of the Chamber and a privy councilor, has nothing but good to

dow embrasure, reading the Little Office of Our Lady with the tears pouring down his face. Cavendish was surprised and asked, "Why, Mr. Cromwell, what meaneth this dole? Is our Lord in any danger that ye lament for him?" To this came the honest answer: "Nay, it is for my own unhappy adventure. For I am like to lose all that I have labored for all the days of my life. But this much I will say to you, that I will this afternoon, when my Lord hath dined, ride to London to the Court, where I will make or mar, or ever I come again."

Cromwell realized that he was in a predicament in which he needed the help of heaven. He may have seen the King that day; more probably he saw only the Duke of Norfolk, the man now most influential in political matters. At any rate we know that through Norfolk's patronage he was nominated to sit as the member for Taunton in the Parliament to meet only two days later. It was in that unprecedentedly long Parliament—one that sat until 1536—that Cromwell's career really began.

He had made a desperate throw of the dice, and it proved astonishingly lucky. As Cardinal Wolsey's agent, Cromwell was not in good standing with anybody; he himself said that he was exposed "to the disdain of all men." How he managed to placate the Duke of Norfolk, the Cardinal's most bitter enemy, is a mystery. The wonder is that he was not arrested as soon as he put in an appearance at Court. We must suppose that he arrived with a number of valuable suggestions, though a complete plan of campaign is hardly imaginable at this stage. Scoundrel though he was, he was known to be an extremely efficient person and to have much political sagacity. At all events he convinced Norfolk and perhaps Henry (with whom he may have had an interview) that he could be of service. From

---

say of his former associate, Thomas Cromwell. He was of course obliged to confine himself to the Cromwell he knew up to 1529, but his personal acquaintance did not end there, for we find him taking the surrender of monasteries under Cromwell and receiving grants of monastic property, even being appointed one of the auditors of the Court of Augmentation. He is to be commended for feeling some gratitude to Cromwell and for avoiding saying anything detrimental about him. But Cavendish was so simple a soul that he may have been unable to see Cromwell's iniquity. Instead he saw what other people often missed—the good nature and even the generosity that Cromwell now and then showed. He certainly credited Cromwell with loyalty to his fallen master.

that time forth he was the go-between of the Duke and the Cardinal, a very delicate position but one that he handled in masterly style.

To act as a go-between was, however, hardly enough; other men might have been used in the same capacity, men less corrupt and, on the other hand, less likely to serve the Cardinal than the antagonistic Court party. A conjectural explanation sometimes thrown out is that Cromwell arrived on All Saints' Day bearing a document which, according to Cavendish, Wolsey had had in his possession, the authorization from the King to perform the very acts for which he had been condemned under Praemunire.

To be fair to Cromwell, this seems extremely doubtful. Had such a document existed, the time for Wolsey to have used it was when he pleaded guilty the previous month in the court of the King's Bench. Cavendish's chronology is rather muddled at times, but it seems clear that if this authorization had existed and been purloined, this would have happened several weeks before All Saints' Day. His words could bear the meaning that the Cardinal's papers had been seized at the time of the seizure of his possessions at York House. Moreover, Cavendish was writing twenty years after the event, when the memory of what had been said and done may have become distorted. Wolsey may have said merely, "But I had the King's permission to act as I did!" and Cavendish may have jumped to the conclusion that this permission had been given under the royal seal and signature.

What is true is that Henry heartily approved of the Legateship Wolsey obtained in 1518 and did all he could to further it. But while it is likely that a good many things were done of which the King knew nothing, but could be regarded as having exceeded the Legate's powers, in general Wolsey was amply authorized and probably had specific authorization, given orally or in writing, for particular acts. But he did not dare to say this; it was more politic to plead guilty and hope for the King's mercy.

Parliamentary action was taken against the fallen minister, including the passing by the House of Lords of what is often described as a bill of attainder (which is not too inaccurate a term for it) but which was, strictly speaking, a bill to disable Wolsey from ever again holding any office. When Parliament met at Blackfriars, Sir Thomas More, the new Lord Chancellor, standing at the right of the King explained that they had been summoned to rectify some abuses, which he did not indicate, and then launched into an attack on Wolsey. "As you see," he said, "that amongst a great flock of sheep some be rotten and faulty, which the good shepherd sendeth from the good sheep, so the great wether which is of late fallen, as you know, so craftily, so scabbedly, yea and so untruly juggled with the King, that all men must needs guess and think that he thought in himself that the King had no wit to perceive his crafty doing, or else that he presumed that the King would not see nor know his fraudulent juggling and attempts. But he was deceived, for his Grace's sight was so quick and penetrable that he saw him— yea, and saw through him—so that all thing to him was open. And according to his desert he hath had a mild correction. Which small punishment the King willeth not to be an example to other offenders, but clearly declareth that whosoever hereafter shall make like attempt to commit like offence will not escape with punishment."

The authenticity of that speech, which is reported by Hall, has been questioned, and it does seem harsh coming from More, who was never one of Wolsey's enemies. But it receives substantial corroboration from other sources, and it must be remembered that the Chancellor was speaking as the mouthpiece of the King and according to instructions. The point that should not be missed is that an assurance was given of a "gentle correction" in this instance, with a warning that others must not expect such lenient treatment.

On December 1, 1529, the disabling bill was presented to the House of Lords and passed by them, signed by seventeen of the peers, with the name of Sir Thomas More, by virtue of his office, at the head of the list of signatories. It was, however, drawn up not by More but by Lord Darcy.

This document contains forty-four articles, not all of which need be considered here. Some deal with trivialities, and at least one is absurd, for it accuses Wolsey of having endangered the King with the "great pox" (or syphilis) by whispering in his ear. Other charges, however, were all too well founded, though only a few specific actions of the Cardinal are mentioned. The thing to bear in mind is that the bill contains what had long been common knowledge and that in the nearly two months since Wolsey had fallen there had been ample time to gather substantiating material when necessary.

Several articles bore on the way that Wolsey had misused his

45

Legateship, but no article charged that he was guilty under Prae-munire for having exercised his Legateship at all. That was something thought of later. In addition to abuse of authority, the Cardinal was accused (Article XIX) of having "by his untrue suggestions to the Pope, shamefully slandered many good religious houses, and good virtuous men living in them," and Article XXI said plainly that, by the methods used against the suppressed monasteries, the Cardinal "and divers of his servants have gotten much riches, and your subjects suffered great wrongs."

This was enough to make Cromwell and even Archbishop Allen of Dublin shake in their boots. To make matters worse there was Article XXIV which read: "The same Lord Cardinal at many times when any houses of religion hath been void, he hath sent his officers thither, and with crafty persuasions hath induced them to compromit their election to him. And that, before ever he named or confirmed any of them, he and his servants received so much great goods of them, that in manner it hath been to the undoing of the house."

Had this bill been passed by the Commons, as it was passed by the Lords, it would hardly have been possible for Cromwell—at least Cromwell—to have escaped hanging. It is therefore a little strange that he should have been the man selected—we cannot but suppose at the King's instance—to make a speech against it. Cromwell probably did use the "witty persuasions" in Parliament that Cavendish mentioned, but what weighed most was the knowledge that the King wished the bill to be dropped quietly. The members did not dare go against him in this matter, greatly as they disliked Wolsey. As for Cromwell, the very fact that he had been put up to defend Wolsey showed he enjoyed the King's favor and would be protected.

One would give a good deal to have heard Cromwell's speech, for it must have been excellent comic entertainment. Yet it was no doubt powerful and plausible. We may be sure that he carefully steered away from the articles that asserted Wolsey's guilt under Praemunire, for Wolsey had already pleaded guilty. It is, however, likely enough that the House of Commons—largely made up of lawyers and hardheaded men of business—realized that Wolsey's condemnation for this offense, though it might be technically correct, was monstrously unjust, and that this inclined them to modera-

46

tion. Similarly we may be sure Cromwell avoided all mention of those articles in the bill that bore against the misdeeds of the Cardinal's agents. The bill was so long that it would not have been possible to deal with its contents point by point. As much would have had to be passed over adroitly, things that less directly concerned Wolsey could have been left out of the discussion.

Cromwell was given a chance of another sort, a chance he would hardly have missed. He might well have pointed out that the article charging Wolsey with having had an uncanonical wife and having married her to Mr. Lee of Aldington was irrelevant; so also was his loading his son young Thomas Winter with benefices and then pocketing nine-tenths of their revenues himself. These deeds were no doubt reprehensible but were not offenses that could be punished by law. And we may imagine that Cromwell contrived to explain away the charges of extortion and undue pressure made on religious houses. Even if this had been done, it was excess of zeal in a good cause, the founding of colleges intended to lift the standard of clerical education. Had the Cardinal's reformation only started a year or two earlier, the admirable results would already have been before everybody's eyes. Though the House was probably far from really convinced, it allowed itself to be convinced—at any rate to the extent of perceiving that it would be injudicious to proceed against the King's wishes.

Henry was of two minds about the permanent degradation of his immensely able minister; for where else could he find anyone nearly his equal? Sir Thomas More, the new Chancellor, though more finely gifted and of vastly superior character, had slight interest in politics as practiced and confirmed himself as much as possible to the judicial functions of his office. Here he had a good excuse: Wolsey had neglected them, so that there was much legal business to clear up. The Dukes of Norfolk and Suffolk were, the one of third-rate talent, the other less than that. Stephen Gardiner, who was about to be appointed Bishop of Winchester, was perhaps close to being first-rate, but he had not as yet fully proved this. Cromwell himself was of course at this time unthinkable for any office, serviceable though he was already showing himself.

The goodhearted, simple-minded Cavendish took Cromwell's defense of Wolsey as being the most generous devotion of a servant to a master fallen into adversity. Others thought so too. And Shakespeare, drawing very largely upon Cavendish, has popularized that version of the matter. While it need not be entirely ruled out, Cromwell must be said to have combined his devotion to Wolsey with a devotion to his own interests. Wolsey himself was grateful, for he was well aware that the country was bitterly antagonistic toward him. This was true of the nobles but even more true perhaps of Wolsey's fellow bishops. They were delighted at his fall, as this freed them from a tyranny under which they had groaned for more than ten years. Du Bellay, the French Ambassador, to whom Wolsey made many confidences, was of the opinion that the Cardinal had surrendered to the King mainly because he preferred to throw himself upon the royal mercy than suffer the animosity of his episcopal victims. As between the King and the Cardinal, the bishops preferred the King, never guessing to what the King's authority would lead. It was an attitude of mind that made it all the easier for the assertion of the royal supremacy over the Church. They may have surlily acknowledged that Wolsey had, according to his lights, sought to uphold the liberties of the Church, but they knew that the episcopate had had no liberty during his administration. They were glad to see him go, fondly believing that the Church in England would now revert to its pre-Wolseian state. The Pope himself was probably secretly glad to see Wolsey go, for the Papacy had had to endure much bullying from the English Cardinal. It was the King who was Wolsey's main hope. And time after time during these crucial days Henry showed his favor, sending him rings, then (secretly) four cartloads of furniture for the bare house at Esher. At the back of his mind flickered the idea that he might have to recall the Cardinal, whom he not only liked but looked upon as indispensable.

An incident recorded by Cavendish is perhaps more illuminating than he imagined. It occurred shortly after Cromwell had been given his seat in Parliament and knew himself to be safe. One day the Cardinal summoned his household into the great hall at Esher and, with tears, explained that he was destitute and so could not pay their wages—that he had, in fact, nothing but the clothes on his back. He had done this because Cromwell prompted him to it, asking, however, for his own wages. The Cardinal's reply was, "Alas, Tom, you know I have nothing to give you or them." Upon which Cromwell made a characteristic remark, revealing his contempt of the

48

clergy, "You have abundance of chaplains that have been preferred to benefices, some of a thousand or five hundred pounds, yet we your other servants, take more pains in one day's service than all your idle chaplains have done in a year."

The remark was not quite uncalled for; Wolsey *had* distributed rich livings to the priests who served him; but Cromwell ignored the circumstance that his own pickings in the suppression of monasteries had been enormous. To emphasize this contempt, he contributed five pounds sterling toward the paying of the servants, and by doing so obliged the chaplains who stood around to make at least equally good contributions. With what poured into the plate that day, Wolsey was able to pay part of the wages that were in arrears.

It might be noticed that Wolsey's servants were devoted to him— not only his chaplains and officers but his menials. He was haughty toward the rich and the powerful, but toward the humble he was kind, as he was just in his dealings with the unfortunate and the poor. These servants of the Cardinal's seemingly were content to continue in his service, even in the badly furnished house at Esher. A few may have slipped away to other employments, but he was still well attended. Cromwell had made sure that their service would continue.

The Council were for getting Wolsey as far away from the King as possible, in the fear that Henry might recall him. Even in late September, 1529, when Wolsey saw Henry for the last time and the Cardinal dropped some innocent remark that priests and bishops should be in the benefices to which they had been appointed and that he intended to go to Winchester, the Duke of Norfolk had growled, "Nay, to your benefice at York, where your principal charge is." The Duke meant that at York the Cardinal would be less likely to establish contact with the King. Early the next year, Cromwell—still plain "Thomas" to Norfolk—carried to Wolsey a message that if he did not go north the Duke would tear him with his teeth.

This, despite Norfolk's threats, was not done immediately. Wolsey moved from Esher to a house he had at Richmond, and it was there, as Cavendish relates, that he noticed on the walls a tile engraved with a dun cow, the emblem of the Tudors, who took this from their suppositious ancestor, the Welsh chieftain Cadwalader.

When Cavendish drew the Cardinal's attention to this tile, he got the comment: "Yea, marry, upon this cow hangs a certain prophecy that perhaps you never heard of. There is a saying that

> When the cow doth ride the bull
> Then, priest, beware thy skull."

It was, no doubt, one of Wolsey's clever impromptus. The bull of course was Anne Boleyn, at that time pronounced Bullen.

From Richmond the Cardinal moved, at the beginning of Lent, to a house Colet had built for periods of retirement on the grounds of the Charterhouse at Sheen. Now Cavendish and Cromwell used to find him sitting every day with a Carthusian monk, making a kind of retreat. He was going to spurn all the follies of the world, and as a sign of this he accepted from the Carthusian a hair shirt, though one may doubt whether he ever wore it. The sight was edifying, and Cromwell took it gravely, though his sardonic temperament could hardly have failed to be amused.

All this time Cromwell was, either by personal visits or letters, Wolsey's link with the Court. Wolsey completely trusted him. "Surely," he writes in one of many pitiful letters, "if you knew what heaviness of mind I am in at present and that the same doth daily more and more increase, I have no doubt that your gentle heart would have compassion thereof." This trust may indicate a failure of Wolsey's powers (he had once come very close to death from sheer grief at Esher), or it may indicate that Wolsey, wonderful as his judgment was when dealing with things in the mass—whole nations, or ideas, or institutions—was weak in his assessment of the individual character. But it may also indicate that Cromwell—at least in his relations with Wolsey, though even there within limits —was actually trustworthy.

Cromwell did what he could, relying upon the means that would have been effective with himself—that of trying to placate the Boleyn faction with pensions drawn from such endowments as Wolsey still possessed but being also careful to make those who received these favors feel grateful to himself. Even so, it helped the Cardinal to some extent. We find Wolsey writing to Cromwell in December, 1529: "If the displeasure of my Lady Anne be somewhat assuaged, as I pray God the same may be, then it should be devised that by some convenient mean she should be further labored, for this is the only remedy. All possible means must be used for the attaining of her favor. . . . I commit me to your wise handling." The upshot was that her brother George, now Viscount Rochford, got an annuity of two hundred pounds sterling from the Bishopric of Winchester, and another two hundred pounds sterling from the Abbey of St. Albans. Similarly Henry Norris, already in receipt of one hundred pounds sterling, had that sum doubled, and Sir John Russell had his annuity of twenty pounds sterling raised to fifty pounds sterling. Lord Sandys, Sir Henry Guildford, and Sir William Fitzwilliam were also pensioned, for no other reason than that they were of the Boleyn circle. It placated nobody, except for the moment, but the Cardinal was so desperate that he could think of nothing better than to try to purchase the good will of his enemies. It is questionable whether in the long run this did much good to Cromwell himself, as the pensions from Winchester had to be continued even after Stephen Gardiner went there as Bishop, and of course much to his annoyance. While the enmity that Gardiner came to feel toward Cromwell had better grounds, probably we can find here a secondary factor.

Though Cromwell was anxious to help Wolsey—for he was aware that the Cardinal might be restored to power—a somewhat contemptuous attitude shows itself in some of the letters he wrote at this time. The following might be accepted at its face value of pious commonplace were there not other letters. After Wolsey's conversion to religion Cromwell wrote to him, "I do reckon your Grace right happy that ye be now at liberty to serve God, and to learn to experiment how ye shall banish and exile the vain desires of this unstable world, which undoubtedly doth nothing else but allure every person therein, and especially such as our Lord hath endowed with His gifts, to desire the affections of their mind to be satisfied; in studying and seeking whereof, besides the great travails and afflictions that men suffer daily, most persons be driven to extreme repentance, and searching for pleasure and felicity find nothing but trouble, sorrow, anxiety and adversity. Wherefore, in mine opinion, your Grace being as ye are, I suppose ye would not be as ye were to win a hundred times as much as ever ye were possessed of." But Wolsey's enemies could not believe that of him, not if he wore a hundred hair shirts. Their one idea was to hurry him to York, where he would not be able to establish any contact

51

with an unstable king who, if he ever saw Wolsey again, might relent.

A coarse and greedy spirit sometimes emerges from Cromwell's letters to his former master. Thus in July, 1530, he writes to tell the Cardinal that he needs more money, that he is actually one thousand pounds sterling worse off than when his troubles began, which must have been untrue. Not only was he, as the distributor of the Cardinal's pensions, greatly strengthening his own position at Court; he was finding rich profits in the moneylending he was able to effect among the courtiers, most of whom found themselves obliged to live far beyond their means.

There is a patronizing tone in some of his letters to Wolsey, and this is very displeasing, even when the advice he is giving (unasked for) is sound. For instance, when Wolsey reached Cawood, in the Archdiocese of York, as he did in the early summer of 1530, he found that everything there was in rack and ruin. He therefore began to do some repair work, pushing this on with some of his old energy and employing 300 workmen. That number were probably needed to make a tumble-down mansion habitable, if this was to be done, as was necessary, in a short space of time. Immediately Wolsey's critics seized upon this: it was a sign that the builder of Hampton Court was still what he had always been. Therefore Cromwell wrote to him in August, "Your modest behavior and humility hath gained ye the love and good report of the country, yet your enemies deprave all. Sir, there be some that do allege that your Grace do keep too great a house and family and that you are continually a-building. For the love of God therefore have a respect and refrain." He says much the same thing in another letter written later in the same month.

These expostulations were uncalled for. Wolsey was making only urgently necessary renovations. The most hated man in England was becoming beloved by all who saw him in his new circumstances. Every Sunday he would ride with some of his clergy to neighboring churches, where he would say Mass and have one of his chaplains preach. Afterward he would administer Confirmation. Nor did he let his pastoral zeal rest with this: he used to invite the local notables to dinner—always bringing this with him, so as to put nobody to expense, and during dinner he would inquire whether any people in that parish were quarreling with one another. If so, he would send for these people and try to patch up their differences. He even let it be known, when the chapter of his cathedral at York came to see him to make arrangements for his long-belated installation on November 7, that though his predecessors had walked on similar occasions on carpets from St. James's chapel, "We intend to go on foot without any such pomp or glory."

His enemies simply refused to believe that he was a changed man. And it is a question whether Wolsey would not have leaped at a chance of restoration to power. It was a fact that he was attempting in a roundabout way to reach the King, and though this may have meant merely that the Cardinal hoped to regain Henry's friendship, it was not unnaturally interpreted as meaning much more than that. Agostini, the Cardinal's Venetian physician, was the bearer of some letters to the French Ambassador in London, letters begging him to get the King of France to intercede for Wolsey with Henry. That much was true and harmless enough. But Agostini, after getting a bribe of one hundred pounds sterling from the Duke of Norfolk, enlarged upon the matter; the Cardinal was, he said, in communication with the Pope and the Emperor—and the inference was that he was doing this by way of working against the royal divorce. It was enough to justify a treason charge.

The Cardinal was arrested three days before the date set for his installation in York Cathedral by one who had been a few years before one of his own gentlemen-in-waiting, Henry Percy, who had succeeded his father as Earl of Northumberland. Wolsey was taken to a house of the Earl of Shrewsbury, where he remained as an honored guest but still under technical arrest, until Sir William Kingston arrived with a band of the royal yeomen, most of them former servants of the Cardinal. Kingston was full of the deepest respect and tried to comfort his prisoner with assurances that no more was intended than to give him an opportunity to clear himself.

Wolsey was not deceived and asked Kingston not to bring him into a fool's paradise. "I know," he added, "what is prepared for me." He was well aware that when Henry struck in this way it was to kill. For a couple of days he was too ill to be moved, and when he got somewhat better he was still ill. By the time he and his escort reached Leicester Abbey, he was a dying man, and he announced at once that he had come to lay his bones there. Lying in his bed, he said to Kingston, "Let me advise you, if you be one of

53

the Privy Council, as by your wisdom you are fit, take heed what you put into the King's head, for you can never get it out again." It was to Kingston also that he made the remark, immortalized by Shakespeare (who has it addressed to Cromwell): "If I had served my God as diligently as I have done the King, He would not have given me over in my grey hairs." To Henry he sent a message advising him to be on guard against the spread of heresy in England. That too was a humble self-accusation. Wolsey had been remiss about this, partly because he had been busy with other things, but more because he had been unable to believe until then that England would ever be a soil in which heresy could take root. Yet no word was spoken, unless it was in the confession he made before death, that showed any compunction regarding the way he had behaved as Legate. Belatedly he had done what most bishops did when they fell out of favor at Court or grew old; he had attended to his diocese, and he had shown that he might have been an excellent shepherd of his flock. But he had weakened the English Church by concentrating all authority in his own hands. He had left dioceses vacant or had given them to foreigners residing abroad as a reward for diplomatic services; he had been highhanded and unjust; and his pride and avarice had been enormous. Yet if (as is possible) he did not realize that these were things of which he should repent, they were not subjectively sins in his case. Probably his relations with Miss Larke were not mentioned; undoubtedly they had been previously confessed, so there was no obligation to go into them again. But there is no need to speculate as to what Cardinal Wolsey did or did not confess on his deathbed: he was not a fool; he knew that in a few hours he would have to answer to God. We may be sure that he confessed everything of which he believed himself guilty.

God may have forgiven him; it is not very easy for us to do so. He had brought the English Church into a condition, by cowing its bishops and clergy, which would enable the King to take over the concentrated authority the Chancellor-Legate had enjoyed. And he had trained in Thomas Cromwell a man who perfectly understood how to bring this about, encouraging him to browbeat, cajole, and trick the heads of religious institutions to extract lands, money, or plate from them. In Wolsey's service Cromwell had come to see that the clergy of England, even when they seemed rich and powerful, were poor-spirited and could easily be subdued

54

by one who came armed, as he was, with the requisite authority. Further he had seen that this authority could be naked tyranny, that the monasteries of England could be terrified into surrender or into proffering huge bribes to be allowed to continue to exist.

Cardinal Wolsey had been, in England, Vice-King and Vice-Pope; it had not yet dawned on Henry that he could be Pope as well as King. But to the man Wolsey had trained, this was already clear, and he was soon to show Henry how it might be brought about. There might never have been any Protestant Reformation in England, had not Wolsey, quite unwittingly, prepared for it by taking as his servant the efficient, the quietly ruthless, and the infinitely corrupt Thomas Cromwell.

Chapter Four

THE SCHEME

In DECEMBER, 1530, Thomas Cromwell was at last free to take things over. Not that he had been waiting for the Cardinal to die, except in the sense that everybody felt as soon as that happened there would be great changes in England. Even while he was out of office and in obscurity, the tremendous force of the Cardinal was remembered; not until he was safely dead could anyone be sure that he would not return to take charge of affairs. In the meanwhile there had been a kind of marking of time, with no decisive action taken. Whatever was done had to be tentative, conditional, in the nature of half measures.

Cromwell as yet was a man of no official standing. For though he gave advice, it was in private, for he was not a member of the Council until the following year. Though it was evident that the King had come to rely upon him a good deal and was finding important use for his services, nobody expected his astonishing rise, perhaps not even Cromwell himself. Wolsey's place as Chancellor had been filled by Sir Thomas More, a man who had accepted it reluctantly and with the stipulation that he would not be called upon to do anything connected with the royal divorce of which, as was well-known, he disapproved. He presided at the Council when the King was not present, and he presided also in the House of Lords. He enjoyed at home and abroad an immense reputation, but this was as a wit, a scholar, a writer, a judge inflexible in his integrity; he was not a politician. As for the Duke of Norfolk, the most influential of the men around the King, he owed his position to the fact that he was the leading figure among the older aristocracy. His talents were not of a high order. He had succeeded, in conjunction with Anne Boleyn, in overthrowing Wolsey; he was incapable of taking Wolsey's place.

The fact that More was Lord Chancellor was of considerable significance. Only once or twice before—and a long time before—had the chancellorship been held by one not a high ecclesiastic. More's position indicated that the lay politician was about to come into his own. Hitherto the best that a layman could hope for was a job in the bureaucracy, and these jobs were not well paid—pitifully badly paid, in fact, compared with the bishoprics with which priest-diplomats were rewarded. Though men of this sort often found opportunities for rich pickings on the side, they did not direct policy. But Cromwell was already directing policy to some extent, if only behind the scenes as yet. He must have recognized that his chance had come.

He had, however, nothing to do with the decision to arrest the Cardinal, about which he may have not known. Even had he known of it, he could have done nothing to prevent it. He may have surmised that Henry had permitted the arrest as a means of finding an excuse for meeting Wolsey again. Wolsey's enemies also may have surmised this, for they were in no hurry to bring him to London and were greatly relieved when the ailing man died. As for Henry, he was so discouraged when he heard of the Cardinal's death that, according to Pole, he was on the point of giving up the project of the royal divorce, as he saw nobody else competent to carry this through. That, too, gave Cromwell his chance: he had thought out a plan of his own, and this he now presented to the King.

It might seem a little surprising that Cromwell, who was still known to be Wolsey's agent, was not suspected of some complicity in what Wolsey was charged with—or, it would be surprising did not Wolsey's enemies know that his friend was no enemy to them. Skillfully Cromwell had contrived to keep a foot in both camps. While credited with being loyal to the Cardinal, it was well understood that he would never carry that loyalty to the point where he would suffer on its account.

The King now was brought to think of him as the practical man

57

who would come to the rescue. While Henry was not yet quite ready to put himself completely in Cromwell's hands, he was at least inclined to believe that he had in him somebody who would find a way of cutting through the intricate webs that canon lawyers and theologians love to weave. The King's innate disposition was to observe all the forms of law, so that it was not until three years later that Henry was brought to a complete conviction that Cromwell was perfectly sound in his judgment, namely, that the only way he could obtain his divorce was by breaking with Rome and ordering an English ecclesiastical court to do what was required. To the last moment he did his best to avoid schism, and while he accepted advice from Cromwell which was, as he perceived, likely to lead to this schism, he continued to hope that a breach with the Papacy could be avoided. Cromwell believed from the outset that the breach would prove to be inevitable. Wolsey's idea that the Pope could be bullied or frightened into doing what Henry wanted had proved a failure. Clement had shown weakness, but he had not yielded. Instead he had tried stratagems and had temporized. That sort of thing might go on forever. Cromwell's policy was that of cowing the Church at home and using it as an instrument against Rome.

He had committed himself to finding a sure means of obtaining a divorce for Henry. And yet that divorce was only a detail in his larger plans. The divorce, in fact, merely provided him with the opportunity he would otherwise have lacked. What he really aimed at was to put the monarchy in England on a new basis, to have it retain the constitutional forms by acting through Parliament but to make the monarchy in effect absolute. And to complete the process the Church had to be subjected to the King.

As Cromwell was at this time operating entirely in the shadows, it may be asked how this can be confidently said of him. It might indeed be inferred from what we know of his steady adhesion to plan and of Henry's unstable character; but where is the positive evidence? Well, we shall catch sight of Cromwell's hand from time to time and grow more and more certain that it was directing everything, even when not actually visible. But there is a letter written in 1540 by Cardinal Pole to James V of Scotland in which he says that at this time, when Henry was on the point of abandoning as hopeless his attempts to obtain a divorce, Cromwell showed him how he could effect his desires: instead of being bound by what was considered right in the schools, he should make himself Head of of the Church.

It should be remembered that Pole, not yet a Cardinal nor even an ecclesiastic, was in England in 1530, and, being the King's cousin and friend, he saw a good deal of him. He was able therefore to speak as one "in the know." This is only one more instance of the familiar fact that the true story as known to an inner intimate circle is often vastly different from the official version given out for popular consumption. But this case is, however, not exactly one of an official story, though many of the moves were planned in secret and often designed to mislead. What can be affirmed is that until Wolsey's death these moves were hesitant and lacking in power, but that after Cromwell's appearance upon the scene they were, while still often secret, according to a consistent design.

The dejection Henry felt after Wolsey's death was not the first of these fits. While Anne Boleyn might, and did, upbraid him from time to time for not pressing on the matter more vigorously, that was useless unless there was some sort of a plan. Wolsey had had one and been confident that it would work, but it had broken down. Even so, Henry had several times appeared to be on the point of recalling him and giving him a chance to try again; but each time there was hesitation, and now the Cardinal was dead. Henry was now willing to let Cromwell see what he could do.

The year 1530 passed in futilities. There was the bad blunder of sending an embassy in January to the Emperor, headed by the Earl of Wiltshire, Anne's father. Wiltshire blundered further by offering Charles 300,000 crowns of Katherine's dowry, only to get the cutting reply that his aunt was not for sale. Then there was the petition to the Pope in July signed by the English nobility and episcopate and twenty-three abbots, something permissible enough, though it used rather threatening terms. It only served to draw from Clement VII a mild suggestion as to the mending of manners. Neither of these ideas is likely to have originated with Cromwell.

By far the best of the ideas of this year was Cranmer's. It was what first brought that obscure Cambridge don into the public eye. He was wellborn but of an impoverished family, gentle, timid, fertile in resources, and invariably pliable to the royal will. He was later to prove himself, in his Book of Common Prayer, one of the greatest of prose stylists. He suggested that the universities of Christendom be canvassed for their opinions. It was taken for granted that these opinions would be favorable to the King, and there were means of ensuring this. In England pressure could be brought to bear on Oxford and Cambridge, and abroad enough of the dissenters could be bought to give Henry a majority vote. Then Clement would have an excuse, which he would be glad (so it was thought) to avail himself of; this would relieve him of the responsibility of making a decision. The trouble here was that the venality involved defeated its own object.

Henry was a man who originated very little. Quick and clever as his mind was, it operated on the surface of things, never going very deep, for he was fundamentally lazy. He was infinitely cunning, but, except in a minor fashion in the arts, he was not creative. Having let it be known what he wanted—at this time and for some years to come, it was freedom to marry Anne Boleyn—he looked to others to find the means for bringing this about. His part in the matter was hardly more than using his devious charm to throw dust in the eyes of the Papacy and of foreign ambassadors. As such he was very useful—perhaps indispensable—but others always had to map out the plan of campaign.

In this case it was Cromwell. Yet Cromwell had to be careful. Henry would have been shocked at the suggestion that England cut itself off from communion with Rome. He had to be led up to this by degrees, and he accepted this solution in the end only because he was gradually put into a position from which there was no escape, short of complete surrender. He had started of course as early as 1515 with rather strong claims as to his authority over the Church; but schism was not in his mind. It was not in his mind even when he later threatened schism; he supposed that threats would bring the Pope to heel. Cromwell maneuvered him; Cromwell managed him.

Cromwell, however, could not have done this were not Henry's mind receptive. At the end of 1529, when Cromwell had little influence or none, Du Bellay, the French Ambassador, was able to write to his King, "The Lords intend, after Wolsey is dead or ruined, to impeach the state of the Church and to take all its goods; which is hardly necessary for me to write in cipher, for they proclaim it openly." Earlier that year Simon Fish's famous little book

The Supplication of Beggars had been widely circulated, there is reason to suppose with Henry's connivance. This estimated that a third of the entire wealth of the country—later Fish said it was nearer a half—was in the possession of the Church. He even worked out some fantastic statistics to show that the friars alone obtained yearly offerings that amounted to £433,333.6.8, arrived at by asserting that there were 52,000 parishes in England, each containing an average of ten households, and that each household might be presumed to contribute a penny every quarter to the five orders. Thomas More promptly replied to him, proving how preposterous such estimates were and remarking that he knew of only seven members of the nobility in favor of dispossessing the friars and monks, and that of those seven three were dead. More, however, was mistaken. The majority of the nobility acquiesced in the spoliation when it was carried out and accepted their share of the loot, even when they had not actively promoted it.

The scheme of spoliation was in the air, especially after Wolsey had demonstrated what could be done. But indeed 120 years earlier Sir John Oldcastle (better known as Lord Cobham) had introduced a bill into Parliament which, after allowing 40,000 priests a stipend of seven marks a year, would have made possible the endowment out of ecclesiastical revenues of 15 new earls, 1,500 knights, and 6,200 squires, with an extra twenty thousand pounds sterling a year for the King. Nothing had come of this, and Cobham had been burned at the stake for the heretic he was. But now there was a revival of interest in his ideas, and Henry sent to Oxford for Wycliffe's books. How good it would be for the clergy to return to evangelical poverty—especially as this would mean additional affluence for his Majesty and the peerage!

Henry's mood changed from day to day, and his ideas were far more moderate and cautious than those of Cromwell. Sometimes an appeal could be made to his cupidity, sometimes to his pride. But Cromwell also knew how to work upon his vanity: the King could take up the work of reformation started by the Cardinal. Henry may even have toyed with the notion that this would give him prestige in the eyes of the Pope. This new service to the Church might bring him the reward he deserved.

If so, such a fancy could have been entertained only fleetingly. While seeking to retain at least a nominal obedience of England to the Pope, he permitted himself to be guided along a road which led far away from Rome. A Florentine in London wrote just after Wolsey's death—that is to say in December, 1530—"Nothing else is thought of on that island every day except of arranging affairs in such a way that they no longer be in want of the Pope, neither for filling vacancies in the Church, nor for any other purpose." Here, as in what Du Bellay wrote at about the same time, there was a certain amount of exaggeration, but it is more than likely that Cromwell's plan of separation from the Holy See was finding many supporters in Court circles. And Cromwell was looked upon as the man capable of carrying this plan through. By the spring of 1531 he was appointed to the Council, where he at once became one of its most influential figures. Two years later Chapuys was able to write to the Emperor that "[Cromwell] has been constantly rising in power, so much so that he now has more influence with his master than the Cardinal ever had; for in the latter's time there were Compton, the Duke of Suffolk and others, to whose advice the King occasionally listened, whereas now-a-days everything is done at his bidding. The Chancellor [the new Chancellor, Sir Thomas Audley] is but a tool in his hands."

The method finally decided upon was to intimidate the clergy under the threat of holding them all guilty under the law of Praemunire. Yet the first intimation of this is in a letter Cromwell wrote to Wolsey on October 21, 1530, which tells him that the prelates are not to be indicted under that statute: "There is another way devised, as your Grace shall know further." This way would appear to have been the renewal of the request by the King, through his agents in Rome, for permission to commit bigamy. Sir Gregory da Casale had written on September 18 to say that this had been suggested by Clement as a solution. Casale was misinformed, as was soon to appear, but it was his letter that led to the dropping of Praemunire.

Such a request sounds too astonishing for credence. It was not, however, quite so shocking as it might appear. From Henry's point of view he was not asking for a dispensation for bigamy but merely to be allowed to take a new wife, leaving the troublesome question as to whether he was or was not married to Katherine undecided. But that Casale grossly misunderstood the matter is evident from a letter written by Dr. Benet, Henry's other agent in Rome, on

62

October 27. This says: "I asked Clement VII if he were certain that such a dispensation was admissable, and he answered that it was not; but he added that a distinguished theologian had told him that in his opinion the Pope might dispense in order to avert a greater evil; he intended, however, to go into the matter more fully with his council. And indeed the Pope has just now informed me that his council (known as the Consistory of Cardinals) had declared to him plainly that such a dispensation was not possible." Such an answer was so inevitable that we can only suspect Clement had been once more playing for a little more time. When Benet's letter reached England, the Cromwellian plan of the use of Praemunire had to be taken up again. It was proposed to make the penalties of the statute apply to the entire nation, clergy and laity alike, which would mean that only Henry himself would escape under the legal fiction that the King can do no wrong. As Parliament refused to admit guilt or to compound with a fine, the laity were, in the end, untouched; but the application of Praemunire against the clergy was rigorously pressed.

Brewer has described Parliament under Henry as hardly more than a court for registering the King's decrees. Though it is true there were occasions when it refused to do so, in general it was very subservient. Wolsey had disliked calling Parliaments at all and did so only under extreme necessity. But under Cromwell a technique not altogether new was perfected: it was that of turning elections into a mere matter of form, for the sheriff on receiving a writ summoned the electors or such of them as he chose to notify and then presented the name he had received from some member of the Council. In Cromwell's own case, as we have seen, he was directly appointed by the Duke of Norfolk on November 1, 1529, to the Parliament that was to meet two days later.

The packing of Parliament at this time has sometimes been denied, on the ground that the evidence is too scanty to affirm it. And it is true that the system of packing had not received the development Cromwell gave it later. But Sir Thomas More, who had been Speaker of the House of Commons in 1523 and presided over the House of Lords as Chancellor from 1529 to 1532, when he received sentence of death three years later, said in his speech after sentence, "And God knows what kind of a Parliament!" as though referring to its venality and subservience as facts too notorious to be questioned. Stubbs says on this point that he has to reject altogether that Henry VIII was "the interpreter in any sense of the wishes of his people: the utmost that he did in this direction was to manipulate and utilize their prejudices to his own purpose. I allow fully the truth of the theory that one great principle of his policy was to obtain for his measures, for all his measures, the acquiescence of his people, and thus to invest them with a safe, irrefragable authority; but I must add that he knew how to turn opposition into acquiescence, or to take acquiescence for granted." F. W. Maitland goes even further when he asserts that "the nation was thoroughly frightened by Henry. But what does demand our notice is that this very tractability of parliaments serves in the end to save and strengthen the parliamentary constitution; parliament is so very tractable that the king is very willing that the king in parliament should be recognised as supreme—it strengthens his hands that what he does should be the act of the whole nation." Finally Sir Courtenay Ilbert writes that "Henry VIII accepted Henry IV's principle that the king should rule through parliament, but worked that principle in an entirely different way. He made parliament the engine of his will. He persuaded or frightened it into doing anything he pleased. Under his guidance parliament defied or crushed all other powers, spiritual and temporal, and did things that no king or parliament had ever attempted to do, things unheard of and terrible." If in later reigns Parliament succeeded in establishing its independence and even a domination over the Crown, this was because the spoliation of the monasteries—with which the Parliament that assembled in 1529 ended its work—created a new landed class whose power became greater than the King's. It was this class that made up the great bulk of the parliamentary membership. And it must always be remembered it was Cromwell, far more than Henry, who engineered all that was done, though of course Cromwell could manipulate Parliament as he did because standing behind him was the awe-inspiring figure of the King.

The subservience of Parliament at this time is indicated by the promptness with which it canceled the King's debts, those extortions euphemistically called an Amicable Loan. The action was all the more deplorable because the royal I.O.U.'s had been used as negotiable notes and were now quite worthless to the purchasers. Professor Pollard, who loses no opportunity to say what he can in extenuation of Henry, blandly explains that had these debts not been canceled, they would have had to be met out of taxation which would have fallen upon many, whereas the Amicable Loan was contributed to only by the well to do. This explanation would be more convincing except that the Crown had large revenues out of which public needs were supposed to be supplied. The debts could have been paid off had Henry only been willing to curb his personal extravagance. In any event taxation would have been more honest. But the fact is that the debts were canceled as a method of purchasing exemption in the matter of Praemunire.

The clergy, meeting in Convocation, also tried to purchase their exemption. When it met early in 1531, they were given to understand that an especially large grant would be expected from them. Accordingly the Convocation of Canterbury, meeting in London, voted £40,000. This was refused as insufficient, whereupon the grant was raised to £100,000. This also was refused unless the clergy acknowledged the King to be supreme head of the Church.

Even that did not mean all the King was to claim later, but it was more than enough to cause great alarm. Baron del Burgo, the papal Nuncio, a layman, went to the assembly to beg it not to give in. But everybody was so terrified that the Nuncio was asked to leave at once. Then Anne Boleyn's brother was sent to them to say that, if they objected to the proposed formula, the title of "the Supreme Head after God" would be acceptable to the King. Of course they saw that this was even more sweeping. And when Warham, the Archbishop of Canterbury, suggested still another formula, "We recognise his Majesty as the singular Protector, and only Supreme Lord, and so far as the law of Christ allows, even Supreme Head," he was met with silence. It was very evident that the assembly did not like the formula, even with its restriction. But as something had to be done, Warham said, "Silence gives consent." At this somebody called out, "Then are we all silent!" upon which the Archbishop declared the motion passed. It did, after all, have a qualification which could be considered as rendering it meaningless. But Chapuys put his finger on the truth when he wrote that it was "all the same as far as the King is concerned if they had made no reservation, for no one will now be so bold as to contest with his lord the importance of this reservation." Nor did it greatly matter that the Convocation of York, sitting under Tunstall, the Bishop of Durham, as Wolsey's place had not yet been filled, accepted the formula on the understanding that it applied only to temporalities and did not affect the Church's spiritual jurisdiction. Though the formula served to soothe troubled consciences, the King had been assured that his clergy would be subject to his will.

Henry, however, had not finished with the clergy. The following year he used Parliament against them, simultaneously getting passed the first Annates Bill—depriving the Pope of his dues from newly appointed bishops—and instigating the presentation of the petition of the Commons against the Ordinaries—ostensibly a plea for reform but actually an attack on the clergy—both of course directed by Cromwell. Yet the Annates Bill was forced through only when the King went to the House of Commons to observe how each member voted. To suspend the actual application of the act for a year suited his purposes well enough, for it enabled him to notify the Pope that it would be permanently suspended if Clement did what was wanted in the matter of the divorce. At the same time he informed the Pope—in complete variance with the truth—that the act had been passed by an indignant people against his personal wishes and that he was doing all he could to try and hold back encroachments on the papal preserves. He felt sure that Clement would give in when his revenues were cut off, for the Annates were the first fruits, the first year's income that a newly appointed bishop paid into the papal treasury. As for Parliament, it had no quarrel with the Pope, with however jaundiced an eye many of its members may have regarded the clergy in England. The Pope had done England no harm, and while there was no very intense enthusiasm for him, Parliament saw no reason why he should be injured in this or any other way.

It was a somewhat different story with regard to the Supplication Against the Ordinaries, though here what seemed spontaneous was actually officially prompted. Even if we did not have several copies of this famous document in Cromwell's own handwriting or at least revised by him, its contents would show who inspired it. Some of the charges, if soundly based, would indicate there was much in the ecclesiastical practices of the times calling for reform. Nobody will deny the crying evils of pluralities, the giving of benefices by bishops to relatives too young to perform their duties, or the charging of excessive fees by the spiritual courts which probated all wills.

But it is not to be believed that "the said prelates and ordinaries daily do permit and suffer the parsons, vicars, curates, parish priests and other spiritual persons having cure of souls within this realm to exact and take of your humble and obedient subjects divers sums of money for the sacraments and sacramentals of Holy Church, as the Holy Sacrament of the Altar, Baptism, Matrimony, Confession, Burials, Weddings, Churchings and such other, sometimes denying the same without they first be paid the said sum of money." While customary fees were usually paid (then as now) for some clerical services—not, however, for Holy Communion or Confession—to demand them as by right in the form of fixed charges is contrary to canon law and plain Christian morals. But of course the real aim in all this was to disable Convocation so that it could not make any regulations without the consent of the King.

The Supplication was presented by a deputation from the House of Commons, and after it had been given to the bishops and they had made their reply, Henry sent for the deputation again and told them, with fine impartiality, "We think this answer will smally please you, for it seemeth to us very slender. You be a great sort of wise men: I doubt not but you will look circumspectly in the matter, and we will be indifferent between you." His "indifference" was of course an incitement to further attack.

As though further to show his impartiality, Henry announced to Parliament on May 11 a new discovery, saying, "Well beloved subjects, we thought that the clergy of our realm had been our subjects wholly; but now we have well perceived that they be but half our subjects—yea, and scarce our subjects. For all the prelates at their consecration make an oath to the Pope clean contrary to the oath they make to us, so that they seem his subjects and not ours." This was sheer effrontery, for any incongruity between the two oaths told against the Pope rather than the King; every bishop, upon receiving his temporalities, swore to renounce any grants made by the Holy See if they should be found injurious to the Crown.

Convocation had by this time been brought to a realization that it was powerless to resist and so five days later made what is called the Submission of the Clergy. This did not pass the House of Lords, where Sir Thomas More, the Chancellor, and Bishop Gardiner led the opposition. But though it did not obtain statutory force for another two years, it went into immediate application because of

Convocation's timidity. The most that its members ventured to do was to indicate that their submission was personally made to King Henry and not applicable to his successors. To him, however, they yielded, because they recognized his "excellent wisdom, princely goodness, and fervent zeal in the promotion of God's honor and the Christian religion"; also because his learning far exceeded "in our judgment the learning of all other kings and princes that we have read of."

What Convocation should have done and would have done had it dared, was to have refused this submission and the Oath of Supremacy, even with its qualifying clause. Henry could not have hanged the entire body of priests in England nor would have ventured to proceed against the leaders of a united clergy. But nobody had any zest for martyrdom, and concerted action was made difficult by the uneasy feeling of many priests that, however disingenuous many of the complaints brought against them, those complaints were, in some instances, not without justification. So they gave in without striking a blow. From thenceforth the King, under Cromwell's direction, forced the English Church to act against the Church Universal. Convocation as well as Parliament was turned into an instrument to be used against the Pope.

The ground had been unconsciously prepared for this by Wolsey. He had tyrannized over the individual bishops and abbots, but he had at the same time done his best to guard the liberties and prerogatives of the Church, taken as a whole; however, what he had actually done was to make that whole extremely vulnerable. After his fall a sigh of relief went up, and the English episcopate enjoyed a year of freedom until his death. Then by steady pressure, one step being taken at a time, the liberties and prerogatives were taken away and with them rather more than half the wealth of the Church.[1]

Even if we did not have Chapuys's statement that the measures mentioned were "Cromwell's devices"; even if we did not have memoranda in Cromwell's writing about drawing up the anticlerical

[1] This expression, "the wealth of the Church," should not be misunderstood. As a corporate body the Church possessed nothing. Each diocese and religious house or hospital or parish church possessed its own endowments, which varied greatly in value. In the aggregate these holdings were large, perhaps too large. But usually the separate endowments were hardly excessive, and in the majority of cases they were almost pitifully small.

bills and getting them passed, we would be able to recognize the Cromwell touch. He kept Parliament in session for a period hitherto unprecedented (1529 to 1536) solely on account of the dispute with the Papacy, for normally a parliament sat for only a few weeks. Even after the breach with Rome in the spring of 1534, the legislature met again at the end of that year to pass laws designed to send such men as More and Bishop Fisher to death. And then it met again early in 1536 to pass the act suppressing the smaller monasteries. All through the process Henry insisted upon all the constitutional forms being duly observed, making his tyranny the more obnoxious by its pedantry. And in nearly everything done the architect of the new structure that was to go up on the existing ruins was Thomas Cromwell.

There was a considerable difference in the point of view of the King and his minister, close as was their collaboration. Henry hoped that every new blow directed against the Church in England would serve to bring the Pope to his knees. The Church in England quickly succumbed; the Church Universal, weakly and badly as it was guided, did not. Yet though by degrees Henry came to think of the Papacy as his enemy, he was essentially a conservative to whom anything revolutionary was abhorrent. But much as he wished to keep religion, and even the local ecclesiastical organization, what they had been, he was determined to have his own way. And working with him, and for him, was the perfect revolutionary, the man utterly without conscience, who could always be depended upon to find the means for effecting what the King wanted.

Cromwell was able to take advantage of Henry's pride and stubbornness and his thirst to augment his authority by representing that his own political philosophy was identical with that of the King. There were sufficient points of contact. The minister with a power that was to be without a previous parallel in history crystallized the idea latent in many minds that the monarch must be paramount in Church as well as State. In the case of most reformers, they are driven by force of circumstances further than they wish. Thus Christiani in his chapter, "The Reformation of the Continent," in *The Cambridge Modern History*, says of Luther that "anxious to restore ecclesiastical discipline, but incapable of returning to the Pope and admitting his error, he saw that the one course open to him was to entrust the control of his Church to the princes. He had begun with a dream of liberty and equality among all Christians, subject only to the Word of God; he was to end with a *State Church*. The dictum of the Protestant historian Harnack is, therefore, well founded: 'The Reformation ends in a contradiction.'" Cromwell, on the other hand, was never under any illusions: a State Church was what he aimed at from the outset. He was not one of those goodhearted, simple-minded people who sigh regretfully at the end of the process, "Well, it has all turned out so differently from what we had intended!" Religious confusion aplenty came later and has steadily increased down to our own time. But what Cromwell effected in his own time turned out exactly as he had intended—or almost so—for he and Cranmer were never able to make Henry go as far as they would have liked. Church and State were put under a single head, in which theoretically the King was, in his political aspect, a constitutional monarch, but in his ecclesiastical aspect, a despot of the kind such as no Pope had ever dreamed of being. The enslavement of the Church was all the more complete in that the royal domination, as conceived by Cromwell, compelled the Church meekly to request further and further degrees of enslavement.

This was not brought about, nor could it be brought about, at a single stroke. From the start it was evident that the Church was bewildered and frightened. But it was still powerful and wealthy, still capable of resistance should it choose to fight. However, what was accomplished by the oath of 1531 and the submission of 1532 made it difficult, if not impossible, for the Church to reverse the course of events, especially as the ultimate end that Cromwell had in mind was carefully concealed.

There were some curious happenings during 1531. Not long after Chapuys wrote to the Emperor on January 23, "The Bishop of Rochester [John Fisher] lately sent to me to say that the King had made new efforts to suborn him and others who hold for the Queen," an attempt was made to poison Fisher. His cook, a man named Richard Rouse, was arrested and admitted having put some powder in the soup but asseverated that he did not know what it contained. Under torture he probably revealed a good deal more; if so, his confessions were suppressed. This was, in the general mind, attributed to the implication of the Boleyn faction in the crime. Henry was so terrified at the idea of poison that he had a bill passed in Parliament in which Rouse's name was mentioned, and with retroactive effect, that poisoners should be boiled alive. And the chronicler of the Grey Friars records, "This year was a cook boiled in a cauldron at Smithfield, for he would have poisoned the Bishop of Rochester, Fisher. He was locked in a chair and pulled up and down with a gibbet at divers times till he was dead." Further color was given to the suspicions against the Boleyns by the fact that a gun—the damage that it did clearly showed it must have been a small piece of ordnance—was fired across the river at Fisher's house at Lambeth, breaking some of the tiles and rafters. It could not be proved that it had been fired from the Boleyns' house, but their house was certainly in the neighborhood from which the missile had been aimed. Fisher thought it prudent to leave Lambeth and return to Rochester.

It was about this time that Henry had introduced into Parliament a bill pardoning the clergy's offenses under Praemunire—their pardon having been purchased by heavy payments from the Convocations of Canterbury and York and also by the Oath of Supremacy —but when the Commons saw that the laity were not included in the pardon they refused to pass it. Chapuys reported, "In the House of Commons . . . it was publicly said that the King had burdened and oppressed his kingdom with more imposts and exactions than any three or four of his predecessors, and that he ought to consider that the strength of the King lay in the affections of his people." Henry, who had undoubtedly been hoping he would be able to force from the laity a grant equal to that made by the clergy, saw at once that it would be inadvisable to press such a demand. He had to be content with the parliamentary cancellation of his debts. Accordingly two bills, pardoning the temporality and the spirituality, were passed simultaneously. But this act of grace of course left the King all the more free to make other demands upon Parliament.

Only about 1533 did it fully dawn upon people—even on so acute an observer as Chapuys—that Cromwell was the real director of affairs. Audley, at first only Keeper of the Seal but a little later Chancellor, was known to be negligible. The Duke of Norfolk was thought of as the King's main adviser. But the general belief— which was carefully encouraged—was that the changes occurring originated with the King himself. Only in this way had they any chance of acceptance. There would have been an uproar had it become known that the baseborn and disreputable adventurer Cromwell was at the back of everything. He had to take care not to emerge from the shadows too soon.

What Cromwell's relations were with Anne Boleyn at this time it would be hard to say. The sprightly young woman with the slender neck and the dark eyes and the long unbound hair (she was not so very young in 1533, probably thirty, which would have made her regarded as almost an old maid) preferred sprightly young men around her, and the heavy, unprepossessing Cromwell would have been of no interest to her. If she was a little afraid of him, it would not be surprising: he was probably present when Cardinal Wolsey gave her a wigging about her early infatuation for young Henry Percy, and he would have almost certainly been present when Wolsey, in the presence of his officers and attendants, told Percy bluntly that Mistress Boleyn was not for him.[2] Yet not until some time later did the King decide, to the great loss of his personal dignity, to enter into competition with the young men with whom she liked to flirt and from whom she was to permit, even after she had become Queen, a freedom not much to her credit. Cromwell would of course have flattered her on such occasions as they met; and she, after thinking of him first merely as a mysterious person often closeted with the King, may have come sooner than most people to a realization that here was the maker of a new England, one with whom her own fortunes were to be closely related.

Chapuys, her enemy, credited her with great courage and intelligence. Courage she undoubtedly had, and intelligence she showed to the extent of playing her cards well, refusing Henry's written and spoken importunities, declining to become his mistress (as her sister Mary had previously been), and demanding nothing less than the position of wife. In this she showed extraordinary tenacity. Except at the start she was not managed by her family, for her uncle the Duke of Norfolk thought she was in danger of overreaching herself. And her father, who had been complacent already about his

---

[2] Cavendish jumped to the conclusion that Henry already had his eye on her. The truth, however, was that he broke off her match with Percy because he wished her to marry the Earl of Ormonde, as a means of satisfying by compromise a claim that her father was asserting to the earldom. This Ormonde marriage would have taken place had not the Butlers asked too much.

72

daughter Mary, feared that Anne might be aiming too high, believing that it might be safer for her to be the King's mistress. But Anne had seen how Mary had been discarded without anything being done for her, and she knew that the same had happened to Bessie Blount, the mother of the royal bastard, the Duke of Richmond. She had made up her mind that she was not going to be treated like that. For some years she had her own apartments in whatever palace the King occupied at the moment, with Queen Katherine under the same roof—until in 1532 Henry rode out early one morning from Windsor Castle never to see Katherine again. Yet Anne, though many regarded her as the King's mistress, steadily held him off until she could be sure of being his wife.

It was through Anne that Cromwell had come into power. For though she had no part in pushing his fortunes, yet had there been no Anne, Cromwell would never have found his astounding opening. The Cardinal had had many powerful enemies, but Anne was the enemy who finally brought him down. In Cromwell's case there was no danger of his arousing her animosity. Rather, when she grew aware of what he was doing, she perceived that all his activities tended to her benefit. She felt no special reason to be grateful to him on this account, as her benefit was only incidental; but at least she had reason to encourage Henry to place his confidence in a man so obviously competent and so full of resource.

It was the same with Thomas Boleyn, now Earl of Wiltshire, and his son George, Viscount Rochford. The Earl had risen coincidentally with his daughters' favors with the king, though it would be too much to say that his rise was solely on this account, as he had been a serviceable official, entitled to some reward, even if an earldom was more than he had a right to expect. He was a man whose grandfather, a Lord Mayor of London, had enriched himself in the wool trade; therefore Thomas Boleyn had been able to marry a daughter of the Duke of Norfolk at a time when he was not yet even Earl of Surrey. The Howards were at the time still in partial eclipse, suffering from the effects of having fought for Richard III instead of the usurping Tudor at the battle of Bosworth. A dapper little man, cunning and cautious, Wiltshire was distinguished in no way except by his love of money and his ability to survive. Chapuys wrote that he and Anne were "more Lutheran than Luther himself," but this was only to say that the Boleyns and their faction were antipapal. In 1533 Thomas Boleyn had served on the commission that found John Frith guilty of holding heretical views about the Eucharist. As in the case of Cranmer, who had been his chaplain and Anne's tutor for a while and was far more responsible than Boleyn in sending Frith to the stake, his own views were probably not unlike Frith's save that they were less distinct than Cranmer's. Yet his so-called Lutheranism merely meant that it was to the interest of his group to throw their influence, of course with all due caution, on the side of the new religious trends. George Boleyn, of all the members of the family, had best cause for being obligated to Cromwell, for he had been the dispenser to him of one of the pensions Cardinal Wolsey had paid out in 1529 in his desperation. There is nothing to show that he felt much gratitude. But of course with the developments that time brought, Cromwell and the Boleyns more and more acted together.

With Sir Thomas More, Cromwell had little to do, though the friendly More was always affable when they met in the Council chamber or elsewhere. But More had resigned his chancellorship in May, 1532. It was shortly after this that he gave Cromwell a piece of advice, which it need hardly be said was disregarded. "Master Cromwell," he said to him, "you are now entered into the service of a most noble, wise and liberal prince. If you will follow my poor advice, you shall in your counsel-giving unto his Grace, ever tell him what he ought to do, but never what he is able to do. So shall you show yourself a true faithful servant and a right worthy counsellor. For if a lion knew his own strength, hard were it for any man to rule him." As More had already discovered, Cromwell was already busy contriving ways by which the lion's strength might be exercised, but he hoped that, even at that late date, a successful appeal might be made to Cromwell's better nature. More continued to hope for a reversal of policy. He knew that Henry did not at heart wish for any breach with the Holy See, though that began to seem the ultimate consequence of what was happening in England, under the advice of Cromwell. As More could do nothing further, he retired and gave himself to the writing of books in defense of the Catholic faith. If England remained orthodox in doctrine, it might yet be saved for Catholic unity.

So it might have been saved, after a fashion, had the Pope yielded regarding the point Henry was insisting on. But yielding there would have brought about a disaster even greater than the one that occurred. The unity could have been only of a formal sort, for the Pope would have had to renounce all real authority and so have discredited his office. As it was, Clement did not emerge from the sad business with much luster, but he had at least shown that the Holy See was a tribunal to which, in spite of his own deliberate dilatoriness and shiftiness, people might appeal, sure that justice would, at however late a date, be done.

All through these years—and in fact, to the end—Cromwell maintained officially an orthodoxy to which he personally attached little importance. He had for a while dickered with Tyndale, whose *Obedience of a Christian Man* perfectly stated Cromwell's own totalitarian view: "One King, one law in the realm; no class of men exempt from the temporal sword; no law except the law of the land." But he had hurriedly dropped his patronage of Tyndale when the translator of the New Testament denounced the divorce proceedings against Katherine. He even went so far as to send Sir Thomas Elyot to the Emperor requesting that Tyndale be extradited, not of course for this reason but because of his heretical views. The Tyndale episode may leave the sincerity of Cromwell's orthodoxy under suspicion, but at least in his official capacity he was orthodox.

It would probably be going too far to suggest that there was hypocrisy in this. Or if there was hypocrisy, it was a negative kind. Cromwell was not, as so often was true of Cranmer, offering ostensible opposition to views which he secretly held; Cromwell considered religion a matter of no importance. The only aim he had was to strengthen the authority of the King and to widen its scope. As the King was orthodox, it was necessary for Cromwell to be orthodox too. And in this he showed a quiet, efficient, dispassionate ruthlessness, which increased as his power increased, but did not fully manifest itself until 1535.

With this ruthlessness went, as one might expect, a cool cynicism, if it is possible to make any clear distinction between qualities which, in Cromwell's case, were so closely interwined. If the cynicism appears first, this was because not until later did he have opportunities to exercise the other of the twin tendencies. Thus writing to the King on June 13, 1532, he expresses satisfaction over the report that the Turks are about to invade Italy; this will be very awkward both to the Pope and the Emperor and therefore to Henry's advantage. The danger to Christendom is nothing to him.

The same spirit manifests itself in a minor fashion when in the same year he writes to the Abbot of Bury, peremptorily ordering him to send the masons and other workmen he is employing to London; the King needs them for his own purposes. And on July 9, 1533, writing to Thomas Allen, the brother of his old crony, the Archbishop of Dublin, he informs him that, if he fails to pay his debts to the King and himself, he will be fined a thousand marks. Ten days later he instructs Sir Anthony Fitzherbert and Walter Luke to delay the hearing of a lawsuit, as the jury seems to be on the point of bringing in a verdict unfavorable to his interests. Four days later again he writes to the King about two Observant friars whom he has had arrested: "It is undoubted that they have intended and would confess some great matter, if they be examined as they ought to be, that is to say by pains." In that month he also tells the Abbot of Woburn that he is much displeased at his having deposed his "well beloved friend," the Abbot of Vaudey, in order to give the office to the cellarer of his own abbey.[3] And on November 8 he orders the Abbots of Fountains and Byland to delay no longer in appointing the Abbot of Rievaulx: "And thereby ye shall not only deserve the King's most gracious thanks, but also have me do for you in all your good causes the best I can."[4] These interferences with monastic discipline must have been a carry-over from the arbitrary administration of Wolsey and help to account for monastic demoralization. Cromwell is already acting as though the King were Head of the Church and he, the King's Vicar-General. Similarly he writes on December 6 to the Abbot of Netley, asking (really commanding) that his friend John Cook be given a lease of sixty years for one of the abbey's farms. In most of these cases one cannot but suspect that Cromwell proceeded as he did because he had received

[3] I do not know how this could be. Every Benedictine abbey is autonomous, and both these abbeys were Benedictine, though of the Cistercian branch. But presumably the abbot of a large community, such as Woburn, was capable of bringing strong pressure to bear in the election of abbots of smaller houses. If the Abbot of Woburn was exceeding his authority, still more was Cromwell exceeding his.

[4] Again the instructions are mysterious. Rievaulx had the right of electing its own abbot.

a bribe. It is also abundantly clear that in 1532 he already possessed dictatorial powers.

Nor was his pressure confined to abbots. On April 24, 1534, he asks Bishop Gardiner to appoint to a living within his gift in Hampshire one whom Cromwell describes as a "dear friend" of his. In this instance, as the benefice was worth only ten or eleven pounds a year, there was probably no bribe; more likely a reward was being given for some service. In the same year he writes on behalf of a Mr. Allen (who may have been the man whom he had threatened to fine if he did not pay his debts) asking that he be given the lease of a farm in Essex. The recipient of this letter was apparently the Abbot of Colchester. Cromwell enforces his request with another; even if the lease had been promised to somebody else, the promise must be broken and the farm go to Mr. Allen.

There were probably many more letters along these lines than those that have survived. What is very evident from them is that Cromwell, even prior to 1535, when he might have claimed some legal sanction for actions on account of his position, was already behaving as though he was Vicegerent. It is also evident that, at least in some of these cases, he was acting not for the King but on his personal initiative. Yet his official standing was not very high—only that of the Royal Secretary and the Master of the Rolls. Cromwell aimed not so much at position or title—he was content that Audley, his tool, should be Chancellor, and he himself obtained his barony only in 1536—but at the reality of power. Very early after Wolsey's death he made himself the most important political figure in England—more important than any of the bishops, more important than any other member of the Council, more important even than the Dukes of Norfolk and Suffolk. He was the man to whom the King had committed the direction of all national affairs.

Chapter Five

THE SCHISM

THE SEPARATION of England from the juris-
diction of the Holy See was effected, and could only have been
effected, in an age indifferent to religion. The suggestion has even
been made by some historians that this was to the advantage of
England: had there been enough people on either side to care sufficiently, the country might have known the ferocity of the religious
wars that drenched France with blood. I mildly remark in reply that,
without wishing anything like that, I regret there were not more
people willing to accept martyrdom. Had they existed, there might
have been no martyrs at all. The presence of a strong opposition
probably would have deterred Cromwell and the King.

But if the opposition to their policy was not vigorous enough to
make itself felt, it must be said that that policy itself had few convinced adherents, apart from the King himself and a handful of
interested people like the Boleyns and their group and men like
Cranmer and Cromwell. The two last named really did believe that
there should be a royal supremacy over the Church, and Henry
was brought to believe this; but the conviction was not of such a
strong sort as to inspire them with a readiness of martyrdom. The
supremacy might have been a political convenience, but everybody
was aware that England had managed fairly well without it for a
thousand years. When in 1556 Cranmer died at the stake and, sixteen years before that, Cromwell died under the ax, it was not in
defense of this principle.

78

H. A. L. Fisher, the author of what is perhaps the best book on Henry's reign, has remarked, "Cynical men do not exploit religion unless religion is already a force; nor do they exploit it successfully unless there is some coincidence, accidental or essential, between the statecraft of the cynic and the enthusiasm of the prophet." That sounds very sensible, but one might ask, just who *were* these enthusiasts and prophets? Early in the reign, even before the advent of Luther, there were a handful of religious eccentrics to whom Wolsey meted out no punishment more severe than that of "bearing their faggot"—that is, to wear on their clothes a distinguishing emblem which showed they had been convicted of holding subversive theological opinions. Later there were a handful of heretics of a more definitely Lutheran tinge—men like Frith and Bainham and Nicholson and Bayfield and Barnes and, after Cromwell had gone, a few others, of whom the most prominent was Anne Askew. But she was prominent only socially and because she stood out by her truculent courage. Of the other heretics only Barnes had much intellectual influence, and even he not an immense amount. The more dangerous Tyndale and Coverdale were careful to remain abroad. Simon Fish, who was an anticlerical rather than a heretic, fled to Holland where he died in 1531 reconciled, it is said, to the Church. Christopher St. German was another anticlerical; Sir Thomas More, when replying to his anonymously published book, surmised that the author, because he had centered his attack on the secular clergy, must be a monk with a personal grudge; his doctrine was not unorthodox.

But with the word "anticlerical" we lay our finger on the trouble. It implies a purely negative attitude, one of dislike for the clergy (for whatever reason), but it need not involve any opposition to the religion of the clergy, however much it may prepare the ground for positive doctrinal opposition. Such people undoubtedly abounded in early sixteenth-century England, but their animosity was directed against the local clergy—more particularly the secular clergy—as these made the odious exactions for the probate of wills, mortuaries, and the rest. Such dislike can of course be very strong and is capable of resulting in fierce outrages; but no flaming principle is involved. Heresy can produce martyrs; of this, mere anticlericalism is incapable.

One is therefore forced to the conclusion that Professor R. H.

Tawney's judgment is, upon the whole, sound when he says, "The classes whose backing was needed to make the Reformation a political success had sold their support on terms which made it inevitable that it should be a social disaster." I say "upon the whole" for there were other factors at work which we are unable to assess very accurately—chief among them remnants of the old Lollard and Wycliffite movements and, in London and the seaports in contact with the Continent, a Lutheran infiltration. This last does not appear to have been widespread or very enthusiastic, except in isolated cases. Though Cromwell contrived to get some bishops of the new school appointed, these had to be careful not to show their true colors. Heresy is hardly discoverable among the nobility at all as a genuine conviction. As for the officials, two cases might be cited as typical: the base Richard Rich lived to make himself conspicuous in Mary's reign for his severity against Protestants; and John Dudley, who made himself Duke of Northumberland during Edward's reign and led the Lady Jane Grey conspiracy, died proclaiming his Catholic faith. Men such as these supported religious changes for no other reason than that they found it to their profit to do so. Such enthusiasm for what I must be permitted to describe as heresy was to be found only among humble and obscure people who had no influence whatever, unless upon people as humble and obscure as themselves.

This was equally true of the vastly larger number of people who disapproved of what was going on. Public opinion counted for little. Moreover, in the absence of all means of information, except a royal proclamation or a sermon (whose content was dictated by the King), nobody could be sure as to just what was happening and still less as to where it was going to lead. When Henry told Chapuys that he was "very watchful of the countenance of the people" and would know at what point he had to stop, he meant only that he was paying attention to what important people thought. He knew that he could disregard what the mass of his subjects were thinking.

Nor of course is it possible for us, after this long lapse of time, to have any very definite knowledge as to what was going on in their minds, though some inferences can be drawn. Anticlericalism, of the kind that we saw surging up during the Hunne affair in 1514, though probably not limited to London, seems to have subsided after that outburst or to have dwindled to nothing worse than a casual grumble about an unpopular priest. There was no antipapalism whatever, so far as we know, among the people at large; and if this tended to increase after 1529, it was due not to the support of the King as against the Pope but to disgust with Clement VII for not having acted more strongly in the defense of the beloved Queen Katherine.

On the other hand there was not much enthusiasm for the Papacy, which had been damaged in public esteem by the Great Schism, when from 1378 to 1417 the Church had rival popes, and, before that, by the Avignon Captivity, from 1309 to 1378, when the Pope had been reduced almost to being a chaplain of the King of France. Nor was there as a rule any very clear concept, even among theologians, as to precisely what was involved in papal authority. Catholic teaching is that papal infallibility was part of the deposit of faith from the foundation of the Church; but infallibility was not defined until 1870, and the ordinary exercise of papal jurisdiction, while a frequent cause of irritation to secular governments, was something of which the populace was hardly aware. A king might have a quarrel with the Pope over some administrative detail, but such a king, even Henry himself, never dreamed of questioning the body of doctrine of which the Pope was the custodian. Spiritual life might be lax, or perfunctory, or somnolent; nevertheless, orthodoxy was all but universal.

It should be noted that even Sir Thomas More, who, as the event was to prove, was prepared to lay down his life in defense of the Pope's supremacy, did not always hold the position he eventually reached. In 1521, if not later, he held, as did most people, that though this supremacy was a convenience, it had come about rather as a historical necessity than as something divinely ordained. It took him, according to his own statement, seven (in another place he says ten) years of thought and study to reach his later conclusion. Humorously he attributed his change of mind to the arguments Henry had used in his book in confutation of Luther.

Part of the strength of Henry's position was that he could claim, with some justice, that he would be a more effective guardian of orthodoxy in England than the Pope. Wolsey as Papal Legate had been negligent in this matter, whereas Henry, though his attacks on heresy were only spasmodic, did from time to time make attempts to suppress it. He even presided in person at one heresy trial. It was this consideration that brought him the support of such orthodox bishops as Tunstall, Lee, Gardiner, and Bonner. And it is worth noting that only one of Henry's bishops refused to accept him as Head of the Church—John Fisher of Rochester; whereas in Elizabeth's reign only one bishop refused her "settlement" of religion—Kitchen of Llandaff, a man of eighty, who may be excused for not finding the force to resist at his age. Yet several of Henry's bishops lived on until Elizabeth's accession—Tunstall and Bonner and Heath, for example. By that time they saw the issue plainly, after the radical Protestantism officially introduced under Edward. As More said to Bonvisi, his Italian friend, it was the papal supremacy that was the basis of everything.

The breach with Rome was regarded with a good deal of trepidation by Parliament, though under pressure it did what was required. Yet this may not have been primarily due to devotion to the Papacy but to a fear of possible spiritual reprisals and political complications. What would be the consequences of an interdict nobody knew, and an effort was made to ward off these consequences by a law that forbade any priest to cease the performance of his functions should an interdict be launched. On top of this was the likelihood that, to carry out a sentence of deprivation against Henry, the Emperor or the King of France (or both) might invade England. At the very least, it was thought, there would be a cutting off of trade with the Low Countries. Cromwell had to bring all his persuasive powers to bear to prove, from personal knowledge gained by his residence in Antwerp, that the merchants there would fear the loss of trade quite as much as Englishmen and stood to suffer even more.

There was still another factor in the case. Sympathy for the ill-usage of Queen Katherine was common even among the sycophantic courtiers and was universal elsewhere. And Anne Boleyn was detested. It hardly needed Cromwell's private secret service to bring in the information that she was popularly known as "Nan Boleyn, the whore," sometimes enlarged into "the goggle-eyed whore." In the August before her marriage she would have been lynched by a crowd of about seven thousand women, augmented by men in women's clothing, if they could have laid hands on her when she was junketing in a villa on the river. Her arrogance, her lightness of tongue, her flippancy, her lack of dignity were anything but queenly. Henry perhaps still considered all this amusing, but her

82

shrewishness had several times made him smart and he had been obliged to bring in her relatives to patch up the lovers' quarrel. A secret resentment against her had been growing, and he went his way only out of sheer obstinacy. He had made up his mind to win this woman, who had refused to be his mistress; even if he had to make her his wife, he was not going to be thwarted.

As it had become clear in 1532 that Pope Clement was not going to act—at any rate not in the King's favor—pressure was brought to bear upon Warham to pronounce the Henry-Katherine marriage null and void, by virtue of his powers as Primate. But Warham, though he had been compliant enough during the early stages of the King's Great Matter, now refused to hear the case. He would not go in the face of the Pope's strict prohibition against any court but his own deciding the issue. He was now over eighty and would soon die. Cromwell talked of hanging him on a gallows as high as Haman's, but Warham stood firm. On his deathbed he prepared a speech which he hoped to deliver in Parliament calling for the repeal of all recent legislation against the Church.

Even if Cromwell was serious in his threats regarding Warham, Henry was aware that drastic action would instantly precipitate what he still hoped to avoid, a breach with the Holy See. While coming more and more to believe that Cromwell had been right all along, he continued to hope that the Pope would be reasonable. But even if he was not, Warham could not last much longer. After his death the situation would be entirely different. On August 24, William Warham died.

For two years Cromwell had been gambling on the constancy of a very unstable man. Henry had needed persuasion and flattery and wheedling to keep his resolution at the proper pitch, but now, with Warham's death, a way was open for Henry to get his divorce and, what mattered far more in Cromwell's estimation, an unqualified supremacy over the Church. He had undertaken to make Henry the richest and most powerful King in Christendom; he would now also make him, so far as England was concerned, Pope as well. To Cromwell the divorce was hardly more than the hinge upon which his plans turned. The totalitarian solution was the one at which he had always aimed. When Wolsey had gathered all the reins of government into his own hands, this had been looked upon only as a temporary state of affairs, one necessary to the schemes of reform

83

he had hoped to carry out. Now that centralization of authority should be made permanent, and the undying monarchy should be put in control. Cromwell had often declared that the sultanate was his ideal—a secular ruler whose sway was absolute and one who was a spiritual head as well. This was what he now proposed to make Henry.

A week after Warham's death Anne Boleyn had the patent of the Marquisate of Pembroke conferred upon her. It is instructive to know that it was drawn as though she were a man, as an indication that she enjoyed it in her own right. What is even more illuminating is the fact that the document did not specify that her heir must be lawfully begotten, the customary form. The implications are plain: though Anne, now that Warham was dead, saw the crown of the Queen within her grasp, yet, knowing Henry as she did, she realized that at the very last moment he might refuse to marry her. If so, she would have her marquisate and the revenues with which it was endowed; and she could pass these on to her bastard, should she bear a child out of marriage.

Another point should be noted. It may be taken as certain that she had not yielded to Henry's importunities until she was protected at least to this handsome degree. We also know that she became pregnant a month before her marriage. One cannot but suspect that Henry wished to make quite sure she was capable of motherhood before he took her as his wife. For much as he wished to possess her, still more did he wish for an heir. That period of September to December must have been one of considerable anxiety to this woman. Physical passion was not very strong in Henry—not nearly so strong as the vanity and obstinacy that grew when opposed. At the very last moment he could have accepted the divorce of which he was now positively assured and married somebody else. If this was cold-blooded, the whole business had been cold-blooded. Dynastic and political considerations were, to his mind, of vastly greater importance than the satisfaction of an appetite he would have found no difficulty in satisfying in other ways.

Cranmer was at the time on a diplomatic mission on the Continent. Yet he, an obscure Cambridge don, with no higher ecclesiastical standing than that of Archdeacon of Taunton, was selected to be the new Archbishop of Canterbury. The news took him completely by surprise. It also greatly embarrassed him, for he had married in

84

Nuremberg, and he knew the King's views about clerical celibacy. But this was an order he had to obey; so, not too quickly, he went home, leaving Mrs. Cranmer in Germany.

Just what Cromwell had to do with this appointment we do not know, except that he was consulted about everything, even when he did not take the initiative. Though Cranmer's name may have been suggested by the Boleyns, Cromwell would have been asked what he thought. He could have answered that Cranmer was entirely pliable, not merely like the other pliable men of whom England was full; for where these did what was wanted with nothing else in mind than to curry favor, Cranmer regarded an order or hint from the King as carrying a religious obligation. Cromwell, who was free of religious prepossessions and carried out the King's wishes because he believed there could be no stable order except under absolute obedience, was himself sometimes glad to employ the Cranmerian argument of religious sanctions because of its usefulness. As to how far the two men were working together at this date is uncertain, but it is safe to suppose that Cromwell looked upon Cranmer's nomination as a very happy stroke, nor is it unlikely that this occurred to him even before it occurred to Henry and the Boleyns.

In backing Cranmer, however, he was defrauding Gardiner of a position which everybody considered as rightfully his. Here was the most prominent of the bishops—at least in the political sense—the kind of man who might have hoped to be, like Morton and Warham before him, Archbishop and Chancellor. In Mary's time he was, in fact, made Chancellor, and missed translation to the See of Canterbury only because Reginald Pole, the Cardinal-Legate, had superior claims. Cromwell thus gave Gardiner a reason for enmity and a hearty dislike for Cranmer, though in each case the animosity was not merely personal but mainly based on distrust of their orthodoxy.

It is true that Gardiner wrote a book after the schism, entitled *De Vera Obedientia*, in which he ably argued in defense of the royal supremacy. Its thesis was that if what the King or Parliament commanded was wrong, submission should nevertheless be given, as the individual conscience was discharged. But his conduct in the reigns of Edward and Mary made it clear that he took this line because no other was possible under Henry. What was already known about him was that, in so far as he dared, he was independent. He had joined with More in having the Submission of the Clergy, made by Convocation in May, 1532, thrown out of the House of Lords. He was one of several bishops—Edward Lee of York was another—who, after having served the King well in attempts to persuade the Pope in the matter of the divorce, perceptibly cooled off as soon as they had obtained their promotion. Such men were not sufficiently obsequious and were therefore passed over, though their title to Canterbury was much stronger than Cranmer's. But only Cranmer could be counted upon to do exactly as he was told; he was appointed to pronounce Henry's marriage null and void.

Even if Clement VII had no very definite reason to distrust Cranmer, Chapuys saw to it that he was warned not to send the necessary bulls. These warnings were disregarded. Partly this was because Henry had allowed it to be understood that he was prepared to accept a commission to sit upon the divorce case in neutral territory, Cambrai having been chosen. The Emperor had been induced to give his consent to this. So the Pope was counting upon some further months of delay. He believed he could also count upon Cranmer's doing nothing contrary to his absolute prohibition of unauthorized hearings or at least of not being indecently precipitate.

What the Pope did not know was that Henry and Anne Boleyn, without waiting for the divorce, had been secretly married on January 25. A little later he did of course hear about Anne's condition. This very fact may even have been one of the reasons for not refusing the bulls. Clement had at first believed—as did most other people—that Anne was Henry's mistress and had counted upon the satisfaction of his passion to eliminate his determination to marry her. Now the Pope could hope that, as Anne actually was Henry's mistress (as he supposed), Henry would soon tire of her. Perhaps the divorce project would be dropped, or if it were persisted in and the court at Cambrai set up, Katherine who had steadfastly refused any accommodation, so long as the rival was the Boleyn woman, might be more amenable if she knew that her supplanter was to be of higher rank and character. All kinds of new possibilities had arisen; such being the situation, Clement decided that it would be inadvisable to antagonize Henry further. Even a remote chance of preventing schism was worth something.

But was this chance so remote? According to what Clement was hearing from his English Nuncio, Baron del Burgo, Henry was a man largely misunderstood. The truth was that he was very friendly to the Holy See. At the opening of Parliament in February, 1533, he had taken the Nuncio with him, causing del Burgo to be seated with special distinction at the right of the throne and losing no chance of the kind of flattery at which he was adept. The Baron was taken in and by sending reports of such happenings to Rome helped unwittingly in the hoodwinking of his Holiness. Even the shrewd Chapuys had begun to wonder whether there was not "some secret intelligence between the King and the Pope."

Nothing was further from the truth. Yet neither the Pope nor the King understood that this marriage would involve a breach with the Papacy; at any rate, they did not understand that the breach would be permanent. Anne had won her point; this woman, conspicuous for nothing except her tenacity, had made an often-wavering Henry carry out her will; she had now married the King and would soon be openly proclaimed Queen. But Henry still hoped that Clement would accept the situation and allow his hand to be forced. No decision had as yet been reached by the Holy See regarding the validity of the King's marriage to Katherine, so Henry could hope that the divorce England's new Primate was about to pronounce—in spite of the Pope's strict prohibition—would be ratified at Rome. And even if Clement refused to budge, his successor might be induced to deliver a new judgment for the sake of peace, if for no other reason. If schism had to come, it need not be beyond repair.

Cranmer, being an astute ecclesiastic, may have judged the question more correctly. He was, however, not a shaper of policy but merely one who carried out the royal will. All one can say of him is that he wished the schism to occur, as he hoped it would give him a chance to persuade Henry to make England more Protestant than Henry had, in fact, any intention of doing. As to that, though, a cardinal tenet of Cranmer's private creed was that the subject was in religion bound to obey his prince as though he were God. Therefore he was prepared to profess orthodoxy, if that was what was demanded of him. Only Thomas Cromwell saw the issue perfectly clearly. Like Cranmer, he was ready to be officially orthodox but merely because he did not think religious doctrine mattered. His sole object was a political one: he meant to make the King paramount over both Church and State. He realized that to bring this about a breach with the Papacy must come. As to whether it remained permanent depended upon political exigencies. The immediate thing was to free Henry from the Pope; if afterward it seemed advantageous to heal that breach, he counted upon its being accomplished on such terms that it would leave the King with a vastly enhanced power over the local affairs of the Church. What he had been working for since 1530 was now on the point of happening.

On March 30 Cranmer was duly consecrated, taking an oath of allegiance to the Pope, one which he had privately disavowed in advance. Simultaneously with this, Convocation was asked to declare its opinion of the Henry-Katherine marriage and overwhelmingly voted it null and void. Though this was only an opinion, it was intended to strengthen Cranmer's hand when he performed what he had been summoned to England to do. And to render Katherine powerless, an act prohibiting appeals to Rome had been rushed through Parliament in the same month. It met with some opposition in the Lower House, but Cromwell, using his technique of terror, saw that it eventually passed. All this while Henry was befooling the papal Nuncio!

There were other elements of comedy in the matter. On April 11 Cranmer wrote Henry a letter from Lambeth in which he most humbly asked that he be allowed to go into the question of his Grace's "great cause of matrimony," explaining that it would be to "the relief of all manner of griefs and infirmities of the people, God's subjects and your's, happening in the said spiritual causes, providing such remedy as shall be thought most convenient for their help and relief in that behalf." He asked to be informed as to the King's pleasure (as though he did not know it perfectly already!), "to the intent that, the same known, I may proceed for my discharge before God to the execution of my said office and duty according to His calling and yours." But though the Archbishop had asked the King "on my knees to pardon me of this my bold and rude letter," Henry sent it back to be rewritten, with corrections made by himself. Cranmer was not to be merely on his knees but "prostrate at the feet of your Majesty," and he was ordered to protest in the name of Christ that his sole motive was to try the case truly and impartially.

The trial, when it opened at Dunstable on May 8, was from start

88

to finish stage-managed by the all-powerful Cromwell, and a post was maintained to keep Cromwell informed of the results of each day's proceedings. What greatly frightened the timid Cranmer was that word should get out of what was afoot.

Dunstable was chosen because Ampthill, where Katherine was living, was only a few miles away, so that she could be summoned to attend and never be able to say that she was not given a chance to be heard. However, Cromwell took the precaution of seeing to it that the only counsel who would have been of any use to her, Bishop Fisher, was arrested on the ground of his having led the opposition in Convocation when the divorce question was discussed there six weeks earlier. And Fisher was kept in custody until the divorce sentence had been pronounced by Cranmer. Even so, Cranmer was very afraid that the Queen, though unsupported by counsel, would put in an appearance and kept sending messages to Cromwell expressing his anxiety. His letter of May 17, when the proceedings were nearing their end is typical; he hoped that "the noble lady Katherine would not change her mind, as that would cause delay." In view of Anne Boleyn's condition delay would have been extremely awkward.

They need not have been so alarmed: there was no danger of Katherine's appearing at Dunstable. She consulted Chapuys on the point, and he told her, very properly, that, as she had an appeal pending at Rome, she should recognize no other court. Indeed, apart from this, to have come before Cranmer would have done her no good, though it would have been an embarrassment to him and Cromwell and something more than an embarrassment to Henry and Anne. But even had the proceedings been strung out, by the use of various legal tricks, until the royal infant was born, it would not have been bastardized. The marriage of Elizabeth's parents had taken place and the declaration made by Cranmer at Lambeth on May 28, that the marriage was "good"—that is, valid—would have sufficed to preserve the child's technical legitimacy. There was not, as in the Campeggio-Wolsey court of 1529, any effort to produce an array of witnesses to show that Katherine's marriage to the King's fifteen-year-old brother Arthur had been consummated; that fact was assumed to have been established. Nor was there need to discover possible technical flaws in the papal dispensation for Henry's marriage to his sister-in-law; in face of the passage in

89

Leviticus, the papal dispensation was held valid. Everything could be—and was—disposed of in the shortest order.

The decree pronounced by Cranmer at Dunstable on May 23, reads in part (it is a rather lengthy Latin document): "We, Thomas, Archbishop, Primate and Legate aforesaid, having first called upon the name of Christ for direction therein and having God altogether before our eyes, do pronounce, sentence and declare for the nullity and invalidity of the said marriage, decreeing that the said pretended marriage always was, and still is, null and invalid, and that it was contracted and consummated contrary to the will and law of God, that it is of no force or obligation, but that it always wanted, and still wants, the strength and sanction of law."

With that the six years' struggle was over, so far as Henry was concerned, though he continued to hope that Clement would accept the accomplished fact. No decision on the royal divorce had yet been reached; there was still a possibility that it would be in Henry's favor. As Cranmer was Primate and, as such, *legatus natus*, perhaps the Pope would allow the Archbishop's sentence to stand, though it had been issued in defiance of the papal prohibition. The marriage, while making Henry and Anne and Cranmer liable to excommunication, would, Henry thought, be recognized, as it would relieve Clement of the responsibility of deciding the issue.

But how could the marriage of January 25 be recognized? It had taken place before Cranmer had pronounced the divorce. It was therefore bigamous. This consideration has led some historians— Lingard amongst them—to conjecture that immediately after the Dunstable divorce Henry and Anne married again. There is no evidence for this, and at least one conclusive reason for supposing that nothing of the sort happened. A second marriage would have been an admission that the first was invalid. But Cranmer declared it "good," though without giving out any particulars as to when it had taken place. We know only from a later, privately made statement that the date was January 25.

A curious fact should be noted. Anne was crowned as Queen on June 1, Whitsunday. But on the previous Easter Sunday, which falls seven weeks before Pentecost and therefore fell that year on April 15, George Browne, the Prior of the Austin Friars, a crony of Cromwell's, went up into the pulpit of St. Paul's and, to the astonishment of everyone present, publicly prayed for Anne as Queen. It must be remembered that Henry did not receive his Cranmerian divorce until five weeks later, and no intimation had been made as yet about the secret marriage. Browne's prayer therefore not only created astonishment but aroused indignation. To a man the congregation walked out.

In conformity with tradition Anne spent the night before her coronation in the Tower, the same apartments to which, under very different circumstances, she was sent less than three years from then. The celebration was, officially, conducted in grand style. She went to the Tower in the barge that had been Katherine's but with her coat of arms removed and replaced by the bogus heraldry of the Boleyns. Hall says that in front of this barge was "a foyst or wafter full or ordnance, in which was a great dragon continually moving and casting wildfire, and round about the foyst stood terrible monsters and wild men, casting fire and making hideous noise." No wonder!

The next day she was drawn to her coronation in a litter by palfreys in white damask, which swept the ground, a golden canopy borne above it making music with silver bells. All the steeple bells of London were rung; every fountain ran with wine; ladies were posted along the way with large bunches of flowers; children sang songs or singsonged little speeches. One of these speeches expressed the hope that as from St. Anne had sprung a fruitful vine, the same would be true of the Queen. The guns of the Tower roared; the trumpets blew; flags were everywhere; no expense was spared. But all this was merely official: hardly a man uncovered as she went by, and the women wore set, scornful faces. Nor did Anne do anything to allay her unpopularity by keeping a bag of gold presented to her instead of flinging it out among the crowd as largess. Cromwell, realizing that it would not have taken much to transform the sullen mood of the people into fury and that this was likely to fall upon him, found it advisable to move his worldly possessions into the Tower for safekeeping.

Henry himself was less alarmed. Though the populace might murder Cromwell or burn his house down, the King and the Queen were quite safe for one simple and sufficient reason. Anne was by now not far from childbirth, and if her child proved to be a son, the greater part of the opposition to the royal divorce would evaporate overnight. People would have gone on believing that Katherine had been shamefully treated, but they would have allowed their belief to sink into inoperative theory in their joy that the kingdom had a male heir. Their joy was instead of a different kind when in the room known as the Chamber of the Virgins in Greenwich Palace Anne gave birth on September 7 to the girl who was to be Queen Elizabeth. In every heart was one unspoken thought: England would never permit her to supplant the rightful heir, Henry's and Katherine's daughter, the Princess Mary. People danced in the streets around bonfires; nor were their expressions of delight over the discomfiture of Anne Boleyn so discreet that Cromwell's spies were unable to discover their real sentiments.

Henry was deeply chagrined. In the interval between his marriage and Elizabeth's birth he had begun again his old philandering, which had been completely laid aside during the long difficult courtship. And when Anne upbraided him, he brutally threw her complaints back in her teeth. Nevertheless when, after Elizabeth's birth, he witnessed Anne's grief (which was not unmixed with vague forebodings), he took her into his arms and comforted her, vowing that he would if obliged beg from door to door, if only he might have her by his side. Her hysteria gradually quieted; what he was telling her was true: the next year a son might arrive.

The previous July the Pope in consistory had annulled Cranmer's divorce sentence and withdrawn his Nuncio from England. But this did not necessarily mean that the sentence of the Holy See regarding Katherine would not be what Henry continued to hope for; here was merely a quashing of what Cranmer had done without authority. Henry trusted to Francis I to plead his cause at the meeting to take place in the autumn between Clement and himself. Any chance of this was ruined when Edmund Bonner pushed his way into the Pope's presence to announce that Henry of England intended to appeal to a general council of the Church, a gratuitous insult not only to the Pope, as he alone had the right to summon such a council, but to the King of France, as he was opposed to the calling of the council demanded by his enemy the Emperor. Even so, Francis did what he could by sending Du Bellay to London. From there he carried to Rome demands of a character that could not be met. Henry would have been glad of a reconciliation with the Holy See but only on his own terms—a complete surrender on the part of Clement, and before Easter.

In spite of this, Henry did not wait to find out what the Pope's reply would be. On the very same day in March in which at long last the Pope's consistory cast nineteen votes to uphold Katherine, with three cardinals recommending further delay, in England the Act of Succession was passed; this cut the last link with Rome, as its preamble repudiated the Pope's authority. Cromwell appeared both before Parliament and Convocation, declaring that the King wished Mary excluded as heiress and Elizabeth received in her place. He was sure, he said, that they all loved his Majesty so much they would not refuse to agree. Whether it was from love or fear, the act passed, and the Convocation of Canterbury on the last day of March and that of York on May 5 confirmed this abjuration of the Pope.

It was a triumph for Cromwell, the embodiment in the laws of England of his political philosophy. Even so, few people regarded the schism as something that would be permanent. Not even the handful of heretics could imagine England as other than Catholic. Yet the orthodox looked upon these events with the gravest misgivings; for once changes in religion began, who could say where they would end? The Primate was suspected of being a secret heretic; Cromwell was also suspected. The one hope was in the King himself: violent, selfish, stubborn though he was, he was known to be sincerely orthodox. Had it not been for this hope, there would have been much more opposition to the royal will and the royal whims. As it was, the sanguine looked forward to the day when Henry's anger would have spent itself and he would become reasonable again. He had been for the first eighteen years of his reign the most steadfast champion among the princes of Christendom not only of Catholic doctrine but of the papal authority. Those good days would surely return. In expectation of this the nation resigned itself to putting up with what it looked upon as only an outburst of temper or as a method of putting pressure on the Holy See.

Chapter Six

THE MARTYRS

WE NOW come to such a reign of terror as England had never known. After the summer of 1535 Henry seemed to discard all restraints; from that time on there was no cruelty from which he recoiled. Potentially he may have been what his too partial cousin, Reginald Pole, called him, the greatest of English kings. From the time of the commencement of the royal divorce proceedings, much of the brilliance with which he had begun his rule showed a tarnish, but after he had tasted the blood of the martyrs, his degeneration was rapid, though he still showed from time to time elements of greatness. Cromwell, the instrument of the terror, was, on the other hand, quite without the King's feline ferocity. He remained, as before, self-possessed and businesslike, always dispassionate and often personally well-disposed toward his victims. His attitude made the terror all the more frightful.

The punishment for most felonies was hanging, but for treason it was hanging with a good many trimmings. There had been so far in the reign few such executions, and the most notable treason case had been the gentlemanly beheading of the Duke of Buckingham in 1521. Even after the disturbances of what was called Evil May Day, four years earlier, it had been regarded as a mark of the royal clemency that only four of the ringleaders in what was, after all, merely a riot of the London prentices, were executed according to the full rigor of the law; the other victims suffered only simple strangulation.

94

Just what did being hung, drawn, and quartered mean? The "traitor" was dragged, bound to a hurdle, from the prison to the place of execution. There, before an immense crowd, he was hauled up in a noose until he lost consciousness, at which moment he was cut down, castrated, and disemboweled. The phrase about making a man eat his heart was no figure of speech; it often happened that a man was not quite dead when his heart—his "cankered heart" was the expression used—was rubbed against his mouth. His entrails were burned at the same time. Then his head and arms and legs were cut off and tossed into the caldron of boiling tar which stood ready to receive them, into which followed his quartered body. His head was set up, parboiled, on a spear on London Bridge and the rest of his remains placed in other parts of the city. It was the extremity of pain and also the extremity of indignity.

The horror was always witnessed by shuddering thousands. Their eighteenth-century descendants used to attend public hangings as interesting spectacles, until it came to be recognized that, instead of serving as a salutary warning, they were merely brutalizing. But the old method of executing traitors really did overawe the public. It was designed to prove how hideous must be the crime that was being expiated in so hideous a death. Those who had witnessed it went away with water in their bones. They had been present at a solemn ceremony that inculcated the duty of loyalty to the person of the King.

Death at the stake was far preferable. Dreadful as was its pain, it was at least clean and without ignominy. Those who endured it were commonly uplifted by the thought that they were testifying to the truth or what they believed to be the truth. And physical mitigation was frequently given by placing a bag of gunpowder on the breast of the man who suffered, so that death came quickly.

The age was a harsh one. Over seventy thousand felons are estimated to have been hanged during the thirty-eight years of Henry's reign. But for some felonies hanging was considered too easy. The law of 1531 prescribed boiling alive for poisoners. And a wife who murdered her husband was liable to be burned at the stake. One such woman was actually executed in this way as late as the end of the eighteenth century. Prisons were normally places for detention, pending trial. There were not nearly enough jails to house felons, so it was more expeditious and cheaper to hang those who, today, might get only a term of a few months. England had no galleys, in which life, though a long-drawn-out misery, gave some reason to hope for eventual freedom. Where loyalty to the King was concerned, an absolute obedience, of the most groveling kind, had to be accorded the brand of totalitarianism Henry had accepted from Cromwell.

What elaborate preparations had to be made for an execution for treason comes out in a bill for the hanging of Friar Stone at Canterbury in 1538. It lists half a ton of wood for the gallows, payment to a carpenter and a laborer who dug the holes in which to place the gallows and to four men for setting them up. Drink, too, had to be provided for these men—thirsty work! Then there was the cartage of the timber for the hurdle from the stable to the prison, and a horse had to be hired to drag the prisoner on this hurdle. Two men were employed to set up the parboiling kettle and to supervise that part of the performance, and a woman had to scour the kettle first. Two other men were engaged to take Friar Stone's quarters to the city gate. There was the purchase price for the halter and also for some straw—this was going to be bloody work. Finally there was the executioner's fee—four shillings and four pence, about five guineas in modern values. The entire cost must have been about twenty pounds sterling. One imagines that at Tyburn, where there was a permanent gallows and a regular hangman, executions were much less expensive.

It is hardly surprising that few people were ready for martyrdom or that those meditating real treason thought a second time before venturing. Even Sir Thomas More, while never making the least compromise with his conscience, took all possible precautions against condemnation and explained, with characteristic humility, that he had not been a man of such holy life as to dare run toward his fate. And John Fisher, at the block, asked the witnesses to pray that he would not falter at the last moment. Yet in these cases the punishment had been mitigated to beheading, though this was something upon which neither man had been able to count.

These matters were under the direct control of Cromwell. It is true that he did not preside at the trials; this function was performed by the new Chancellor, Audley, who was theoretically Cromwell's superior but always did as he was told by Cromwell. He is described by Lord Campbell, who himself became Lord Chancellor in 1859, as "having only commonplace abilities, sufficient, with cunning and shrewdness, to raise their possessor in the world. . . . He was of a comely and majestic presence; and by his smooth manners and systematic anxiety to give offence to no one, he acquired general popularity, though known by those who had studied his character to be unprincipled, false and deceitful." Campbell concludes, "Such a sordid slave does not deserve that we say more of his vices or demerits."

The first group of martyrs was found among the Franciscan Observants, though in the beginning they received what might be considered leniency, their houses being merely seized and given to the subservient Augustinians. But though some of them were treated so roughly in prison, often with torture, as to die, a formal sentence of death for treason was not given to any of them until some time later. The reason for this leniency, such as it was, must have been that Henry remembered that their main house, the one adjoining Greenwich Palace, had been founded by his father and that it was in the Friars' chapel that he had been baptized and married to Katherine of Aragon. The Queen had been a Franciscan tertiary and often used to rise at midnight to be present at the chanting of Matins and Lauds. Henry himself, without going to that length, owed much of his early piety to these men.

The Observants showed themselves extraordinarily courageous. Their bold speaking to Henry must have been due to their belief that by this he might yet be turned aside. And that might have happened had others been as bold. Unfortunately theirs was almost an isolated case and so was of no effect. A couple of years later nobody dared to speak at all. But in the spring of 1532 their Guardian, William Peto, who in Mary's reign was made a cardinal and replaced Pole as Legate, when preaching before the King one Sunday took as his text: "Even where the dogs licked the blood of Naboth, even there shall the dogs lick thy blood, O King." Henry was very angry but did nothing except put up a Dr. Curwin (afterward to be Archbishop of Dublin) to reply the following Sunday. Then Curwin was interrupted by a friar named Elstow; in fact, several indignant voices shouted the preacher down. Cromwell had these men summoned before him and told them that they deserved to be tied in a sack and thrown into the Thames, only to get from Peto the calm reply: "Threaten such things to rich and dainty folk, which are clothed in purple, fare deliciously, and have their chiefest hopes in this world. We are joyful that for the discharge of our duty we are driven thence. With thanks to God we know that the way to heaven is as short by water as by land, and therefore care not which way we go." This happened in 1532 before the schism had occurred, so Cromwell did not proceed to extremities. Peto and Elstow were allowed to retire abroad, and later a good many other Observants, through the connivance of Wriothesley, got away to France or Ireland or Scotland.

It is interesting to note that Cromwell was working upon a dissatisfied lay brother in the Greenwich community, a man named Richard Lyst, and used him as a spy. We also hear in a letter that Cromwell wrote to the King on July 23, 1533, that he had arrested two Observants named Cornelius and Hugh Payne. He expresses the opinion that they could be forced to confess "some great matter, if they be examined as they ought to be, that is to say by pains." I do not find that this, in spite of Cromwell's recommendation, was actually done; the time for such things had not quite come.

The great storm did not break until the following year with the affair of Elizabeth Barton, otherwise known as the Holy Maid, or the Nun of Kent. Though she may not have been, strictly speaking, a martyr, at least she was used in an effort to trap men who were martyred. Cromwell and Cranmer between them did a very nice piece of work.

Elizabeth had been a servant girl subject to fits, but after being cured—she said by the Blessed Virgin—she entered a Benedictine convent at Canterbury where, as this was stationed on the main post road between London and Dover, she was visited by many people who were impressed by her holiness and what were supposed to be her prophetic powers. As nuns in those days, at least in England, were not usually strictly cloistered, Sister Elizabeth received visitors freely and even made visits herself to prominent people, including Wolsey, Warham, and the King. In her interview with Henry she appears to have spoken her mind plainly, and he decided not to be offended. When he asked Sir Thomas More about her, he said he found in her divinations no more than what "a right simple woman might speak of her own wit." Regarding her sanctity, More said he would not presume to pronounce. Eventually it occurred to Cromwell, however, that because of her celebrity she might be used to intimidate those who were standing out against the royal divorce. She had been so indiscreet as to prophesy the King's death seven months after his marriage to Anne Boleyn, and that made her technically guilty of treason. Her associates could be implicated in this crime; and anyone who had ever had any contact with her might be charged with misprision of treason—that is, with failure to inform about a treason of which one is aware.

Cromwell assigned her trapping to Cranmer, who sent for her and, in his gentle wheedling way, found means of getting her to make damaging admissions. His Dean of Arches, Dr. Richard Gwent, who was present at the interview, wrote in admiration to Cromwell that the Archbishop "doth but yet dally with her, as if he believed every word, and as soon as he has got all he can out of her she shall be sent to you."

This was not done at once; for Cranmer interviewed her in July, after which she returned to her convent. Not until September was she arrested and lodged in the Tower. There she was treated with unusual consideration, subjected to no tortures, but merely asked the questions a candid soul would answer forthrightly. Cromwell learned at once that she had had dealings with the Marchioness of Exeter, Bishop Fisher, and Sir Thomas More.

The Marchioness's connections with her turned out to be trifling. But as Fisher had not reported what she had said to him—as it was what she herself had told the King—he was held guilty of misprision of treason. Fortunately More was able to prove that, though he had once been persuaded to meet her, he had taken the opportunity of warning her to confine herself to spiritual matters and not to touch on anything that might be considered politics.

In spite of this, when a bill of attainder [1] against Elizabeth Barton was read in Parliament in February, it contained the names of Fisher and More. Fisher compounded with a fine of three hundred pounds sterling, but More for the moment escaped because the Council warned Henry that the House of Lords intended to hear the ex-Chancellor in his own defense and would almost certainly acquit him. Though such a rebuff would have been most damaging,

---

[1] Attainder, it might perhaps be explained, was a statutory abrogation of civil rights and had been formerly used merely as a means of getting Parliament to confirm a sentence passed by a court of law. Under the ingenious Cromwell, it was often used as a substitute for a judicial trial.

Henry was still set on going to the House of Lords and forcing them to vote More's attainder, until Cromwell and Audley whispered in Henry's ear that he would be well advised to do nothing just then. They undertook to find "meeter matter" before long. This was provided when at the end of March the Act of Succession was passed with its preamble rejecting the Pope's authority.[2]

It should be noted that the previous November Elizabeth Barton had stood on a platform outside St. Paul's with the five priests accused of being her accomplices and had read a confession, saying that "she never had vision in all her life, but all that ever she said was feigned of her own imagination, only to satisfy the minds of them which resorted unto her, and to obtain worldly praise." Just how that confession was obtained we do not know, except that it was not through torture. Cranmer may have done some more coaxing, and we know that (strange though it may seem) Cromwell was often trusted by those who should have trusted him least. A guileless young woman may have accepted their promises as made in good faith, and indeed in November, 1533, it was apparently thought that the confession was enough, as it thoroughly discredited the Nun of Kent. She was no longer dangerous, if she ever had been. Sir Thomas More, who may have been one of the crowd, congratulated Cromwell, saying, "You have done to my mind to your great laud and praise a very meritorious act in bringing to light such detestable hypocrisy, whereby other wretches may take warning and be feared to set forth their own devilish dissimulated falsehood under the name and color of the wonderful work of God."

Elizabeth and those arrested with her in September, 1533, were detained in the Tower, as they might be useful in forcing submissions. Here the sequence of dates is illuminating: the Act of Attainder was passed on March 12, 1534; the Act of Succession on March 23; More and Fisher were arrested on April 13; Elizabeth and her five friends were executed at Tyburn on April 20. This culminating deed was done clearly with the intention of intimidat-

[2] Cromwell was well aware that More had an impregnable defense. For More had written him at great length setting out in detail his connection with Elizabeth Barton and enclosing a copy of a letter he had written to her. Cromwell went into the facts and found that they were substantiated at every point. It would have been foolish for Henry to have disregarded Cromwell's warning.

ing More and Fisher, who had refused to take the oath repudiating the Pope, or anybody else who might be disposed to follow their example. The execution of a nun was something new in English history. The poor young woman, according to Hall, made an affecting speech just before being hanged, saying, "Hither am I come to die, and I have not only been the cause of mine own death, which most justly I have deserved; but also I am the cause of the death of all these persons which at this time here suffer. And yet I am not so much to be blamed, considering that it was well known unto these learned men that I was a poor wench without learning; and therefore they might have easily perceived that the things which were done by me could not proceed in no such sort; but their capacities and learning could right well judge that they were altogether feigned. But because the things which I feigned were profitable unto them, therefore they much praised me, and bare me in hand that it was the Holy Ghost and not I that did them. And I, being puffed up with their praises, fell into a pride and foolish fantasy with myself, and thought that I might feign what I would, which thing hath brought me to this case, and for the which I now cry God and the King's highness most heartily mercy, and desire all you good people to pray God have mercy on me, and on them that here suffer with me." Though that may have been somewhat embroidered by Hall, Elizabeth Barton probably said something like it. She was an unbalanced young woman and had been encouraged by men who were either themselves unbalanced or thought her predictions, whether or not divinely inspired, would serve a good purpose. Cromwell had been very clever in the way he managed to make her indiscretions useful to himself.

The chief victim aimed at, however, had been far too circumspect for anything to be discovered against her. This was Queen Katherine. Cromwell did not give up because he had been unable to extract anything about her from Elizabeth Barton. We find him writing to the King about two Observant friars who had recently arrived in England, sent there, he says he is credibly informed, by William Peto. He had been told that these men had visited the Princess Dowager (Katherine's official title now), but he suggests leaving them at large in order that "their further practices might be perceived and their cankered intents might be thereby deciphered." But when at last they were arrested, at the moment chosen by himself, and tortured, Cromwell failed completely to establish any relations between Katherine and Elizabeth. He admitted this to Chapuys.

It is instructive to note that, in this same letter to the King, Cromwell goes on to speak of a merchant in London with whom these friars had been associating. He is having this merchant carefully watched and expects soon to have information upon which he can arrest him, "if he be worthy to suffer to make others beware in time." He explains that this would be worth doing, as the man is "of good substance." The government, meaning Cromwell, was aiming only at prominent people and was content to let alone the host of obscure men and women who might have been charged, merely on the ground of their having consulted Elizabeth Barton, of having conspired with her. Moreover, those found guilty of treason or misprision of treason forfeited all their property to the Crown, so only people of social standing and "good substance" were worth bothering with.

This does not mean, however, that obscurity and poverty were always a protection, even though they had been in the case of the popular following of Elizabeth Barton. Thus on July 13, 1534, we find Cromwell writing to the Earl of Shrewsbury ordering him to have tried a hermit he is sending him in the custody of the bailiff of Chesterfield. Cromwell says that the hermit denies having spoken the treasonable words of which he stands accused but that he encloses the indictment he had drawn up and wants the trial to take place locally, "before the Justice of the Assise and to the example of all others to be punished according to the right and the King's laws." This nameless wretch is only one of many such people who perished in the terror now beginning. The question of their guilt or innocence was of little interest to Cromwell; what mattered was that they should serve as examples. The verdict of guilty, it will be observed, was predetermined.[3]

[3] This must be stressed because Mr. Kenneth Pickthorn, the author of two otherwise valuable studies on Tudor government, tries to explain away the memoranda Cromwell made in 1539 that the Abbots of Glastonbury and Reading were to be tried and executed locally with their accomplices. According to Mr. Pickthorn all that Cromwell meant was that he *supposed* they would be found guilty. These memoranda will be quoted later. But it is perfectly evident that as early as 1534 Cromwell was ordering convictions and executions.

We have several other instances of much the same kind during 1534. On September 6, Cromwell addresses a letter to three priests, named Roger Reynolds, Robert Wolf, and John Kytch of St. John's Hospital, Huntingdon, sending it no doubt by the guard that is to take them to London, ordering them to appear before him to answer the charges lodged against them: "Fail ye not thus to do as ye will avoid further peril and inconvenience." What happened to these men history does not record, but it is not difficult to guess. Cromwell did not go to the trouble of inquiring into alleged treason unless he had settled the disposition of the case in his own mind.

There is no need to do any guessing about the case that follows. On October 17 Cromwell writes to the Privy Council about another man, merely described as an ill-disposed person. His instructions are that "the said person be not put to death till we may know the whole and profound bottom of his cankered heart." The situation is really terrifying: the man is not only condemned in advance; he is to be tortured before being put to death, in the hope that he may implicate others. As we have what can be only a small portion of Cromwell's letters—an average of only twenty a year spread over seventeen years—it is impossible not to presume that there were many other instances of his meting out punishment right and left, mainly for the purpose of striking terror.[4]

Fortunately we know with great completeness the story of the great men he struck down, who, because of their position, had to be proceeded against with some show of legality. Their story must now be told. In it Cromwell may always be glimpsed moving behind the scenes, directing everything that went on.

The Act of Succession, passed in March, 1533, secured the Crown to Anne's daughter, Elizabeth, or her son, should she bear one. This act, standing alone, would have caused no trouble. It was admitted on all hands that Parliament had a right to legislate on the succession, though it would have been a very hardy person who would have

---

[4] To be precise, there are 351 letters in Merriman's collection. However, with few exceptions they were all written during the last ten years of his life, which would give an average of thirty-odd letters a year. So indefatigable a worker must often have written that many in a week. However, there are reasons for supposing that Cromwell preferred to commit as little as possible to writing and transacted most of his shadier business in personal interviews. He was an adept at covering up his tracks.

been sure that the provisions of the act would have been respected after the King's death. But the preamble to the act asserted the legality of Anne's marriage and by doing so, rejected the Pope's authority. Because Clement simultaneously pronounced in favor of Katherine's marriage, the King retaliated by exacting a very stringent oath. It was one prescribed not by Parliament but by the Council, which means that it was drawn up by Cromwell. It was he who put "teeth" into it from which nobody could escape.

Long before 1534 was out, Clement died. Even when he was on his deathbed, Henry tried to make him retract his decision, as though this would be the Pope's last chance of salvation, which the royal egotist probably believed. His successor, the Farnese Cardinal, who took the name of Paul III, was a man who had always been friendly to Henry, though not so partial as to be prepared to ask his cardinals to reverse Clement's decision. Yet with nothing less than that reversal was Henry going to be content, especially now that Cromwell was dangling before him that glittering allure of plundering the monasteries. Paul was not a great man; he was fairly able, good-tempered, less hesitant and devious than Clement had shown himself, but unfortunately too sanguine about resolving the quarrel between Henry and the Holy See.

Though the new Pope let it be known that he was willing to welcome any advances of the King of England—which should have been thought of as an advance on the part of the Pope himself —Henry did not consider this enough. Taking umbrage, he had passed on November 4 the Act of Supremacy, in which those who refused the King his title of Supremacy over the Church were made guilty of treason, which act was, however, not to go into effect until February 1. As further protection to the recusants in the Tower, Parliament insisted on inserting twice the word "maliciously." Only those who showed malice in refusing the King his title were to be guilty. As malice would, it was thought, be something hard to prove, Parliament imagined that it had made the statute innocuous—something about which Parliament was shown to be vastly mistaken.

Yet even after this act had gone into effect, that is, on April 10, 1535, Henry was still seeking a reversal from Paul of Clement's sentence. For on that date Cromwell wrote to Sir Gregory da Casale both in Latin and English—the Latin letter to be shown the Pope —"Affirming (as ye write) that the said Bishop of Rome of his duty and office ought to approbate and confirm this present matrimony, albeit it depended upon the validity of the dispensation made by Julius." Then, after making it clear that the King was going to stand his ground, "like a good and virtuous Catholic prince afore God and the world," Cromwell goes on, "Yet his Majesty doth in such sense interpret your letters that (as appeareth by the same) the said Bishop of Rome beginneth now somewhat to savor and feel the justness and equity of the said cause, and partly to stand with the King's majesty in the same. Wherefore if the said Bishop of Rome do indeed bear so friendly and sincere good mind and will towards the King's Highness (as ye do write), or rather if he love the truth, as it becometh every good man to do, setting apart all hatred and affection, it is his part to show the same now to the universal world in this most just and righteous cause by his own public testimony and approbation." [5] All of which means that the Pope—studiously referred to as "the Bishop of Rome"—as a preliminary to any *rapprochement* was to declare Henry completely in the right and Clement completely in the wrong.

This was not the first time that Casale had jumped to totally false

[5] This letter was of course written at the instance of the King and represents his point of view rather than Cromwell's. Yet Cromwell, as he was to show a year later, realized more keenly than Henry did, the political dangers that might arise from the breach with Rome. Any reconciliation with Rome effected at this time would have been no more than formal and would not have been permitted to hamper the absolutism at which Cromwell was aiming. Had the Pope's supremacy been restored, it would have been only nominal. The Annates and the other revenues he received from England would, no doubt, have been paid as formerly, and it could have been explained that the royal supremacy extended only to temporalities. For nearly two hundred years the English kings had nominated the bishops appointed by the Holy See to English bishoprics, under the Statute of Provisors. The legal fiction that would have eventuated would probably have soon broken down. On the other hand, had Henry and Cromwell been really sincere about the matter, something like the Concordat made between Leo X and Francis I in 1515 was quite possible. This proved to be a workable compromise, and Henry was in a position in which in all likelihood he would have obtained even better terms than those conceded to Francis. Such a concordat would have saved the monastic system, though in all probability a partial suppression (called reorganization and adjustment) along the Wolseian lines would have been permitted. And even a concordat that was mainly to the advantage of the King might have sufficed to bring England safely around a dangerous corner.

conclusions. He had done so before in 1530 in writing that Clement was going to give Henry a dispensation for bigamy! Though Paul III had very good will toward Henry, it was impossible for him to accede to the King's demands. When that fact became known in England, it was decided that More and Fisher, who had been detained in the Tower for over a year, must yield or die.

It is now necessary to go back a little way. On April 12, 1534, Bishop Fisher and Thomas More (the only layman summoned that day) were told to go to Lambeth Palace to take the oath which would be presented to them. Each man, appearing separately before Cromwell, Cranmer, Audley, and Benson, the Abbot of Westminster, refused. But they were treated with the utmost courtesy, and the commissioners did their best to make them change their mind, Cromwell protesting with a great oath that he would rather lose his son than have More refuse. When the ex-Chancellor remained firm, he was invited to take a walk in the palace gardens and think the matter over again. He came in with his mind unchanged.

Even with this the commissioners were reluctant to proceed against Fisher and More. Cranmer therefore wrote a letter to Cromwell, suggesting that, as they were willing to swear to the succession and objected only to the preamble to the act, they be allowed to take the oath in a modified form. It need not be announced that this had been done, he explained; the public could be left under the impression that the oath had been taken without any qualification. Cromwell replied a day or two later that the compromise was unacceptable, offering as the King's opinion, what may have been his own advice: "that that manner of swearing, if it should be suffered, might be an utter destruction of his whole cause and also to the effect of the law made for the same." He was naturally afraid that the subterfuge would come to light, as "it might be taken not only as a confirmation of the Bishop of Rome's authority, but as a reprobation of the King's second marriage." In this Cromwell was of course perfectly sound, although Cranmer had proposed as a solution merely that they make no affirmation on these points but simply be allowed to retain their private opinion in silence.

As they had expressed no opinion of any kind before the commissioners on April 13, their imprisonment was of very questionable legality. For that matter, they could not be prosecuted even under the act that followed in November, for malicious speaking against

the King's supremacy could not be charged against men who refused to speak at all. They were therefore from time to time visited
by Cromwell and other members of the Council, in attempts either
to persuade them or to trap them into an incautious word. But nothing was accomplished. In this way they remained in prison for fifteen
months, not uncomfortably housed, allowed to walk in the Tower
gardens, to correspond with their friends and to receive them there,
and even to write books. It was in the Tower that More produced
the most gay-hearted of his works, *A Dialogue of Comfort against
Tribulation*, his famous letters to his daughter Margaret Roper,
some scraps of satirical verse, and his unfinished *Treatise on the Passion*. To contemplative minds such as theirs their detention was not
unpleasant, though it goes without saying that they would have
preferred to be free, and always hanging over them was the fear
that they might be tortured to force them to speak.

At last means were found for bringing a charge of treason against
them. Though Cromwell was behind what was done, he entrusted
the management of the affair to Richard Rich, the Solicitor-General
and a future Chancellor. It might be suspected that the infamous
tricking of these men should be laid to Henry's charge, were it not
his habit to allow the dirtier bits of work to be done with only his
vague knowledge of what was going on. Having expressed his wishes
in general terms, he left the means of accomplishing them to his
subordinates, absolving himself of any responsibility for what they
might do.

At the time of the affair of the Nun of Kent Cromwell wrote
Fisher in February, 1534, in reply to a letter that Fisher had written
him—one that has disappeared. We can infer what Fisher had said
only from Cromwell's rejoinder. It was an effort to maneuver the
Bishop into a position where he would be obliged to admit his guilt
and throw himself on the King's mercy. Cromwell tells him, "I think
verily that your declaration made by these letters is far insufficient
to prove that ye deserve no heavy words." At the same time he
maintains that he did send him no heavy words, "but words of great
comfort, willing your brother to show you how benign and merciful
the prince was. And that I thought it expedient for you to write unto
his Highness and to recognise your offence and desire your pardon,
which his Grace would not now deny you in your age and sickness." He goes on to accuse Fisher with having another motive in

attending what might be called the Nun's séances than the one he had attributed to himself, which was a mere desire to test her credibility. "Think you, my Lord," he says, "that any indifferent man, considering the quality of the matter and your affection, and also the negligent passing over of such lawful trials as ye might have had of the said nun and her revelations, is so dull that [he] cannot perceive and discern that your communing and often sending to the said nun was rather to hear and know more of her revelations than to try out the truth or falsehood of the same." If this can be called guilt, then Fisher had put himself in a position in which he appeared to be guilty of misprision of treason. The upshot was that Fisher was attainted of this crime, made subject to the forfeiture of all his goods and the imposition of imprisonment for life. However, these penalties were not enforced, and Henry and Cromwell no doubt considered that they were letting him off lightly by imposing only a fine. They believed also that he would never venture to refuse the oath tendered to him on April 13.

The incarceration that Fisher had to endure for refusing this oath, while not particularly severe, was hard on one so old and in such poor health. On December 22, 1534, he wrote piteously to Cromwell, "I have neither shirt nor suit, nor yet other clothes, that are necessary to me to wear, but that be ragged and rent too shamefully . . . and now in mine age my stomach may not away but with a few kinds of meat, which if I want I decay forthwith, and fall into coughs and diseases of the body, and can not keep myself in health . . . I beseech you to have pity on me." As Cromwell did not want him to die but to submit, he had doctors visit him but did not essentially mitigate the rigors of his confinement, rather counting upon these to break down his resolution. It was Bonvisi, the wealthy Italian merchant, who sent him more delicate food and a daily bottle of wine—the latter being consumed for the most part by the attendants at the Tower. Presumably, it was also Bonvisi who saw to it that he got some warm clothing.

As nothing else served, tricks were played on him. Fisher was told that More had submitted, just as More was told the same of Fisher. It was true that Dr. Nicholas Wilson, one of the King's chaplains who had been committed to the Tower with them, broke under the strain. But More and Fisher held steadily to the line that, no matter what anybody else did, conscience had to be served. At last a trick was used that succeeded; Richard Rich was sent to Fisher, telling him that he came authorized by the King to ask him, in his capacity as bishop, his opinion regarding the royal supremacy. Immunity was guaranteed whatever he might say. Under such circumstances Fisher did not feel that he could refuse—and so gave the Crown a reason, hitherto lacking, for proceeding against him.

Just before this Paul III, with the best intentions in the world, made a serious blunder. At the consistory of May 21, 1535, he had created Fisher a cardinal, believing that this would please the King. Further to show his good will, he elevated to the purple at the same time Jean du Bellay, who had always been a man who had favored Henry, and Girolamo Ghinucci, who had served him at Rome as an ambassador. The imperialists, however, in order to make Henry suspicious of Francis, spread the false report that Fisher's cardinalate had been bestowed at the request of the King of France. It was in vain that the Pope declared he was ready to give an attestation in writing that everything had been done on his own initiative and that neither Francis nor anybody else had intervened in Fisher's behalf.

Henry was very angry and sent Cromwell to the new Cardinal to ask if he would accept the red hat if it were sent. Fisher answered, "Sir, I know myself unworthy of any such dignity, that I think of nothing less than such matters; but if he so send it to me, I will work with it by all means I can to benefit the Church of Christ; and in that respect I will receive it on my knees." When Henry heard what Fisher had said he roared, "What, is he yet so lusty? Well, let the Pope send him a hat when he will; but I will provide that whensoever it cometh, he shall wear it on his shoulders, for head he shall have none to set it on!" So he was hurried to his trial where, after receiving sentence, Fisher said, "I think and always have thought, and do now lastly affirm, that his Grace cannot justly claim any supremacy over the Church of God as he now taketh upon him, neither hath [it] been seen or heard of that any temporal prince before his day hath presumed to that dignity."

Apparently the only reason that the King did not give himself the savage satisfaction of sending a cardinal to the ignominious death of Tyburn was that Fisher was so frail that he would have died on the hurdle dragged at the horse's tail.[6] So the ax had to suffice. Fisher was imperturbable, and when his servant, having heard a report that his master was to be executed that morning, failed to prepare his dinner, Fisher told him, "Make it ready as thou art wont to do, and if thou see me dead when thou comest, then eat it thyself; but I promise thee if I be alive, I mind by God's grace to eat never a bit the less." When the day of execution did arrive on June 22 and the Constable of the Tower, Sir William Kingston, wakened him at five, Fisher asked him to allow him an hour or two more of sleep. Then, as the air was chilly to one now only a walking skeleton, he put on his fur tippet to go to the block, saying to those who told him that there was no need of it, as he was to die within the hour, that he intended to take care of his health to the very last moment.

He had to be carried down from his cell in a chair and in the same way to the scaffold; but mounting it he said, "Nay, masters, now let me alone; ye shall see me go up to my death well enough myself, without help." And he did, the witnesses marveling, for he was, as one of them recorded, "a very image of death, and, as one might say, death in a man's shape and using a man's voice."

Standing on the scaffold beside the block, he made a little speech, begging the prayers of those present that he should not falter "at the very point and instant of death's stroke." He then prayed for the King and the realm of England. William Rastell, who was present and from whom most of these details are drawn, said that everybody was astonished at the resonance of Fisher's voice, for his words could not have come with a louder, clearer force from the youngest man there.[7] In this way, serene in his courage, the most

---

[6] It is sometimes said that this is the only instance of a cardinal being sentenced to death by a secular court. This is not quite accurate. During the reign of Pius IV, Cardinal Carlo Carafa, the unworthy nephew of the previous Pope, received the death sentence and was executed. However, when Pius V came to the throne, he saw to it that there was a judicial rehabilitation, for, though the Cardinal may have been guilty of the crimes of which he was accused, his prosecution had been vindictively unfair in many respects and was in large part prompted by Spanish political interests. We have recently seen, under a modern totalitarian regime, how very close a cardinal can come to a death sentence from a secular court.

[7] William Rastell was More's nephew and in 1557 was the editor of his uncle's *English Works*. Made a judge in Mary's time, he went into exile in Elizabeth's reign for the sake of religion. He is known to have written a life

venerated bishop in England died. It was the feast day of St. Alban, the promartyr of England.

Early in May, five other priests were dragged to Tyburn. They were three Carthusian priors—John Houghton, Augustine Webster, and Robert Lawrence—together with Richard Reynolds, a Brigittine, and John Hale, a secular priest. Their trial was a kind of test case; as such it is highly significant.

John Houghton had taken the oath, after a short sojourn in the Tower, allowing himself to be persuaded to this by Archbishop Lee of York and Bishop Stokesley of London. He had looked upon his action as making himself anathema, in the hope that the rest of the monks of the London Charterhouse would be unmolested. But when the new and more stringent act went into effect on February 1, the Prior of Beauvale in Nottinghamshire (Lawrence) and the Prior of Axholm in Lincolnshire (Webster) went to London to discuss the situation with Houghton and to decide on their course of action. They concluded that they had best lay their case before Cromwell, who had recently been appointed Vicar-General for the King over the English Church. One catches a hint here, as we shall catch it many times later, that they regarded him as kindly and fair-minded.

They were promptly disillusioned. When they called at Cromwell's house at Stepney on April 13, as soon as he discovered why they had come, he refused to listen to them but put them under arrest and sent them to the Tower. However, a week later, instead of going to see them at the Tower, as might have been expected, he invited the Carthusians to the Rolls. Present were several members of the Council as witnesses, with John Ap Rice, whom we shall encounter again soon, to notarize the evidence. Upon the priors refusing the oath of supremacy they were sent back to the Tower, where they were joined by Reynolds and Hale.

Hale's case was somewhat different from the others, as he was accused of denouncing the King's manner of life: as to that the four

---

of More, but it has been lost, except for the pages that relate to Fisher and the Carthusians. These are so vivid and so precise in detail that one mourns the disappearance of what must have been a remarkable performance. In 1535 he was a law student and because of his interest in the legal aspects of these trials, as well as his sympathy for the accused, followed them with close attention.

monks had expressed no opinion but said that they could not take "our sovereign Lord to be supreme head of the Church, but him that is by God the head of the Church, that is the Bishop of Rome, as Ambrose, Jerome and Augustine teach." They reiterated this when they were arraigned but denied they were guilty of treason. How could they be, as the statute twice made malice a necessary part of the treason, and they had no malice? Reynolds told the judges at their trial on April 26 that the vast majority of the King's subjects believed as they did. When asked who these people were, he replied, "All good men." As the jury was reluctant to convict, their verdict was deferred until the following day.

The jury's objection was that malice was not present in the refusal of the King's supremacy. The judges, however, ruled that it was impossible to deny the supremacy except maliciously, and when the jury still remained obstinate, Cromwell, after sending them a message that they must convict, went to them "in a rage," as Rastell says, and threatened them with death. There was nothing for it except to bow to the royal will, but they did so most reluctantly and "were afterwards ashamed to show their faces."

While the five priests were waiting in the Tower for execution, Cromwell, through his agents, worked on the other monks in the London Charterhouse. One of these agents, John Whalley, had to write to Cromwell to tell him, "It is no use for one Mr. Rastell to come there. He pleads indeed that you wished him to resort thither," but he says that the monks laugh at all that he says.[8] As to these monks, Whalley reports that there is no question but that "they be exceedingly superstitious, ceremonious, and pharisaical, wonderfully addict to their own *mumpsimus;* nevertheless, better and more charitable it were to convert them, than to put them to the extremity of the law." As they remained steadfast, a little later another batch of them were sent to Tyburn, including Sebastian Newdigate, the brother of Lady Dormer, who was afterward married to the Spanish Duke of Feria. Newdigate had been a courtier and a crony of the

[8] This presumably was John Rastell, More's brother-in-law and the father of William. He was rather remarkable in various ways, but the most remarkable fact about him is that he was alone in his family in adhering to the side of the King. In spite of this he maintained some independence (or was it merely eccentricity?) for in 1536 he was arrested for having attacked the paying of tithes and died in prison the following year.

King's, who admired his prowess in the tilting yard. When he joined the Carthusians, his sister went to Prior Houghton and told him that Sebastian was unfit to be a monk, as he could not eat fish without vomiting. In similar forthright style she told Sebastian that she would as soon see him hanged as a monk. Hanged he was, though there is a story that Henry, in an attempt to save him, went to the Tower to try to persuade him to be reasonable. He stood firm; accordingly on June 19 he and two other Carthusians followed the three priors to Tyburn.

Still another batch of Carthusians perished in 1537. On June 14 of that year we have a list of five of them who had already died from the rigor with which they had been treated in Newgate prison, another two who were on the point of death, two others who were sick, and one who had recovered. It was one of the sick, however, who was the sole survivor; this was a lay brother named William Horne, and he survived only to be hanged at Tyburn on August 4, 1540.

I have deliberately anticipated events by introducing this later group. As they were chained to the wall in such a way that they could never get a moment's rest or do anything for themselves, Sir Thomas More's adopted daughter, Margaret Giggs, married to Dr. Clement, one of the royal physicians, used to go to the prison in the disguise of a milkmaid to feed them and clean up their ordure. On the thirty-fifth anniversary of More's execution she died in exile for the Faith at Mechlin, and saw standing around her bed the monks she had so heroically befriended. At once she knew that they had come to summon her.[9]

When the first batch of Carthusian martyrs were being tied to their hurdles, Sir Thomas More was standing at the window of his cell talking to his daughter Margaret Roper. Margaret had doubtless received Cromwell's permission to visit her father that day because he knew what else they would see. This was something that would certainly appall Margaret, and her horror might serve to

[9] This incident is related in the manuscript life of her daughter (a nun), which is preserved at the English convent at Bruges. A good many of the More circle had gone into exile with her in Elizabeth's reign, among them her husband and William Rastell and John Harris (with his wife Dorothy Colley, who had been Margaret Roper's maid), and John Heywood, the poet and dramatist.

shake her father. Instead More turned to her saying, "Lo! dost thou not see, Meg, these blessed fathers be now as cheerfully going to their deaths as bridegrooms to their marriage. . . . Thy silly father, Meg, like a most wicked caitiff hath passed the whole of his miserable life sinfully." He was soon to obtain his own palm of martyrdom.

Here I cannot refrain from quoting (I hope not too maliciously) a remark made by Pollard in his *Henry VIII* that whereas the King "embodied an inevitable movement in politics . . . Fisher and More stood only for individual conscience." Even if there is such a thing as inevitability in politics, which I would strenuously deny, Pollard's dictum seems to me highly immoral. However, it must be said that though Pollard always tries his best to defend Henry, his sense of decency does periodically assert itself. On the very same page with the sentence just quoted occur the judgments: "The nation purchased political salvation at the price of moral abasement" and "In Henry's reign the spirit of English independence burned low in its socket, and love of freedom grew cold." What this great but very prejudiced scholar really means of course is that no infamy was too large a price to pay for the blessings of the Protestant Reformation; I have no idea what the "political salvation" can be unless it is this. Even conceding the "blessings" for the sake of the argument, this is nothing but to assert what is called the Jesuitical principle that evil may be done if good may ensue. I happen to be one who regards the Reformation as not only a religious but a social disaster; but even were it to save Christendom from such calamity, I cannot admit that evil should be condoned. Katherine of Aragon could have saved England for the Catholic side by a little equivocation. She understood this well enough, and she refused. There is the true principle. The history of Henry's reign is mainly redeemed by the martyrs that appeared; England itself may yet be redeemed by them.

These are the men whom all unite to admire. And of them all none is so universally admired as Sir Thomas More. He is a man of whom every one of his biographers has written with warm affection, for his personal integrity, his charm, his gentleness, his kindness, and a family life that managed to be happy in spite of the sharp-tongued Dame Alice, stepmother to More's children and one of the great characters in English literature. Had he not been the kind of man he was, he could still have been the head of the English government at this time. But he had resigned in 1532, hoping to be permitted to live in quiet retirement, writing books in confutation of heresy. The very fact, however, that he had been Henry's intimate friend meant that Henry was now bent upon his destruction, as he always attributed a darker tinge of malice to anyone whom he had favored and who in any way came to oppose him. Cromwell and the unspeakable Rich were in this matter merely his instruments, though in More's case, as in Fisher's, the King may have deliberately blinded himself to what was being done, so that he could retain in his own mind a conviction of perfect rectitude. But while Henry's is the chief responsibility, the mind that suggested the means by which Fisher had been trapped and by which evidence was fabricated against More was almost certainly Cromwell's.

If Fisher had been circumspect, More had been even more so, for his legal mind had seen from the beginning that in silence alone was there any security. So long as he refused to make any expression of opinion regarding the validity of the royal claim to supremacy over the Church, he was safe—safe unless there was resort to torture; in that event, as we can see from his letters to Margaret, as well as to a priest who wrote to congratulate him when a report was being circulated that he had yielded, he could not be sure but that some incriminating word would be dragged out of him. To guard against this possibility, he let these people know in advance that they could set down any apparent change of opinion to the pressure of unbearable pain, to his human weakness; his opinion could never change.

So scrupulous was he that not even in the most confidential conversation with Margaret would he open his mind on this point. He did not doubt that she would guard any such confidence with her life, but he wanted to be able to say with absolute truth that not to a living soul had he declared himself. He was questioned over and over again by Cromwell and his agents, cajoled and threatened, but he smilingly maintained his reserve. He affirmed also that he had never advised anybody as to the course he should follow, nor had he criticized anybody who differed from him. He must have suspected that many of the most prominent people in the country were not acting in good faith—Tunstall and Lee and Gardiner, to go no further—but he was not going to say so or even to judge individuals in his own mind. He left each man to his own conscience; all that he asked was to be allowed to act according to his.

At last, on July 1, Sir Thomas More was put on trial at Westminster Hall. Sir Richard Rich, the prosecuting counsel, contrary to all legal rules, went himself into the witness box to give the evidence that was to doom More. And it was so doctored as to be perjury. He told of a conversation he had had recently with the accused, in which, when Rich had asked whether More would accept him as king should this be the decree of Parliament, the answer had come, "Yes." But More had gone on to ask Rich a question of his own. "Suppose that Parliament would make a law that God were not God; would you then, Master Rich, say that God were not God?" Up to this point the conversation was in all likelihood reported correctly enough. But then Rich went on to say that More had added, "No more could Parliament make the King Supreme Head of the Church."

More, conducting his own defense, said he was more sorry for Rich's perjury than for his own peril. Turning to his judges—made up of the leading peers and the chief members of the English judicial bench—he asked them if it was credible that he could have said such a thing to Rich—a man whom they all knew to be of infamous life and a liar—when he had refused to disclose his opinion to the Council or the King. The question answered itself.

As in treason trials the law demanded that there be at least two witnesses, Rich put into the box the two men, Thomas Palmer and Sir Richard Southwell, who had accompanied him on the day of the interview. It is somewhat to their credit that they would not corroborate Rich. But neither would they gainsay him. Evasively they answered that they were at that moment busy making bundles of More's books and so had not heard what he had said. Nevertheless Rich's unsupported word was allowed to stand, and it was upon this that More was found guilty.

Then More spoke out: England, being only a small part of the universal Church, could no more make laws for the whole than could London alone make a law for all England. The government of the Church could not belong to any temporal prince but only to the See of Rome, "a spiritual pre-eminence by the mouth of our Saviour Himself, personally present on earth." He appealed to the accepted

Catholic belief and said, "Therefore I am not bounden, my Lord, to conform my conscience to the Council of one realm against the general Council of Christendom." He declared further, "No more might this realm of England refuse obedience to the See of Rome than might the child refuse obedience to his own natural mother." When Audley, presiding as Chancellor, told him that his malice was now manifest, More answered that there was no malice in this. But he had well understood that he would not be protected by that qualifying word in the statute. Now as his long silence had failed to save him, he was speaking as plainly as possible.

Then sentence was passed upon him, and he saluted his judges—several of them friends of his, and all of them men who wished him well—hoping that they would meet merrily in heaven. And he went out of Westminster Hall with the edge of the ax turned toward him.

There was no certainty that he would not be dragged to Tyburn, as were the Carthusians, for though he had been Chancellor, he was not of noble blood. But he was by far the most distinguished of Englishmen, and even Henry would not risk the odium of making him suffer the ignominious death ordinarily meted out to traitors. So five days later he was led to the block on Tower Hill, going there calmly and jesting on the scaffold itself.

There are same marvels recorded of his burial. The King had granted as a special favor that More's relatives and friends might be present. But it is uncertain as to where his remains were laid, except that it is virtually certain that his head, after being taken down from London Bridge, was preserved by his daughter Margaret and buried in the Roper vault at St. Dunstan's, Canterbury. His body is supposed to rest in the little church of St. Peter's ad Vincula in the Tower. But though no doubt it was originally buried there, a manuscript life of Fisher in Latin in the British Museum—one apparently written during the reign of Mary—says that the body was buried in the More tomb in Chelsea church, perhaps transferred there by permission of the Catholic Mary.[10] Apart from the documentary testimony to this, there is a fact that inclines me to believe More's remains are at Chelsea. It is that, though the church was completely demolished during the Nazi bombings of London, the More tomb, alone of all that it contained, was left intact.

Another marvel is related by Thomas Stapleton, who says that

[10] Such is the belief of both Bridgett and Chambers.

he was often told about this by Dorothy Colley, the wife of John Harris. She had gone with Margaret Roper to get More's body, but they discovered when nearing the Tower that they had forgotten to bring money with which to buy a winding sheet. Margaret, greatly distressed, asked Dorothy to look in her purse again; then the precise amount needed for the winding sheet was found. This incident may be rejected on a priori grounds or be susceptible of a natural explanation. But it is at least as well attested as are most historical facts.

All Christendom was horrified when news came of the execution of Fisher and More. So Cromwell found it advisable to write in September, 1535, to Sir Gregory da Casale, explaining for the Pope's benefit that these were men guilty of high treason. This being the case, he professes to wonder that the Pope should be indignant at their just sentence. But as Stubbs remarks, these executions "seemed to have proved to the King himself that no scruples should ever hereafter touch him." At any rate no scruples ever did.

Chapter Seven

THE PERSECUTION

$\mathfrak{H}$ENRY'S DISAPPOINTMENT that the child Anne bore seven and a half months after marriage was a girl soon became evident by his attitude toward the Queen. He began to revenge himself for the long years he had wasted in sterile fidelity. Now that his passion had been satisfied, it was replaced by the resentment stored up during the courtship by Anne's arrogant behavior toward him. She was even more arrogant toward others, and this resulted in a lessening of the influence of the Boleyn faction. Even had she borne a son—which would of course have made her secure—the nation would still have groaned over the prospect of being ruled by Anne and her brother as regents, when the old King died.

In addition, her allies abroad were cooling toward her. If for no other reason than that the Emperor was her declared enemy, the King of France had professed himself her friend. Yet when, shortly after the passing of the Act of Supremacy at the end of 1534, Chabot de Brion was sent over as the French envoy, he was rather studiously cool toward her, and ostentatiously cordial toward Chapuys. Nor did Anne's behavior toward Chabot help matters. Sitting by her side one evening, he saw the King going down the hall to fetch a gentleman whom he wished to present to the Queen. Suddenly, Anne broke into a shrill peal of laughter, which Chabot, very much offended, supposed was directed at him. She tried later to explain that it was because she saw the King lost in conversation with her rival of the moment and quite forgetful of what it was he had meant to do. But Chabot, who did not understand Anne's strange make-up or that her nerves were very much on edge, did not really believe her. He continued to suspect that she had ridiculed him.

It was about this time that Thomas More in the Tower one day asked his daughter Margaret how the Queen was. He got the answer, "In faith, father, never better"; but said in his turn, "Never better, Meg! Alas! Meg, alas, it pitieth me to remember into what misery, poor soul, she shall shortly come." He knew how unstable Henry was and that Anne's hold over him was already precarious; it was not difficult for his acute mind to foresee her inevitable end.

Anne herself probably realized that the King's affection for her —if "affection" is the right word—was being transformed by degrees into positive dislike, but she was not intelligent enough to estimate the danger in which she stood. Otherwise she would not have been so indiscreet as to provide her enemies with a handle by the flirtations in which she indulged with some of the young courtiers. Her lack of dignity—it was nothing worse—caused much unfavorable comment. So also did the vindictiveness she always showed to Katherine, whom she continued to regard as a rival, and to the Princess Mary, whom she knew the people of England would prefer to her daughter Elizabeth, whatever the Act of Succession might say. Some extenuation may be found in her sense of insecurity. But she was only adding to the indignation that the country felt; she was increasing her own danger.

All she could indulge in was petty persecution of Katherine and her daughter. And though that persecution was not, in the event, bloody, there was always the possibility that it might become so. Of Katherine she used to say, "I will be her death and she mine," and Chapuys had to warn the "Princess Dowager" to guard herself against assassination. He also reported that Anne had threatened, at a time when the King was intending to visit France, that in his absence she would have Mary executed. Her brother, Lord Rochford, warned her against such wild talk, but she retorted that she would really do it, even if she were to be skinned alive for it. Had Katherine wished to take advantage of her own popularity and the unpopularity of Anne (which to a large extent recoiled on the King, who reproached her for it), she could very easily have done so.

What Katherine did, however, was only to stand steadfastly by her refusal to recognize her divorce or Henry's new marriage. When commissioners were sent to her shortly after Cranmer's decree at Dunstable to inform her that she must accept the King as Head of the Church and be content to be known in future as the widow of Prince Arthur, Henry's elder brother, she asked that she might read to herself the long document that had been read to her. Then she sat at her desk and crossed out every reference to herself as the "Dowager" and insisted, as she had done at the interview, that she was still Queen of England. She would have no servant who would not address her as such; truth was truth and must be honored; she said, "I would rather be a poor beggar's wife and be sure of heaven, than queen of all the world, and stand in doubt thereof by reason of my own consent." She was not contending for vain glory, but she would not slander herself by confessing that she had been the King's harlot for twenty-four years. "The cause," she concluded, "I cannot tell by what subtle means has been determined here within the King's realm, before a man of his own making, the Bishop of Canterbury, no person indifferent I think in that behalf; and for the indifference of the place, I think the place had been more indifferent to be judged in hell; for no truth can be suffered here, whereas the devils themselves I suppose do tremble to see the truth in this cause oppressed."

Chapuys, the Imperial Ambassador, was busying himself in organizing the many disgruntled nobles as the leaders of a rebellion against Henry for the restoration of the rights of the divorced Queen and her daughter. He believed that the acquittal by his peers of Lord Darcy, shortly after Anne's coronation,—something virtually unheard of in treason trials—had proved to the peers their own strength. Because of this they might be all the bolder to act again.

He had to proceed with the utmost caution, for Cromwell's spies were everywhere, and Cromwell, by striking at the right moment at one or two of the leaders of the conspiracy and bringing them to the block, could cow the others. It was not safe for Chapuys to give private interviews to those with whom he was in touch. They had to send their wives to his house or meet him themselves, as though by chance, in an open field, where there was no danger of being overheard, or to proceed by signs. Thus Lord Darcy sent him a penny on which was enameled the arms of the Poles; that meant that the Princess Mary should marry Reginald Pole. Darcy's next gift was a dagger; Chapuys understood this to mean that rebellion was being prepared.

Though Darcy did not name all the sixteen earls and barons who would rise, he managed to let Chapuys know that all the nobility of the North could be counted on, with perhaps the exception of Northumberland. Lord Montague and his brother, Sir Geoffrey Pole, were ready in the West, as was also the Marquis of Exeter. Wales, already restive under recent attempts to bring it under English law, was only waiting the signal to rebel; in fact, Wales or Cornwall were thought of as the best places for the Emperor to land his army when he sent the expected aid.

In all this Chapuys was a good deal too sanguine. Though there was undoubtedly considerable disaffection, it had not come to the necessary boiling point. And several of the essential factors for a successful rising were absent. But Chapuys painted the picture in its rosiest hues in order to obtain the approbation which Charles was most reluctant to give. The Ambassador told the Emperor that probably no nobles would adhere to the King except the Boleyns and the Duke of Norfolk. Even the Constable of the Tower, Sir William Kingston, was counted upon and would prove invaluable in the early stages of the outburst. Norfolk himself might come over as soon as he saw that the rebellion was going to succeed; and it could not fail. This was even more true of the Duke of Suffolk, now married (for the fourth time) to the daughter of Maria de Salinas, the Countess of Willoughby, a former lady in waiting to Katherine. And the adhesion of Lord Edmund Bray and the Earl of Rutland and Sir Thomas Elyot, until recently Henry's Ambassador to the Emperor, and Sir Thomas Burgoyne, the Duke of Buckingham's son-in-law, was thought very likely. The scheme seemed really foolproof.

Charles, however, would never give any definite promise to send even a small invading army. Instead he always pointed to the difficulties he was encountering in this or that part of his empire. Though—if what Chapuys said was reliable—the rising would succeed even without Charles's assistance, Charles knew that, once it had started, he could hardly keep out of it. And he did not want to be dragged into what he considered a dubious adventure. He was therefore consistently cold where Chapuys was enthusiastic, and this was discouraging to everybody.

The main difficulty, however, was not Charles but Katherine. She resolutely refused to have anything to do with a rising. She felt that she had already done England much harm, and she did not wish blood to be shed in her cause. Over and above this, she held that she owed Henry obedience both as his subject and his wife. She would not even go so far as to countenance the plan to have Mary abducted to the Low Countries and married there to Reginald Pole. It was in vain that Chapuys assured her that there would be hardly any risk. Mary was then living at Eltham, near the Thames estuary. She could be met when out riding by a band of horsemen and hurried to the ship waiting for her. Everybody could be counted upon to connive at her escape. But Katherine believed that Mary's flight would be the signal for the rising, so she would not agree. As Katherine would be in no sense a party to what was planned, the ingenious conspiracy being hatched by Chapuys lacked a focal point.

Her mode of life at Buckden, where she was transferred from Ampthill after her divorce, is described by Harpsfield as one of great solitariness, full of prayer, almsgiving, and ascetic practices. When she was not at her devotions, she spent her time with her gentlewomen embroidering vestments for churches. There was a room in the house with a window opening into the chapel, and at this window she spent a large part of every day and also of every night, leaning upon the stone sill, her tears making it so wet that it seemed washed by rain. Though there were cushions upon which she could have knelt, she removed them to kneel upon the hard, cold flags. She was praying for Henry, whom she thought of as a good man misled by evil councilors—Cromwell being mainly in her mind. She prayed that her husband might return to God; she prayed in fear that he lose his soul and in fear of the souls that were being lost on his account. She firmly believed that strong papal action against Henry would have the effect of bringing him to his senses,[1] and she

---

[1] Judge Caribites has defended the papal dilatoriness in his *Clement VII and Henry VIII*, on the ground that the delay was providential, by allowing the Jesuits to come into being before the breach with Rome had occurred. I cannot see the force of this argument, as even if we take August 15, 1534, as the birthday of the Society it was not until several years later that the Jesuits began their counteroffensive. See pp. 212–213 of his book.

kept writing vigorous letters to Clement urging this. But she would have no other sword drawn except the sword of the spirit.

Cromwell's spy system brought him information as to what was afoot. He had agents in Katherine's household, the Emperor's Council Chamber, and even the Roman Curia, as well as a host of sharp-eyed observers in England. But, though the air was murky with suspicion, he could never get hold of anything definite enough to warrant a charge of treason. Moreover, without dismissing the possibility of a rising, he felt that he might safely discount it. Henry told his Council: "The Lady Katherine is a proud, stubborn woman of very high courage. If she took it into her head to take her daughter's part, she could quite easily take the field, muster a great array, and wage against me a war as fierce as any her mother Isabella ever waged in Spain." But he was well aware that her loyalty to him would never permit this.

Officially Henry disapproved of murder, though unofficially he countenanced the unsuccessful attempts made on the life of Cardinal Pole and the successful attempt made on the life of Cardinal Beaton in Scotland. But he much preferred a coloring of legality when he wished to remove an obstacle. There came a time in 1535 when it was seriously considered whether he should not arraign both Katherine and Mary for high treason. Neither of them were in the least guilty, as he knew, but as in that year it seemed for a while as though Charles might invade England—in which event the country would burst into flame—he believed it would be as well to remove the incentive for invasion and rebellion. The plan was abandoned only because the risks were too great. Were Katherine and Mary tried, it would have had to be before peers known as, for the most part, their adherents. There was a similar obstacle to attainder. It was much safer to allow nature—encouraged to operate by the lodging of Katherine in one house more unhealthy than the last—to do what was desired. But Katherine knew what was being meditated and wrote to Chapuys, "I am told that the next Parliament is to decide whether I am to suffer martyrdom. If it is to be so, I hope it may be a meritorious act. . . . There is no punishment from God except for neglected duty." About the same time she concluded one of her letters to Mary, saying, "I set not a rush by it; for when they have done the uttermost they can, then I am sure of the amendment. . . . We never come to the kingdom of heaven but by troubles."

124

The occasion of this danger was that in the fall of 1535 Charles at last had his hands free and could have invaded England had he chosen to do so. He had won the great victory of Goletta in North Africa, a victory which when reported to Henry and Cromwell by Chapuys made them look, as he maliciously records, "like dogs who had tumbled out of a window." They both gave their insincere congratulations by word of mouth that day, and Cromwell wrote on September 10, and again on the thirtieth, expressing the King's great joy at hearing of the Emperor's triumph. But it is not without significance that, though in the first of these letters he had given a half promise that Chapuys should be allowed to visit the Lady Mary, the second letter asks that the visit be postponed. He and Henry considered it inadvisable that Chapuys be in direct communication with the Princess then of all times.

Similarly Chapuys was prevented from seeing Katherine until she was on her deathbed the following January, when a visit could be of no political consequence. Indeed, Katherine's death was going to mean, it was hoped, that Henry would be able to end his quarrel with Charles. Cromwell, though he did not have any animosity toward either Katherine or Mary, several times expressed the pious hope that one of them or both would die, so as not to embarrass him in his plans. On the very day news came that the divorced Queen was dead, he tried to take advantage of this fact by writing to Bishop Gardiner and Sir John Wallop, the English ambassadors in France, instructing them to explain to Francis that he had better lose no time in meeting Henry's demands; otherwise he might be forestalled by the Emperor, who now had no reason not to heal the breach brought about by Henry's treatment of Charles's aunt.

It was widely believed at the time that Katherine had been poisoned, and in our own time Paul Friedmann has argued with considerable weight that such was the case. But when he says, "The events which followed Katherine's death would be inexplicable if she died in the ordinary course of nature. The government acted again and again as if it knew that a murder had been committed," one may still answer that these actions can be explained on other grounds. For instance, the detention in England of Jorge de Ateca, the Bishop of Llandaff, who had been Katherine's chaplain, of her physician, de la Sá, and other attendants may be readily accounted for by Cromwell's not wishing to have them go abroad to spread stories about the ill usage the Queen had received. Furthermore, the condition of her heart, which was black with a growth attached, as noticed by the chandler who embalmed her body, suggests cancer. In the sixteenth century one heard a great deal about slow poisons, and Friedmann suggests that the Queen received repeated low doses which exhausted her constitution and so made her susceptible to other diseases.

After Anne Boleyn's fall there was open talk of her having poisoned her rival, but Merriman says, very truly, "If the Queen was murdered, there is every reason to think that Cromwell was chiefly responsible." As for Henry, when a great crime was about to be perpetrated, it was his way to walk about with his hands in his pockets and his chin stuck into the air, whistling as though he did not have the faintest idea of what was going on. Dirty work might be done, so long as he was kept in ostensible ignorance.

But to say that Cromwell found Katherine's demise convenient is not at all the same thing as to say that he hastened it, unless it was by having the "Princess Dowager" lodged in the unhealthy Buckden and then at the even more unhealthy Kimbolton. Whether we dismiss the chandler's description of the heart—as given by a man without any medical knowledge—or accept it, it would not necessarily rule out the poison theory. But one question still has to be answered: how was poison administered and by whom? Katherine, following Chapuys's advice, shut fast all the doors and windows of her room at night. But she did even more: she would eat no food except that prepared by her trusted ladies in waiting over the fire in her bedroom. Chapuys was a very accurate reporter of facts, but his suspicions must not be regarded as proofs. He did not put it past Henry to murder his daughter as well as his wife, and few will put murder past Cromwell. Yet I believe both men were entirely innocent in this case. Katherine's death must be set down to natural causes.

When news of her death reached Rome, it was hoped that Henry would now be reconciled with the Holy See. Paul III renewed his expressions of good will. It would have been easy to regularize Henry's marriage to Anne. So far from the Emperor wishing to create complications, he instructed Chapuys, who had been Anne's enemy so long as Katherine was alive, to give her his backing now. Her miscarriage on the day of Katherine's funeral made him believe she would never bear another living child; and he was sure that

126

Mary would be accepted by the English people in preference to Elizabeth, in spite of the Act of Succession.

Unfortunately this was the worst of all possible moments for a reconciliation with Rome. Parliament was to be brought into session again early in February, and the main business was to consider a bill authorizing the suppression of the smaller monasteries. With hundreds of manors now within Henry's grasp, or soon to be, and with Cromwell dangling before him the glittering prospect of an immense booty of plate, the last thing in the world the King wanted was even a formal submission to the Pope, as this would make it impossible for him to proceed at once to plunder. When Cromwell only a very little later changed his mind about this and advocated coming to an understanding with the Pope, since this was one of the conditions the Emperor laid down for a firm alliance with Henry, it was Henry who demurred. He reasserted in the strongest possible terms his supremacy over the Church and seized his opportunity, now that Mary lacked the moral support her mother had given, of forcing her submission.

But before coming to this, it should be said that in February plans were renewed for Mary's flight to the Low Countries, which hitherto had been opposed by Katherine and discouraged by the Emperor. Now it was the Emperor who sent a special agent to England to arrange the matter with the help of Chapuys. But the situation had changed; it would have been difficult to have arranged an abduction, so carefully was Mary guarded at Hatfield. Moreover, the Emperor found reasons for changing his mind once more and decided that it would be more to his advantage to seek Henry's friendship. In this Mary was the principal sufferer.

Ever since Mary was a baby there had been various marriage projects for her, but they had come to nothing, first because until this time she had been too young for marriage, and afterward because her statutory bastardization stood in the way. Foreign princes objected to accepting a bride with even a fictitious stigma attaching to her. The rumor whispered in 1536 that she might be married to Cromwell was certainly quite false. The whole thing seems to have been based upon the fact that Cromwell had a ring made for her, one with a Latin inscription on it reminding Mary of her duty toward her father. In any event Cromwell was not permitted to give her the ring, for Henry, when he heard of it, took the ring away from Cromwell and presented it to his daughter himself. It is impossible to imagine that Henry would have accepted as his son-in-law a man so despised by the nobility; and he knew that the moment he died all England would rise against the hated "King Thomas." Chapuys mentions the rumor only to say that he does not believe it.

Cromwell's function regarding Mary was quite different: it was to combine persuasion and threats to force her submission to her ·father. Anne had attempted this, alternating between spiteful ill-usage and lavish promises, only to be repulsed steadily. It is doubtful whether Mary would ever have submitted while Anne was alive, for her pride forbade her to give Anne, her mother's supplanter, such a triumph. But when Anne, like her mother, had passed from the scene and in Jane Seymour there was a new Queen, unaffectedly kind, the submission, though humiliating, was at least one that would not pain Mary's mother, the dead Katherine. Pressure was therefore at once applied, in the reasonable certainty that what had previously proved impossible would be brought about.

Cromwell, as has been said, was Henry's agent in this. The wheedling Cranmer would have been of no use in Mary's case, as she detested him, both as a heretic and as the man who had divorced her mother. But Mary seems to have been one of the many people who trusted Cromwell. She frequently addressed him as though he were the only friend she had in official circles. Thus after Anne's death she wrote, saying, "I perceive nobody durst speak for me as long as that woman liveth which is now gone, whom I pray God of His great mercy to forgive. Wherefore, now she is gone, I am the bolder to write to you for one of my chief friends. And therefore I desire you, for the love of God, to be a suitor for me to the King's grace."

And Cromwell did intercede for her, though in his own fashion, using her daughterly affection as a lever to extract what the King wanted. He got Henry to agree to receive a letter from her, and this letter Cromwell himself composed, sending it to her to copy. But what came back from Hunsdon on June 10, 1536, was not abject enough, as it did not acknowledge the King as Head of the Church or her mother's marriage to have been incestuous—because she had previously married Henry's brother. So Cromwell had to compose another letter for her to copy—this time word for word—and dispatch to the King. As a promise of general obedience was insufficient, Cromwell told Mary sternly, "With your own folly you

128

undo yourself, and all that have wished you good; and yet I will say unto you, as I have said elsewhere heretofore, that it were a great pity ye should not be an example in a punishment, if ye will make yourself an example in the contempt of God, your natural father, and his laws, by your own fantasy. . . . Wherefore, Madam, to be plain with you, as God is my witness, like as I think you the most obstinate and obdurate woman, all things considered, that ever was. . . . If you will not with speed leave all your sinister counsels, which have brought you to the point of utter undoing, without remedy, and herein follow my advice, I take leave of you for ever, and I desire you never to write or make any means unto me hereafter. For I will never think you other than the most ungrateful, unnatural, and most obstinate person both to God and your most dear and benign father."

This was a very broad hint, which Mary perfectly understood, that if she persisted in her attitude her father would proceed against her as he had proceeded against More and Fisher. Chapuys had long before given his opinion that Mary (and for that matter, Katherine) should take the Oath of Supremacy and say anything else required of them, if it became a question of extreme necessity. He saw that point had been reached, and he undertook to have the Pope informed that she acted only under duress, in which circumstances he could be counted upon to absolve her. Mary was not so much afraid for herself as of doing anything to infuriate her father further. Opposition always made him all the more insistent; so she hoped that by compliance he would soften toward her and perhaps return, now that Anne was gone, to the Roman obedience. Even if he did not, she had to try to save her life, as there was a very strong chance that she would eventually become Queen, in which case she would restore England to Catholic unity.

Under no circumstances would Katherine have submitted; rather than that, she would have died a thousand deaths. It was different with Mary; she was a young girl, all alone among enemies. And though she was to prove that she had great courage—she had already proved it—she did not have Katherine's indomitable heroism. Accordingly she agreed to sign whatever instrument Cromwell drew up for her.

When she did so, she disdainfully refused to read over the conditions imposed, thereby impressing it upon everybody that her act was merely formal. But she placed herself in subjection to her father's laws; she admitted his supremacy over the Church; she acknowledged that her mother's marriage was against God's laws and man's. And of course there was the customary embroidery about her being "most humbly prostrate at the feet of your most excellent Majesty."

Even after that the King was far from satisfied. Though officially Mary was restored to favor and found in Jane Seymour, as later in Catherine Parr, a stepmother who befriended her, Henry remained suspicious, and not without reason. He realized that Mary's submission was merely on the surface, without conviction. What he demanded was wholehearted assent of her mind. He therefore continued to treat her scurvily, giving her hardly enough to live on, so that at the end of 1539 she had to write again to Cromwell, saying that her father allowed her only forty pounds sterling every quarter. As Christmas was approaching, Cromwell was begged to try and get the King to increase this amount. "And thus, my Lord," she told him, "I am ashamed always to be a beggar unto you; but that the occasion at this time is such that I cannot choose." This niggardliness toward the King's daughter came when the King was richer than ever before, with the loot of the last and wealthiest of the monasteries pouring into his hands. One cannot but pity the poor girl, especially for the humiliation it must have been to make this appeal to Cromwell, the man who had forced her submission. Mary wrote to him because he was all-powerful. But it must also be said that throughout the whole business we can discern that she, like so many other people, believed that Cromwell was at heart good-natured. This is hard to understand, but it must be allowed for. That people believed him to be kind stands as a profound puzzle in studying his life.

Chapter Eight

THE LOOT

WHAT SHOULD be said first concerning the initial Cromwellian suppression of monasteries is that it closely followed the Wolseian model. It was of course on a much larger scale, nearly 400 monasteries falling under the law passed early in 1536, as against the 30 that Wolsey dealt with. But in each case the professed intention was the good of the monastic institution, its reform by reorganization and regrouping. Of course in each case there was a secondary reason that was really primary—with Wolsey the endowment of his colleges at Oxford and Ipswich and with Henry the augmentation of the royal revenues, on the understanding that these were to be used for beneficent public purposes. In neither case was there any intention of seizing everything that the suppressed monasteries possessed but only superfluous goods. Ample provision would be made for such monks and nuns as were ejected when they had been placed in other religious houses. After this had been done, without any real suffering on the part of religious communities, the monastic institution itself would be improved and strengthened, and the King would have at his disposal revenues which he could use for national defense, the maintenance of roads, bridges, and sea walls, the endowment of chairs at the universities, and the establishment of those nineteen new bishoprics that Wolsey had projected.

It could also be plausibly said that in some instances the monastic estates were being badly managed, and it was certainly true that many of them were encumbered with debts. And again the Wolseian argument was used that there were too many small monasteries in England, in which the number of monks or nuns had declined below the minimum of twelve deemed necessary for the resonant and stately chanting of the office in choir. Finally the Wolseian method of vilifying the monasteries he wished to suppress was resorted to, though one of the main charges against the Cardinal in the disabling bill of 1530 was that he had given the English clergy a bad name at Rome.

Henry may have brought himself to believe that he intended only good toward the monasteries—for he was a profound self-deceiver—but one must wonder, in that event, why he entrusted the business to Thomas Cromwell who was well-known, while in Wolsey's service, as a great taker of bribes and ruthlessly extortionate. Henry must have conveniently forgotten the past and remembered only how efficient Cromwell had shown himself in recent years and that he was the man most experienced in the kind of work now to be done. In January, 1535, the King appointed him his Vicegerent over the Church with virtually unlimited administrative powers. No time was lost in making it clear to the bishops that they held office only at the King's pleasure and that His Majesty (or Cromwell himself) could make or unmake them as he chose. This was enforced later in the same year with a prohibitory letter sent to all the members of the hierarchy to make no visitations of monasteries within their jurisdiction. Cromwell intended to see to this himself, and he would brook no interference. Now even the formerly exempted religious houses—those which did not fall under the jurisdiction of the bishops—were taken over by him, as the King had superseded the Pope in England.

Cromwell was of course much too busy to make these visitations in person, so he appointed a number of agents—about whom we shall hear more in a little while—whose instructions were to assess the value of the monasteries and to inquire into the moral and religious conditions in the various houses to which they were sent. The object was to collect defamatory evidence against the smaller houses, those to be suppressed under statute when Parliament met early in 1536, in order to induce Parliament to pass the desired legislation.

Cromwell's agents were rather late in settling down to their work, partly because Cromwell was occupied during May and June with the trials of the two groups of Carthusians and of More and Fisher. But the delay was also because it had been believed up to that time, from the misleading reports that Sir Gregory da Casale had been sending from Rome, that Paul III was disposed to reverse the decision of his predecessor regarding the royal divorce. Not until those hopes had been shown to be groundless did Cromwell proceed with full rigor against his victims. For the same reason he held his hand regarding the monasteries. Though the Act of Suppression was already on the statute book, it merely permitted the King to take over certain monasteries; it in no way obliged him to take over any. The Pope might be willing to make concessions to the King to save the threatened religious houses.

The preliminary visitations, when at last they occurred, were all between July, 1535, and January, 1536. But in so short a period it was simply not possible to make anything approaching a thorough investigation. Just two things were sought at this moment: an appraisal of the value of the monastic estates (often put at too low a figure for a reason which will appear in a moment) and blackening information about the religious.

As to this last it must be noted that the charges against the monks and nuns never came from the outside, as would have been the case had they borne a bad reputation, but always from the inside. The procedure was to induce a religious to accuse the superior or some other member of the community of evil conduct—it also served as well when somebody could be induced to accuse himself. Broken under the hammer of terror and softened by the promise of a reward—a position or a pension—enough admissions were made for Cromwell's purpose.

Here three points might be noted, in addition to those already made. First, the majority of the moral delinquencies charged against the religious were of secret vice, something which it need not be said is very hard to discover. Second, when nothing whatever could be unearthed, the inference was that everybody was acting in collusion to conceal it. Third, when the suppressions actually began in 1536, conducted by commissions made up of the local gentry who were familiar with local conditions, in every known instance they presented a very different picture of the state

133

of the monasteries from that so hurriedly and luridly drawn by Cromwell's agents.

We hear, but not until Elizabeth's reign, of a "Black Book" produced in Parliament chock-full of the details of monastic misbehavior. That no such book exists today has been confidently accounted for by Froude on the ground that Bishop Bonner was ordered to burn it when Mary was on the throne. The assertion is quite gratuitous, and indeed Froude on this subject is most unfair, for after telling us that monastic crimes were too nauseous to dwell upon, he nevertheless continues to dwell upon them for thirty pages or more. The fact is that this "Black Book," if it ever existed, could have been merely a summary of the reports sent to Cromwell by his agents, and many of these we have. But even they do not seem to have been presented to Parliament, which, as the preamble of the acts indicates, chose to accept the charges as proved on the King's naked word: he has "knowledge that the premises be true."

The rest of the preamble to the act should be quoted. It reads: "Forasmuch as manifest sin, vicious, carnal and abominable living, is daily used and committed among the little and small abbeys, priories, and other religious houses of monks, canons, and nuns, where the congregation of such religious persons is under the number of twelve, whereby the governors of such religious houses spoil, consume, destroy, and utterly waste their churches, monasteries, principal houses, farms and granges, to the high displeasure of almighty God, the slander of true religion, and to the great infamy of the King's Highness and of the realm, if redress should not be had thereto; and albeit that many continual visitations hath been heretofore had by the space of two hundred years and more, for an honest and charitable reformation of such unthrifty, carnal and abominable living; yet nevertheless, little or none amendment is hitherto had, but their vicious living shamelessly increaseth and augmenteth . . . so that without such small houses be utterly suppressed and the religious persons therein committed to great and honorable monasteries of religion in this realm, where they may be compelled to live religiously for the reformation of their lives, there can be no reformation in this behalf: in consideration hereof the King's most royal Majesty, being supreme head on earth under God, of the Church of England, daily finding and devising the increase, advancement, and exaltation of true doctrine and virtue in the said Church, to the only glory of God, and the total extirping and destruction of vice and sin; having knowledge that the premises be true, as well as by the accounts of his late visitation as by sundry credible informations; considering also that divers great monasteries of this realm, wherein, thanks be to God, religion is right well kept and observed, be destitute of such full number of religious persons as they ought and may keep; hath thought it good that a plain declaration should be made of the premises, as well to the Lords spiritual and temporal as to his other loving subjects to the Commons in this present Parliament assembled. Whereupon, the said Lords and Commons, by a great deliberation, finally be resolved that it is and shall be much more to the pleasure of almighty God, and for the honor of this His realm, that the possession of such religious houses, now spent, and spoiled and wasted for the increase and maintenance of sin, should be converted to better uses; and the unthrifty religious persons so spending the same be compelled to reform their lives."

That is an astounding piece of rigmarole, but it is clear that the suppression proposed was at least as much for economic as for moral reasons—to prevent alleged mismanagement. It also seems to guarantee the continued existence of the larger abbeys, which are given a clean bill of health, and even promises them greater strength. But not appearing in the preamble is the fact that the decision as to what houses are to go does not depend upon the number of monks or nuns they contain—for the point about at least twelve religious in each house being necessary carries weight—but upon the decisive question of income. Those monasteries and convents whose rental values are less than two hundred pounds sterling a year are to be (or may be) extirpated; the rest are to be spared. Parliament, in other words, was invited to believe that those with less than two hundred pounds sterling a year must be vicious and those with an income above that amount are morally and spiritually all they should be.

How did such a bill pass the House of Lords, where sat twenty bishops and thirty of the greater abbots, who in combination could outvote the temporal peers? The answer is that many of these were "excused" attendance—which means that they were, in effect, ordered to stay away. But of the abbots present some no doubt thought the act would be for the advantage of the large and wealthy establishments over which they presided. As for the House of Commons, which was largely made up of rich merchants, knights of the shire, and lawyers, they had already scented that the monastic expropriations were for their profit. Yet even among the Commons there was a good deal of opposition until the King began to talk of having his bill or of having some of their heads. They therefore salved their consciences with the reflection that monastic conditions must be bad if the King said they were. They also persuaded themselves that the act was what it professed to be, one for the benefit of monasticism as an institution. Doubtfully, but because there was nothing much they could do about it, they allowed the act to pass.

The public mind had been prepared by the sending out of three kinds of preachers. One group denounced the monks as "hypocrites, sorcerers, and idle drones" (sorcerers being thrown in to blacken such monks as might be giving themselves to study). Another group were to tell the people that "the monks made the land unprofitable." Here in some instances there was a too easygoing management of monastic estates, and the rents charged on them were lower than the rising costs of living demanded. The third set of preachers—and these were the one whose argument had by far the most popular appeal—told their audiences that "if the abbeys went down, the King would never want for any taxes again." Nothing, as events were soon to show, could have been less true.

Yet the Cromwellian policy was to give the King such vast manorial holdings that from this first spoliation (which was all originally contemplated) the King's income would have been (or should have been) almost doubled. With his increased wealth and the vast number of new tenants owing him direct feudal service, it was supposed that he would be invulnerable against any possible combination of nobles. He could have dispensed with Parliament, regarded as the fountain from which special subsidies flowed; and when it did meet, Parliament, as managed by Cromwell and turned into an instrument for ratifying the King's will, could have been counted upon to be all the more tractable because it would not be asked to vote special taxes.

The policy of Henry's father had been that of weakening the nobility and as such had been eminently successful. The son could go further and remove forever the power of the nobles as a force that might be used against the Crown. Had Cromwell been serving under Henry VII instead of Henry VIII, he might well have accomplished all that he set out to do. But instead of having as his king a man who was cautious, systematic, businesslike, and even parsimonious, he was acting for a man who had nothing of his father in him except his greed for money. But Henry VIII's idea of money was not something to save but to spend, and in the most reckless fashion.

He had always been extravagant—first because the wealth left him by his father encouraged him to spend freely but also because of his weak character, with its desire to show off. And he was surrounded by people who considered that they had claims upon him because of the help they had given him in his struggle with the Papacy. Not only the Boleyns and the members of their faction had to be provided for but a great many other influential people whose support of this new policy had to be rewarded in substantial fashion. It very soon became apparent that the King would not be able to retain all the spoils of the monasteries for himself. Cromwell was obliged to show him that, though this might seem disappointing, it was really an advantage. It was an extension of his methods with Parliament—implicating the powerful elements in what was being done.

Not even Cromwell, however, could have been really happy about the results. He never envisaged such a distribution of the monastic lands as occurred. Not to any great extent while Cromwell was alive were the monastic lands sold, as they were later, at prices absurdly below their true value; that came about mainly because of the wars at the end of the King's life, wars which Cromwell had always been careful to avoid. But even under Cromwell the snowball was set rolling which afterward released an avalanche. The King was certainly immensely enriched, but the nobles—especially the new men among them—and the officials were enriched still more. Nor did the older nobility, even their most orthodox members, see any reason why they should not get their share of the monastic plunder.

The matter is closely connected with that land hunger which had seized Tudor England. This had manifested itself in the en-

137

closure movement, something which Henry had tried to check, though without much success.[1] But that movement had, so far, manifested itself only among those who were already landowners, and some of the most notorious enclosers, as Sir Thomas More points out in his *Utopia*, were holders of monastic property. As land during the agrarian revolution of the time had suddenly acquired a greatly increased value because of the profits to be derived from the sale of English wool, there was all the more eagerness to acquire land as the most profitable of investments. The commercial class as a body was naturally very much in favor of this.

Something more has to be said. Even apart from the profit of obtaining lands for sheep raising (and there was, after all, a limit beyond which this would not be profitable, as sales were not indefinitely to be extended), many rich merchants and lawyers with social pretensions sought lands, so as to become country gentlemen. Now was their opportunity. They were quick to seize it. Such people bought from the Crown at a bargain even when they paid twenty times the yearly rental income on the valuation of under-assessed estates. They realized that they could raise the rents of their tenants. But to court favorites or useful tools, many of these estates went as a free gift or at a nominal price. What was finally accomplished proved—though not in Henry's time—ruinous to the English monarchy. The Machiavellian and totalitarian Cromwell started something which was, in the long run, destined to make the King the salaried servant of his kingdom.[2]

The whole ecclesiastical endowments of England were officially estimated as being £320,000, or about £8,000,000 in modern values, in yearly revenues. The larger half were those possessed by

[1] It might be desirable to explain this. During the Middle Ages fields had been open and had been cultivated in narrow strips. Enclosures meant simply that such holdings were grouped together and surrounded by a hedge or a fence. It made possible sheep farming on an unprecedented scale, for the sake of their wool, and the dispossession of tenants no longer needed for farms not put under the plow.

[2] I am not arguing that the eventual result was not good, though as to this I have some mental reservations. But the good was reached only after a long and devious process. If it was eventually obtained, it was despite Cromwell's policy, of which, indeed, it was the complete opposite. England, where totalitarianism began, is now the one solid bastion in Europe against communism. But to explain how this happened would call for another book.

the monasteries. But of the 376 monasteries and convents which fell under the act of 1536—because they had revenues of less than £200 a year—123 were spared, either because they found powerful protectors or, more often, because they compounded with the Crown and gave large bribes to Cromwell and his agents. This composition was profitable, as it normally consisted in the payment of two years' income for the privilege of continuing, which continuance was guaranteed in perpetuity. What actually found its way into the royal treasury was £32,000 a year, a large amount, but hardly half as large as it should have been. In short, the proceeds were relatively meager. It is this fact which explains what was to happen afterward.

The monasteries, especially the smaller ones, were often in a tangle of debts. The King had a way of ordering that a pension that he should have paid was to come out of one of these religious houses. Moreover, the founders of these monasteries had often stipulated, not unreasonably, that impoverished members of their families should be taken care of by their foundations. There were also annuitants, who (as usual) lived longer than was expected. In all kinds of ways there were drains on these monastic revenues. The financial difficulties in which the religious houses found themselves help to explain why they gave up so easily. Several of these establishments made a voluntary surrender before the passage of the act of 1536. Though passed under pressure, one cannot say that it was illegal; however, it is easy to guess at the kind of pressure that was brought to bear.

While Henry was enriched, he was also swindled. Cromwell had learned the technique of this under Wolsey, and his agents—many of them men who had served Wolsey—knew the technique almost as well as he did. Now he had to wink at their proceedings. He was compelled to do so for the simple reason that he was in a position of extracting much larger bribes than theirs. He was subjected to a kind of blackmail, even while he subjected them to blackmail. Their official salary (and even his) was not very large; it was taken for granted that such people would support themselves—as Cromwell had done under Wolsey—mainly through the perquisites of their office. Sir Richard Rich, however, who was appointed the head of the Court of Augmentation, the office dealing with the mass of business arising from the suppression, was paid what was for those days a fabulous salary, though he had rich pickings on the side.

The chief of Cromwell's agents at this time—and they were in his service for a long while—were Dr. Richard Layton, Dr. John London, Dr. Thomas Leigh (all ecclesiastics), and the Welsh notary, John Ap Rice. It would be hard to say which of them was the most corrupt, but Layton seems to have been the most dreaded, not only by the unhappy religious whom he used to browbeat but by his fellow commissioners. They all spied upon one another and ran with tales of complaint to Cromwell. Layton, according to Leigh, was at one time threatening his life, and he certainly was instrumental in having London convicted of perjury and notorious immorality, for which he was cast into prison where he died. They were as unsavory a set of scoundrels as can be imagined. While it is possible to believe—from our general knowledge of human nature—that individual monks and nuns in those days were not all that they should have been, it is impossible to accept any unsupported statement coming from men of this type. Even when he happens to be telling the truth, a known liar is not to be believed.

Agents of another, and better, sort were John Hilsey, the Provincial of the Dominicans, George Browne, Cromwell's old acquaintance at the London house of the Austin Friars, and Richard Ingworth, another friar—all of them rewarded with bishoprics. Their job was to reduce the five orders of friars into submission. At this time there was no project for suppressing their houses, as the friars, unlike the monks, had little in the way of manorial holdings. But as they formed a compact body with their brethren on the Continent, it was specially important in their case that they should swear the Oath of Supremacy. Few friars refused this outright, but many fled the country. It might be noted how even these agents were in dread of Cromwell. Ingworth, for example, though he could call Cromwell in a letter of February 6, 1538, "his singular helper for XII years past" and showed himself remarkably assiduous in the performance of his assigned duties, was nevertheless not energetic enough to please his master, who charged him with having a friar's heart still. Poor Ingworth had to call heaven to witness that, so far from this being the case, he had laid aside all wish to follow his monastic rule more than a year before he had been able to lay aside his habit.

The friars' submission was all that was demanded of them at this time. But they, like the monks and nuns, were subjected to annoying regulations by the agents who were sent out after the passage of the Act of Suppression. Though 123 out of the 376 houses that came under the law were spared, for these life was made so miserable that many of them, as well as some other monasteries, were willing to surrender of their own accord. The agents carried with them 86 articles of inquiry, a copy of which exists with corrections in Cromwell's hand, and 25 injunctions to which they had power to add. We know from the correspondence between the Vicegerent and his agents that the injunctions were intended to force the religious to ask for the dissolution of their houses and that they as individuals be dispensed from their vows. As very few of them did so—for the vast majority preferred to put up with the deliberate system of annoyances, in the hope that eventual relief would come—Cromwell took it upon himself to dispense all those under the age of twenty-four, whether they wished it or not.

The insincerity of this monastic reform appears in the fact that everything possible was done to disrupt existing discipline while loud complaints were raised that discipline was lax. Any infraction of the injunctions could be reported to Cromwell or his agents, with the result of course that the rule of the order became difficult to enforce against subjects encouraged to insubordination. Not only was this so, but as there was to be only one gate of ingress or egress from a religious house and that closely guarded by Cromwell's officers, it became all but impossible for monks or nuns to attend to affairs on the monastic farms or even to care for their kitchen gardens. As the farms were often scattered over a considerable area, they became neglected; and yet it was the neglect of the monastic estates that had formed one of the main accusations against the religious. Such members of the community as were willing to act as Cromwell's informers—there were not many of them, but here and there they did exist—were rewarded with a dispensation from some of the more onerous monastic duties—particularly the night office—with consequences that can be readily imagined.

As the law did not oblige the suppression of all the houses with an income under two hundred pounds sterling a year but left this to the discretion of the King (which in practice meant Cromwell), pleas for respite began at once. Thus William Aleyn, the Abbot

141

of Waverley, wrote heart-rendingly on June 9, 1536, "beseeching your good mastership, for the love of Christ's passion, to help me in the preservation of this poor monastery, that we your bedesmen may remain in the service of God with the meanest living that any poor men may live with in this world. So to continue in the service of almighty Jesus, and I pray for the estate of our prince and your mastership. In no vain hope I write this to your mastership, forasmuch you put me in boldness full gently, when I was in suit to you last year at Winchester, saying, 'Repair to me for such business as ye shall have from time to time.' Therefore, instantly praying you, and my poor brethren with weeping eyes—desire you to help them; in this work no creatures in more trouble, and so we remain depending upon the comfort that shall come from you—serving God daily at Waverley."

That appeal had no effect; Waverley was one of the first houses to be suppressed. The simple-minded Abbot had trustingly appealed to Cromwell in the belief that he was his friend. He did not realize that if he was to be listened to at all, he would have to come forward with a large sum of money for the royal treasury and a suitable bribe for the Vicegerent. There are many cases of such bribery recorded, but doubtless there were many more of which all trace has been lost or carefully covered. Thus Cromwell informs the Prior of Coxford that his house has been saved by his efforts and demands what he euphemistically calls a loan of forty pounds sterling. And, following the Wolseian technique, he put up offices for sale. An instance of this was when Lady Margaret Sandys had a candidate for the position of Abbot of Worcester and undertakes, in his behalf, that "he will give you in ready money as much as any other man." For the position of Prior of the same abbey, Richard Gresham, the great land speculator, offers one hundred pounds sterling for the appointment of his nominee. And a monk named Marmaduke Bradley offered six hundred marks if Cromwell will make him Abbot of Fountains, which Cromwell did. Froude, unable to deny the venality, says that it is to be extenuated on the ground that it was open!

Nor was this bribery—it was often really a form of blackmail —limited to payments from the heads of religious houses. The bishops, being under the Vicegerent, sometimes took pains to curry favors with substantial sums of money. Cranmer, for instance, paid

Cromwell forty pounds sterling a year, for what reason does not appear, unless Cromwell's spies had found out about Mrs. Cranmer, whose existence could be reported to the King. On the other hand Rowland Lee, the Bishop of Coventry, when asked for one hundred pounds sterling for the grant of a priory, said he had already promised this to another man and in any case could not spare the money. But then Rowland Lee was acting as Governor-General of Wales and performing ruthlessly efficient service there for the King. He was therefore able to show some independence.

Now and then, however, Cromwell performed kindly acts out of good nature. An example of this comes out in an undated letter, written in all probability in 1537, by a John Clansey, in which Cromwell is informed that the Dorothy Clansey who was a nun at St. Mary's of Shaftesbury, though she had been entered there as his daughter, was really the daughter of Wolsey. Mr. Clansey therefore begged that she be allowed to remain and not be turned out like the others who were under twenty-four. "In doing this," he says, "your mastership shall do a very charitable deed." She was accordingly allowed to remain until the dissolution of the abbey in 1540, when she received a pension of £4.13.4 and lived on at least until 1553. But this was, after all, the minimum that Cromwell could do for the daughter of his former patron.

There are other instances of much the same sort, nothing very striking to be sure, but still indications that the man had his kind moments. Thus we find him lending forty pounds sterling to Margaret Vernon, the Prioress of Little Marlow; and she wrote to tell him, "Your visitors have been here of late and have discharged three of my Sisters. The one is Dame Catherine, the other two are the two young women that were last professed, which is not a little to my discomfort. I most humbly beseech you to be so special good master to me, your poor bedeswoman, as to give me your best advertisement and counsel, what way shall be best for me to take, seeing there be none here left but myself and this poor maiden." Cromwell then invited Dame Margaret to lay her grievances in person before him at his house in Stepney. But when she went there, she found so many visitors that she could not get to the great man. The upshot, however, was that he took her under his protection to the extent of making her governess to his son Gregory.

He had, however, no hesitation in using his authority in a most improper way, the brutal highhandedness of one too powerful to be checked. Stow, in his *Survey of London*, tells an astonishing story about this: "On the south side and at the west end of this church [that of the Austin friars] many fair houses are builded, namely in Throgmorton Street, one very large and spacious, builded in place of old and small tenements by Thomas Cromwell, Master of the Rolls etc. . . . This house being finished, and having some reasonable plot of ground left for a garden, he caused the pales of the gardens adjoining the north part thereof on a sudden to be taken down, 22 feet to be measured forth right unto the north of every man's ground, a trench to be cast, a foundation laid, and a high brick wall to be builded. My father had a garden there, and a house standing close to the south pale, this house they loosed from the ground and bare upon rollers into my father's garden 22 foot, ere my father heard thereof: no warning was given him, nor any other answer when he spoke to the surveyors of that work but that their master Sir Thomas commanded them so to do, no man durst go to argue the matter, but each man lost his land, and my father paid his whole rent, which was six shillings and eightpence the year, for that half which was left. This much of mine own knowledge I thought good to note, that the sudden rising of some men causeth them to forget themselves."

If Cromwell ventured to behave like this in private life, sure that no legal action brought against him would have any effect, his conduct when acting under the color of legality was still more ruthless. In May, 1535, he writes to Dr. London that he is to "request" the Fellows of Magdalen College to elect Thomas Marshall and to see that the man who had been head of the college, Thomas Knolles, resigns. Dr. Knolles had promised to do so but was now pleading that it was against the wishes of the Fellows. In the same way Cromwell forced in 1539 the election of George Cootes as Master of Balliol, a man of disreputable character, but who no doubt, like Dr. Marshall, gave Cromwell a handsome present for his service.

Dr. Layton had a grand time of it at Oxford and wrote in high glee to Cromwell, "We have set Duns in Bocardo [the town prison] and have utterly banished him from Oxford for ever, with all his blind glosses. . . . The second time we came to New College, after we had declared your injunction, we found all the great quadrant court full of the leaves of Duns, the wind blowing them into every quarter." Dr. Leigh was similarly engaged at Cambridge, abolishing the study of scholastic philosophy and also of canon law and making many quite arbitrary regulations regarding the courses of study to be followed by the monastic students there.

Cromwell may have had some right to reorganize studies at Cambridge University, as he succeeded Bishop Fisher there as Chancellor. Even so he often acted *ultra vires* flagrantly, not only within the university but toward the mayor and corporation of the town, for he twice peremptorily ordered them to allow the university to use the tolbooth, which was not under his jurisdiction but theirs. The fact is that Cromwell rarely bothered himself about other people's rights. He just seized what he wanted, and nobody dared to say nay.

His meteoric rise is indicated by the list of his offices. Beginning as a privy councilor in 1531, he was made later that year Master of the Jewels and in the next, Clerk of the Hanaper and Master of the King's Wards, obtaining the position of Chancellor of the Exchequer in 1533. In 1534 he was appointed Secretary to the King and Master of the Rolls, and 1535 saw him the King's Vicar-General and Lord Privy Seal. In 1536 he was created Baron Cromwell and in 1537 a Knight of the Garter. He was pre-eminent, with a power such as no politician in England, not even Wolsey, has ever possessed.

It is not necessary to list the monastic properties that came into his hands. Though he had his choice of these, his share and that given to his nephew Richard Williams (who had taken his name and was to be the great-grandfather of Oliver Cromwell) did not much exceed that of some others. He found it prudent to be fairly moderate here. But a great deal more in the way of plundered plate fell to him than anybody else, because he was quietly purloining it. In enriching himself so vastly, he may have felt that he had justification, for his titles and positions needed the reality of wealth to support them. Moreover, he had to maintain a secret service at his own charge, and this was costly. Though this increased his personal power and was freely used for that purpose, it could also be said that it was for the royal authority. He never lived in the princely state assumed by Wolsey, and, greedy though he was, he made careful calculations as to how far he could safely go. Too large a hoard would only serve to make him further hated and envied. If his enemies ever could obtain the ear of the King, Henry might find in his wealth a reason for pulling him down, in order to confiscate his possessions.

Perhaps it was also prudence that made him do something that Stow, who had little reason to like him, records, namely, that at Cromwell's house 200 poor people were fed daily. But perhaps this was not so much due to prudence as to his conscience. He must have remembered from time to time that with every monastery he suppressed hospitality and relief of the poor diminished. When the first monastic estates were disposed of to the new owners, some effort was made to attach the old obligations to the purchasers but as these obligations were almost always neglected, Cromwell may have been trying to atone. However this may be, he should in fairness be given credit for this private charity.

He should also be credited with interesting himself actively in the passage in 1534 of the Act Concerning Farms and Sheep. It was one more effort made by the government to restrict the enclosure movement. But though Cromwell, when writing to the King, said this act would be the most beneficial "since Brutus' time," it was rather liberal toward the landowners, as it permitted the keeping of 2,000 sheep and demanded that only the eighth part of any farmer's land be put under the plow. That particular obligation was often got around by the drawing of a single furrow across a field, thus making it arable land, and then sending out the sheep to graze there. As Sir Thomas More wrote in his *Utopia* in 1516, sheep were still eating men.

Even such a slight brake as this act may have been momentarily on the making of enclosures for sheep raising, it soon became ineffective because of the suppression of the monasteries. Though some of the monks had enclosed, they for the most part were inclined to follow the old customs. With the arrival of the land speculator and the exacter of exorbitant rents, the dikes against avarice began to break at every point, with the King and the courtiers setting the worst example. Probably Cromwell had foreseen this, for he had made his first fortune in wool and appears to have retained a financial interest in his former business.

Cromwell also probably foresaw that the limited suppression of monasteries permitted by the act of 1536 would not be the end of the matter. This would seem to be borne out by the fact that the

146

usual rate of lump payment to the Crown made by such monasteries as were respited was roughly their revenue for two years. Thus St. Mary's Convent at Winchester, which had an income of only £180 a year, paid almost double that amount to the King and then was reestablished only after some of its best possessions had been taken away. Similarly the nuns of Lacock in Wiltshire, whose income was £168, paid an exemption fee of £300, and St. Mary's, Chester, which maintained thirteen nuns on an annual £66, paid £160. Sums as large as these could hardly have been paid except by the houses going heavily into debt.

Though Cromwell guaranteed permanent continuation, he must have had at the back of his mind the idea that it was really only going to last for two years. This being the case, it was worth the King's while to grant respite, for he would obtain, without any further trouble, two years' rental value in a single payment and then be able in the end to enjoy the whole property. Such actions show singular cruelty and bad faith. And on top of these official payments went others to Cromwell himself and to his agents.

Chapter Nine

THE FRAME-UP

IT WAS well understood during the sixteenth and seventeenth centuries that the profession of politics was extremely dangerous and that the unsuccessful politician was likely to end under the headsman's ax. The woman who had caused the upheaval so perished, as did her brother, only their circumspect father escaping. The Duke of Norfolk's son was liquidated by rivals of the Howards, the Seymours; and the Duke himself was saved only by the accident of the King's death a few hours before the time set for the execution. Both Seymours died on the scaffold in their turn, the younger being destroyed by his elder brother, and their supplanter, John Dudley, the Duke of Northumberland, died in the same way, having played for too high stakes. Usually there was no special disgrace involved. A politician against whom the tide had turned did not lose (as with us) the election, but his head. In fact, it might almost be said that a family was not really distinguished unless it could boast a few members who had suffered this fate; it was realized that a charge of treason was often a mere formality.

Nor were the family fortunes necessarily affected. Edmund Dudley, put to death with Empson in 1509, was attainted as a matter of course. Yet Henry pushed his son John forward. Even when Cromwell fell in universal obloquy, his son Gregory's possessions were, in part, protected. This, though Thomas Cromwell was, of

148

all politicians, the one most loathed by all classes of society. Nor has history rehabilitated him, as in the case of Anne Boleyn, the subject of this chapter. Or if "rehabilitated" is too strong a word to use, at least it has found her almost certainly innocent of the specific crimes of which she was accused. But if this be so, extreme odium falls on Cromwell for deliberately contriving her doom.

Some kind of excuse may perhaps be found for him in the circumstance that the pass had been reached when it was either his head or hers. Although his rise had been accidentally due to her, she had not promoted it as she had promoted Cranmer's. Cromwell was therefore not bound to her by ties of gratitude; rather she should have been grateful to him as the man who had succeeded, after Wolsey had failed, in devising means by which Henry could obtain his divorce and Anne could become Queen. But even after the largest allowances have been made, Cromwell's action against her remains very base. It was all the more Cromwellian in that it was completely devoid of personal rancor.

Anne's position had been uncertain for some time. Henry had quickly tired of her and had started his philandering again, only to get his wife's shrill reproaches. But she could hardly have known how very insecure she was or that Henry, not long after the birth of Elizabeth, had made cautious inquiries as to the possibility of a divorce. When he was told that, while a divorce could no doubt be contrived, it would mean that he would have to take Katherine back, in glum fury he dropped the project. Anne shortly afterward announced (and perhaps believed) that she was pregnant, and though that was soon seen to be false, she really was advanced in pregnancy when, early in January, 1536, word came of Katherine's death at Kimbolton. Henry dressed himself in yellow from cap to shoes, and so did Anne. Her joy was that her rival had gone. Henry's joy, though not unmixed with personal resentment against Katherine, was mainly due to the fact that her death brought him relief from political embarrassments.

Anne had always been unpopular, and even members of her own family, including her uncle, the Duke of Norfolk, became alienated by her arrogance. Nor did she make herself any more popular by her treatment of her sister. Poor, soft, good-natured Mary Boleyn had for a while been the King's mistress, marrying shortly before or shortly afterward a man named Carey. But she had been a widow for some years, and when she appeared at Court, it was soon evident that she was in a condition in which no widow of long standing should be. Anne was most indignant, taking a high moral tone, but really more actuated by the circumstance that Mary was pregnant while she was not. Summarily she was ordered away in disgrace.

It is worth noting that Mary's appeal for mercy was addressed to Cromwell, and her letter to him written in September, 1534, shows that she thought of him not only as all-powerful but as a man to whom she could trustfully tell her story. She explained that she was secretly married to Sir William Stafford, a gentleman usher to the King. Her letter is very touching. Obviously she was a much better woman than her sister. "It is not unknown to you," she tells Cromwell, "the high displeasure that both he and I have both with the King's Highness and the Queen's Grace, by reason of our marrying without their knowledge, wherein we do yield ourselves faulty, and acknowledge that we did not well to be so hasty, nor so bold without their knowledge. But one thing, good master secretary, consider, that he was young and love overcame our reason; and for my part I saw so much honesty in him that I loved him as well as he did me. . . . So that for my part I saw that the world did set so little by me, and he so much, that I thought I could take no better way but to take him, and to forsake all other ways, and live a poor honest life with him. . . . For well I might have had a man of greater birth, and a higher; but I assure you that I could never have had one that I should have loved so well, nor a more honest man. . . . And seeing there is no remedy, for God's sake help us; for we have now been a quarter of a year married, I thank God, too late to call it again. . . . But if I were at liberty and I might choose, I assure you, master secretary, for my little time, I have spied so much honesty in him, that I would rather beg my bread with him than be the greatest queen christened. And I verily believe he is in the same case with me; for I verily believe that he would not forsake me to be a king." She asks Cromwell, therefore, to intercede for her and her William, with Henry and the Queen, as also her uncle, the Duke, and her brother, Lord Rochford. It was in vain; the Staffords had to retire from the Court in disgrace.

Something much worse than this was soon to come on her sister Anne. On January 20, 1536, Norfolk went to tell his niece that the King had fallen from his horse. Henry was not in fact hurt, nor was Anne disturbed. But when a few days later she was brought to bed and bore, prematurely, a dead boy, she bitterly blamed her uncle for the abrupt way she said he had broken the news to her. That stillborn child sealed her fate. Henry knew only too well that one miscarriage is likely to lead to another. Anne would have been saved had she produced a male heir capable of living; but only this could have saved her. Henry, with all the brutality of his character manifest, looked down upon the weeping woman and said coldly, "I will talk with you later." What he said (if anything) we do not know, except that we can be sure that it was far from kind. He regarded her as finished. By now he was sick and tired of her. As she did not love him, she probably did not give him the "satisfaction" he expected, and there is reason to believe that he did not give her much. Kindhearted Mary Boleyn had not loved him either, but she would have wanted to please. All Anne was concerned about was the achievement of her ambition.

It should have been sufficient for Henry to have divorced Anne. He had a good case against her. But the fact is that he had stored up resentment—even prior to marriage—against the Boleyn woman for her shrill upbraiding. He had complained to Norfolk that Katherine had never talked to him as Anne had done, for though Katherine was forthright and not always tactful, she was very much of a lady—something that Anne, in spite of her Howard and Ormonde blood, was not.

That Anne was likely to fall was generally known in the courts of Europe and was regarded by them in varying ways. The Pope's idea was that Henry should simply discard her, as the marriage had never been recognized by the Holy See (or anywhere outside of England), and marry Madeline, the daughter of Francis I. Naturally the Emperor did not wish that. Though he had several candidates at hand to take Anne's position, his conclusion, after mature thought, was that Chapuys should give Anne all the backing in his power. It would be better to keep her as Henry's wife than to have him take another who might bear him a son, about whose legitimacy there would be no question. Charles was thinking in terms of Mary's interest but still more of his own.

In England the death of Katherine was immediately seen to be a matter of which political capital might be made. Gardiner and

Wallop, the ambassadors to France, were at once instructed to veer off from Francis, as a reconciliation with the Emperor would now probably result. However, they were to dangle this prospect before Francis, in case he should feel inclined to outbid Charles. Anne would have been deeply disturbed had she known what was going on, for though she had slight knowledge of political affairs, she was not without shrewdness. Her instinct would have told her that she was in considerable danger.

Anne had been in some danger, though this was not acute, ever since she had disappointed Henry by bearing a girl in early September, 1533. Two months later Chapuys had asked Cromwell quietly whether he was willing to work against the Queen (the lady whom in his dispatches he called the Concubine). It was while they were out hawking together, and so out of earshot, and he reported that Cromwell had listened without horror to his suggestion but had shaken his round head, and said that the time had not come. The answer implied that he might be receptive at a future date.

That date had now arrived. In September, 1535, Cromwell had been with the King at Sir John Seymour's house, Wolf Hall, in Wiltshire and had noticed Henry's attentions to Jane Seymour, his host's daughter, who had formerly been a lady in waiting to Queen Katherine. A casual gallantry of this sort ordinarily would have meant little, but its seriousness was impressed upon Cromwell by subsequent events. Perhaps protected by a genuine chastity but certainly coached by her brothers, Jane had been most circumspect. She had refused to receive a purse of gold the King had sent her, rejecting it on her knees with the maidenly remark that, if the King liked to give her something toward her dowry when she married an honest gentleman, his gift would then be acceptable. She also refused to meet the King unchaperoned, so Cromwell had to move out of his room in the palace—one connected by a private stairs with the King's apartments—in order to allow it to be occupied by her brother Edward and his wife. Cromwell was made aware that Henry was all the more anxious to rid himself of Anne, now that he had a woman with whom he wished to replace her.

Cromwell had no knowledge of ecclesiastical law, though all the canon lawyers in the kingdom were ready to do his bidding.

As a practical man he found another way of dealing with the question.

Chance gave it to him, a chance that seemed at first to be of immense peril to himself. Yet at first he did not think of this chance as being in the least related to Anne but simply as a wonderful opportunity in foreign affairs. He had never been pro-French but always imperialist, if only for the reason that Henry's quarrel with the Emperor hindered trade between England and Charles's dominions. He was therefore more than willing to welcome a reconciliation between the two sovereigns.

In February, 1536, Chapuys had had a heart-to-heart talk with Cromwell, sounding him as to the possibility of an alliance with the Emperor. But since the terms included a league against the Turk as well as the "great Turk" Francis and Henry's return to the Roman obedience, Cromwell suggested that they deal with some minor point before proceeding to those of major importance. He at any rate gave Chapuys the impression that he was prepared to consider the major demands. Because the encouragement was not very great, the Emperor wrote to Chapuys on March 28, advising that he do his best to support the tottering Anne Boleyn.

The following month Charles changed his mind. By that time he had been brought to see that Anne was a horse not worth backing. So he switched to what Chapuys had proposed in February— though of course Chapuys had been obliged to be tentative at that time. In return for an alliance against Francis and the Sultan, he would bring about a reconciliation of Henry with the Pope.

Cromwell was all for closing with that offer. His opposition to the Holy See had never been a matter of conviction but only of expediency. For the sake of political security he would have ceased the English opposition, though of course on terms. Reconciliation with the Pope would naturally have involved at least a modification of the plan of suppressing the monasteries. But as this had hardly begun, a certain amount of suppression (to be regarded as reorganization) could probably have been arranged for under agreement with Paul III, just as a certain amount had been arranged under agreement between Wolsey and Clement VII. On both sides the advantages obtainable were worth the making of some concessions.

Unfortunately when the Emperor's proposals were submitted to him, Henry was touched on the sore point of his vanity. Though he wished to rid himself of Anne, he could not bring himself to admit (to the slightest degree of implication) that he had been wrong in divorcing Katherine. The Emperor had opposed this divorce; by doing so, Henry preposterously said, the Emperor had tried to keep him in a state of mortal sin. Even more preposterously, if possible, he said that the Emperor had shown himself unspeakably ungrateful, for to whom did he owe his imperial title except to Henry himself? As a preliminary to all overtures he demanded a written apology from Charles. Also he should either have the papal sentence quashed or give a statement that it had been obtained only because of the imperial threats. Henry was in one of those moods when he was prepared to rebel against everybody. Those who knew him and were watching him in his interview with Chapuys took it as an ominous sign that he kept drumming his fingers on his bovine thighs.

After listening to Chapuys—but ranting more than listening—Henry called Cromwell and Audley into the window recess and asked the Imperial Ambassador to repeat in their presence the overtures he had made. After Chapuys had done so, he left the King and joined Sir Edward Seymour in a distant part of the great chamber where, though Chapuys could not hear all that was said, he saw that the King was arguing angrily with Cromwell. After a while Cromwell said that he was thirsty and needed a drink, so he left Henry and Audley and sat on a chest out of sight where wine was brought to him. He was almost apoplectic with rage and chagrin. When Chapuys left, he was overtaken by Cromwell, who made no attempt to conceal that he considered the King's obstinacy as the height of folly. A chance was being thrown away that might not come again.

So upset was Cromwell that, as soon as he got to the Rolls, he went straight to bed. He felt positively ill, and he kept to his bed for several days afterward. He realized that the rejection of his advice might mean that the King would discard him for another counselor. But the situation was really worse than that: he knew that Henry was quite capable of regarding his advice as treasonable. Cromwell therefore utilized his diplomatic illness, not only for keeping out of sight but for maturing a plan. By April 24 he had this all worked out: he would reinstate himself with the King by demonstrating again that he and he alone was capable of carrying out the royal wishes. The decision regarding Charles would have to be accepted; but Cromwell would obligate Henry to him by getting rid of Anne. He was not going to bother with the long-drawn-out jugglery of canon lawyers but would use the decisive method of the ax. His coup was to be of the most spectacular kind imaginable: the Queen was to be incriminated of the most promiscuous adultery. For good measure Anne was to be accused of incest with her brother. George Boleyn, if allowed to escape, would seek his revenge and so had to be destroyed. Thomas Boleyn could be counted upon to seek nothing but the sparing of his own hide: he was not dangerous.

Everybody at the Court knew that Anne was very vain. She was not only vain; she was undignified and indiscreet. After marriage she had not dropped her admirers but had liked to have them around her saying silly things, to which she responded with an equal silliness. Cromwell perceived how he could fabricate from this idle levity an accusation of adultery. If it be asked why Cromwell sent five men to the block with her, when one would have sufficed, the answer is that, to make his charge plausible, he had to implicate a group. Her attentions, as was well-known, were not confined to one man. As it was, there were two other men arrested—Sir Thomas Wyatt and Sir Richard Page—who were afterward released. That also gave plausibility to the accusations brought against her: nobody was to be condemned who was not guilty; an impartial justice was to prevail.

Cromwell did not go to the King, saying that he meant to bring the Queen down; he merely asked for permission to set up a commission to inquire into a conspiracy against the King's life. Though one cannot but suspect that Henry sensed what was afoot, he asked no questions—such as would have been normal, especially in so grave a matter—but granted Cromwell all necessary powers and in the amplest fashion. Armed with these, Cromwell at once proceeded against Anne Boleyn. This was to be his signal service to Henry.

No very skilled investigators were called for. Cromwell had his spy service, and it was of course employed. But already he had at hand enough damaging information against Anne—some of it going back prior to her marriage, although this was not used. That the

155

woman was flirtatious is true, but that was merely part of her vanity. I personally believe that nothing more could be justly charged. The person who should have been executed in her place was Thomas Cromwell. He was her murderer and the murderer of five lively but harmless young men.

The trap was sprung on May 1, just eight days after Cromwell had been authorized to set up his commission. This included the two Dukes of Norfolk and Suffolk, the Lord Chancellor, and a number of the leading peers, also members of the judiciary. One would imagine that so formidable an apparatus could not have been established without some of its members asking its purpose. Yet even to the commission the only word given was that it was empowered to examine every kind of treason, by whomsoever committed. The terms were unprecedentedly sweeping and implied that a great quarry was being pursued. But as to the quarry no hint was given, though there must have been surmises. Cromwell had already gathered plenty of evidence or knew where it could be obtained.

He found it advisable to start with a definite confession, and this he obtained before the end of April from the one victim, among those he had selected, who could be counted upon to break down, a man of soft fiber who would not stand up against the application of torture. This man was Mark Smeaton, a lutanist at the Court, a gentle, ineffectual soul, petted as such by the Queen and the King, both of whom admired his warblings. The other men, being gentlemen, were hardened by warlike exercises and pride. But poor little Smeaton would wither at a look; he would say all that was required. He admitted adultery with Anne.

It was with the knowledge of Smeaton's confession in his mind that Henry went in the company of Anne to Greenwich, where a May Day tournament was held. Among the challengers that day were two men who were to be charged with adultery with the Queen, Sir Henry Norris and Lord Rochford. Oblivious of their fate they went through their performance and were cheered by the spectators. Nor did Anne, sitting by Henry's side, have any suspicion as to what was in store for her.

The King left a little early, allowing Anne to find her own way back to London. On the way there he encountered Norris, whom he called to him and told that he was accused of being the Queen's

156

paramour. Poor Norris, long a favorite of Henry's—but as such under Cromwell's dislike—roared out a denial. This did not serve him; he was put under arrest.

Anne was arrested the following day and, with her, her brother, Lord Rochford. On the fourth, William Brereton and Francis Weston were sent to the Tower, Weston, it would seem, mainly because Anne had mentioned his name in unguarded talk. The next day Thomas Wyatt, the poet, and Richard Page were apprehended but were soon released. It would not have been credible to have charged Anne with too much promiscuity. The number of her lovers was eventually reduced to five. These men, it was clearly understood from the start, were to die with her.

The accusations against them (and Anne) were preposterous. Froude, Henry's doughty defender, accepts them as proved, and some Catholic historians, because of their hatred of Anne, seem to agree. Friedmann, while rejecting the adultery charge and that of incest, hints darkly that Anne may nevertheless have been guilty of still worse crimes, by which, I suppose, he means that she was a poisoner. But suspicions are not proof: we must confine ourselves to the crime for which Anne died, that of high treason, specifically, making it possible to have a spurious heir foisted upon the King.

These accusations of adultery were very definite, with dates assigned to the offenses. For instance, Anne is supposed to have had relations with Norris on October 12, 1533, and with Brereton the following December 8—that is, shortly after the birth of Elizabeth. Apart from the extreme improbability of this happening at such a time, is it to be believed that the precise dates would be remembered, even by the criminals? The crowning touch was that Anne herself solicited her lovers, who consented only with reluctance! Though perhaps even this is exceeded by the "proof" against Lord Rochford; he and his sister had been alone in a room for two hours! This information was supplied by Rochford's estranged wife, who was to show herself a few years later a very corrupt woman. All the government really had to go on was what was wrung by torture out of the minstrel boy, Mark Smeaton.

He and three others of the accused were tried on May 12 in Westminster Hall, Audley presiding. All four were of course found guilty by a packed jury of men in the King's service, or in debt to Cromwell, or known to be enemies of Anne. But with the exception of Smeaton, who had already made a confession, all refused to admit guilt.

Again with the exception of Smeaton, the men were of good family, though not of such rank as to have expected simple beheading. That, however, is what they got instead of the usual punishment for treason. One cannot but suspect that a kind of deal was made with Smeaton that, if he repeated his confession on the scaffold, this grace would be given him, and he did say something that could be understood in this sense: "Masters, I pray you all pray for me, for I have deserved the death." With them perished on May 17 Lord Rochford, who had been given a separate trial the previous day.

An effort was vainly made to save Weston, who had influential friends. His father was undertreasurer, a position once held by Sir Thomas More. A couple of years later, this Sir Richard Weston was to be the godfather of another Thomas More, the Utopian's grandson. But of course the logic of the matter demanded that none of those found guilty should be spared.

Rochford was tried alone, in the semiprivacy of the Tower rather than before the immense audience that crowded Westminster Hall. He defended himself with such dexterity that bets were being made at long odds that he would be acquitted. But he was under no illusions as to this; when a question was handed to him in writing and he knew that he was not supposed to read it aloud because of its nature, he took his revenge by letting everybody present hear what he had been asked. It implied that Henry was deficient in virility.

Anne was tried (also in the Tower) on the same day as her brother and before the same commission, in each case presided over by the Duke of Norfolk, the uncle of the accused. Cromwell appeared as counsel for the King. Anne was reported to have told Norris that she would marry him after the King had died, from which it was deduced that they wished his death and had conspired to bring it about. She was also charged with having given Norris some lockets, and these were presumed to have contained poison to administer to Katherine. As though this were not enough, she was accused of making fun of Henry's poetry and of the style in which he dressed! It would be hard to think of evidence more flimsy, but of course her condemnation, like that of the five men, was a foregone conclusion. Among the panel of peers that found her guilty

158

was her old flame, the Earl of Northumberland. He had long since turned an enemy, but sad emotions welled up in him and he was taken ill and had to ask to be excused from sitting when Rochford was brought in.

Henry had so pleasant a time before the trial and executions that it disgusted even those who most hated Anne. His levity was not only in the worst possible taste but very suspicious. Officially it was given out that he was overwhelmed with grief, but Chapuys wrote that he had never seen a man who wore cuckold's horns more pleasantly. Every day the royal barge was seen on the river, with musicians providing merry airs, and all London knew whom the King was visiting. To top it all, one evening when at supper at the Bishop of Carlisle's palace, he told the company that he had long foreseen that Anne would end in this way and had written a tragedy on the subject, which he produced.[1]

Cromwell, the contriver of what had happened, wrote on May 14 to Gardiner and Wallop, telling them for the benefit of Francis I at whose Court they were serving, "The Queen's abomination both in incontinent living and other offences against the King's Highness was so rank and common that the ladies of her privy chamber and her chamberers could not contain it within their breasts." If that was so, we might ask how it was that they were able to contain it so long, for the alleged offenses went back to 1533. Writing to Gardiner and Wallop again on July 5, Cromwell said, "The confessions were so abominable that a great part were not given in evidence but were kept secret." This was quite untrue: the only confession was that extorted from Smeaton, and the only bit of evidence that the prosecution tried (unsuccessfully) to keep secret was the question read aloud by Rochford.

Cranmer was, or believed himself to be, in mortal danger with the fall of his patron. This perfectly suited Cromwell, who had an unpleasant duty for him to perform, so he deliberately increased the Archbishop's terror in order to make him more amenable. He therefore sent Cranmer a command to wait at Lambeth for further instructions. This was on May 3, on which day the Archbishop wrote Henry a long letter, a masterpiece of its kind, as it ostensibly

[1] Chapuys got an account of this from the Bishop. As the tragedy does not exist, it may be surmised that the Bishop ventured to hint that it would be more seemly to burn it.

defends Anne with every other sentence and for the rest deplores that the King has had to suffer such grief on account of a woman. "If she be found culpable," runs one passage, "considering your Grace's goodness to her, and from what condition your Grace of your only mere goodness took her, and set the crown upon her head, I repute him not your Grace's faithful servant and subject, nor true unto the realm, that would not desire the offence without mercy to be punished, to the example of all other. And as I loved her not a little for the love which I judged her to bear towards God and His Gospel, so if she be proved culpable, there is not one that loveth God and His Gospel that will ever favor her, but must hate her above all other; and the more they favor the Gospel, the more they will hate her; for there never was creature in our time that so much slandered the Gospel. And God hath sent her this punishment for that she feignedly hath professed His Gospel in her mouth, and not in heart and deed." [2] Then, perhaps in fear that the King's enthusiasm for the Gospel might diminish, now that Anne was about to depart, Cranmer reminds Henry that his "favor to the Gospel was not led by affection unto her, but by zeal unto the truth."

Before this letter was actually sent, Cranmer was told to meet Audley and Lord Oxford and Lord Sussex and the Lord Chamberlain in the Star Chamber. He may have read his letter to them in proof that he was not of the Boleyn faction; it was probably then that he was told what was required of him. Upon his return to Lambeth he added a postscript: "What communication we had together I doubt not that they will make the true report thereof unto your Grace. I am exceedingly sorry that such faults can be proved by the Queen, as I heard by their relation." By this whatever little reservation there had been in the body of his letter was withdrawn; Cranmer accepted Anne's guilt as something completely proved. He had by now been brought to the point where he was ready to do anything.

He had to do something exceedingly humiliating, and finding

[2] The sense in which the word "Gospel" was used should be explained. It did not mean Protestantism, for that was not tolerated in England. Still less did it have the meaning which some modern Protestant sects—those that like to call themselves "evangelical"—attach to it. It appears to mean hardly more than the Henrician gospel of absolute obedience to the monarch and the repudiation of all papal authority. That was at least its core.

means for doing it must have taxed even his ingenious brain. He had pronounced the marriage of Henry and Anne valid (though entered into before the dissolution of the Henry-Katherine marriage); now he had to pronounce the second marriage invalid. The discovery of the grounds for doing so was left to him, though in all likelihood the hint was dropped that a precontract might be established between Anne and the Earl of Northumberland.

That did not work; the Earl absolutely refused to admit the existence of this impediment. It has been suggested that he lied, with the motive of saving his own head, for otherwise a charge of treason might have been brought against him for not disclosing the fact in time. That he took an oath on the Blessed Sacrament has some weight; what has more, before he started his wooing of Anne his family had affianced him to Lady Mary Talbot, to whom, most unhappily, he was now married. The precontract argument simply broke down. Northumberland may have committed some perjury as to details, but the main facts stood.

Cranmer was sent to interview Anne in the Tower. She admitted the precontract, in which she may have been in good faith, for Percy had probably concealed from her his engagement to Mary Talbot. But Anne certainly had large inducements to make such an admission. Cranmer promised her that if she was cooperative her life would be spared and she would be allowed to go to Antwerp. After her interview with him she confidently announced this as settled.

Did Cranmer betray her? I do not think so, low as is my opinion of his character. I believe that he was acting in good faith, though of course under the spur of terror, a terror that must have increased when the precontract basis for a divorce collapsed. If there was bad faith here, it was shown by Cromwell and the King—Henry as usual making somebody else do his dirty work for him.

Another way was open to Cranmer. Henry could have said that when he was married to Anne on January 25, 1533, he was still legally married to Katherine. But this of course would have been an admission of bigamy, so that way could not be taken.

Some basis for a divorce had, however, to be found. And we can imagine many consultations on this difficult problem before the solution was hit upon. Even had Chapuys not discovered the facts about which he wrote to Granvelle on July 8, we might infer them;

there was only one possible ground for an annulment—a defect in the dispensation under which Henry and Anne had married.

That dispensation had been issued in 1528 by Clement VII. It permitted either party to marry—provided that the King's marriage to Katherine was declared invalid—whatever the impediments might be on either side. Specifically this was a dispensation for Henry to marry Anne Boleyn, although he had contracted an affinity by his former relations with her sister. But papal dispensations now had no force in England; that plea sufficed. A divorce court was set up, and Anne was provided with advocates, men who could be counted upon not to do too much for her. The business was soon disposed of.

The action on Henry's part was odious and spiteful, as it meant that Anne died in the knowledge that her daughter Elizabeth was bastardized. It was also stupid. For now, after his frantic efforts to strengthen his dynasty, he had reduced himself to the position in which he had only three bastard children, though of course Mary was not regarded as one by the vast majority of people at home or abroad. But it is not impossible that he was not so much stupid as cunning. He may have thought that by debarring Elizabeth from the succession, the road was left open for Henry Fitzroy, Duke of Richmond. If so, he was to be disappointed; the youth died the following July 23.[3]

Anne, in the Tower, was informed that she was to be beheaded—a grace, as the sentence had made her liable to burning at the stake. She was, as usual, wild in talk, loose-lipped, hysterical. But she expressed some remorse for the way she had treated Mary, and she asked that the Blessed Sacrament be exposed for her in an adjoining room. There she spent hours in prayer. Her execution had to be delayed a day because she fancied that it would be less painful to have her head cut off by the swordsman at St. Omer than by the axman employed at the Tower. On the morning of her execution she sent for Sir William Kingston and asked him to be present

---

[3] He had been made Duke in 1525, when he was six. Three years later he was suggested as a husband for Mary, as it was thought that a dispensation could be secured for this. But he was of course too young at that time for marriage. Later it was proposed that Ireland be made a kingdom and that the young man be crowned as its sovereign. Then, if he were already a king, England might be all the more willing to accept him on Henry's death.

when she received Holy Communion. Both before and after this solemn act she declared on the salvation of her soul that she had never been unfaithful to the King. Chapuys, who hated her, believed that oath. It is now accepted by virtually all historians.

In a faint voice she made a short speech on the scaffold, accepting her death according to law but making no admission whatever of guilt. Her stepson, the Duke of Richmond, was there to see her die. So also was the Duke of Suffolk, though her uncle Norfolk excused himself. Cromwell, who had brought her to this pass, was present as one of the official witnesses. He did not flinch from such things.

That very day Cranmer gave the King and Jane Seymour a dispensation on account of the rather remote consanguinity that existed. Jane was so very distant a cousin that this seems to have been unnecessary, but Henry's mind was of the pedantic kind that demanded a compliance with all formalities. Besides, the legitimacy of Jane's offspring might otherwise be challenged. Ten days later Henry married Jane. Anne's attainder, which implicated all England with the King, through the instrument of Parliament, followed soon afterward.

Cranmer was on a very hot spot. He still feared that with the fall of Anne he might also fall, despite his recent services. He spent the morning of Anne's execution nervously pacing the long lawns of Lambeth Palace, until he heard the cannon shot that announced that Anne's head had fallen. He could not be sure what else might not happen now. Like many other people in England he imagined that there might be a reconciliation with Rome. It was no doubt something of a relief to him when he was summoned later in the day to give the requested dispensation; that the King asked him to perform this duty showed he was not meditating any immediate reunion with the Holy See. Cranmer knew Jane to be a nullity; he also knew that her brothers, who were to count a good deal, were on the side of the "Gospel." Moreover, Thomas Cromwell had emerged from this affair with greatly enhanced power. With Cromwell there, Cranmer felt safe.

Chapter Ten

THE PROTEST

HARDLY HAD Cromwell safely emerged from the peril he had stood in because of the rejection of his foreign policy—a peril escaped by the cutting off of heads of half a dozen people who had nothing to do with the matter—than a new peril was encountered, one even more dangerous as it was a rebellion by declaration directed not against the King but some of the King's ministers. Whatever combination of names was mentioned, one name was always there—that of Cromwell. This spontaneous protest—not really to be called a rebellion—demanded the removal of Cromwell, and it was understood that this meant his execution. The Pilgrimage of Grace had a fine war song; and two of its lines specify:

> Crom, Cram and Rich
> With the three L's and the Lich. . . .

meaning Cromwell, Cranmer, and (obviously) Rich, "the three L's" being Longland, the Bishop of Lincoln, Drs. Layton and Leigh, and "Lich" standing for Rowland Lee, the Bishop of Lichfield.

As we have seen, the death of Anne removed what seemed the worst obstacle to reconciliation with the Holy See. The act suppressing the smaller monasteries had been passed early in 1536, but it had not been put into general operation because in March and April Cromwell was dealing with a possible new departure in foreign policy. Then in May he had been occupied with bringing down Anne Boleyn and regaining his own threatened authority. There was a general expectation that great changes would be seen now that the Boleyns had been exterminated. Paul III on May 27 sent through Sir Gregory da Casale new conciliatory messages, and early in June Cardinal Campeggio's brother was dispatched to England. It was perhaps rather tactless of him to make this visit ostensibly to ask for the restoration of the Cardinal to his See of Salisbury, but that very fact indicates a confidence at Rome that the troubles were about to blow over. Nor was it at all impossible that this would have happened had not Henry been faced with an insurrection. After dealing with it—by first lulling the rebels into a false security by promises he did not intend to keep and then by savage reprisals—he was in no mood to accept peace feelers from the Pope who was, in his opinion, at the bottom of what had just happened. Having been thoroughly scared, he feared that any moderation would be taken as an admission of fear. So he showed his courage by hanging several thousands of helpless men and by remaining obdurate toward Rome.

Still another factor operated. Though the suppression of the smaller monasteries had not as yet proceeded very far—not so far as to have created an insurmountable obstacle to reconciliation— the moment when a greedy man was on the point of obtaining a vast augmentation of his income was the last moment when he was going to endanger his advantage. Cromwell, who perceived into what extreme peril he had allowed himself to be drawn in April, would be more careful in the future. He was now ready to do anything that the King wanted. But he was not, as was generally supposed, the man actively promoting the policy the country so heartily disliked: he was hardly more than one who perforce acquiesced in it.

There was nothing he could do to make himself less unpopular among the mass of the people. He did, however, try to win over his enemy Gardiner by telling him as early as May 14 that of the three hundred pounds sterling "out among these men," the Bishop was to have two hundred pounds sterling, with the rest "bestowed on the Vicar of Hell," Sir Francis Bryan. This meant that Gardiner got back two-thirds of the amount that had been paid since 1530 in the form of pensions from his diocese of Winchester. It is not very remarkable that for so small a favor he was not especially grateful. As for the country at large, there was a great deal of discontent, and Cromwell was blamed for everything. It had rained almost continually since the execution of the Carthusians, more than a year previously, spoiling most of the crops. Taxes were already high, and new taxes were being imposed. The Statute of Wills and Uses—greatly restricting the right of bequest—after having been twice rejected by Parliament had at last passed; it was everywhere considered obnoxious. The number of holy days that Cromwell had reduced by injunction—and there probably was an excessive number of these, especially in harvest time—was another cause of complaint. Princess Mary's bastardization was bitterly resented. But while the motives of the insurgents (if they can be called such) were mixed, the main grievance was the ejection of the monks and nuns. It is perfectly clear that by the people among whom they lived the religious were respected and beloved. But it must also be said that, at least at the outset, there was no formal demand for reunion with Rome. Instead there was a call for the removal of bishops suspected of heresy and of "villein" blood from the Council.

The rising began at Louth in Lincolnshire at the beginning of October. All that happened at first was that a group of men, hearing a rumor that the plate of their parish church was to be seized, set a guard on it night and day. Their leader was a Thomas Melton who, because of his trade, came to be known as Captain Cobbler. This little demonstration was enough to raise the whole county; within a couple of days a crowd estimated variously as being from forty to sixty thousand was with them.

These men met with weapons in their hands, but with no intention of rebelling against the King. Yet they might have turned into real rebels had the Lady Mary given them the approval she refused. The King's councilors—especially Cromwell—were denounced, but always there were protestations of loyalty to Henry himself. Nothing more was intended than a demonstration. They wished to lay their grievances before the King; that was all.

Such a demonstration would have been formidable except for one fact: the mob had no leaders, except for the Abbot of Barlings, Dr. Mackerel, who was not a military man, and some local gentry who had been forced to join under the threat of death. The value of such leadership can be imagined. From the outset it was plain that the interests of the working men and the gentlemen were not

166

the same. So bewildered and angry did the common people become that they were at one moment on the point of killing all the gentlemen. They would actually have done so had not these so-called leaders taken refuge in a church and then slipped away by a side door. We can scarcely wonder that they rode off in a body to meet the royal army now advancing under the command of the Duke of Suffolk.

It was not a large force that the Duke had been able to muster, and most of his men sympathized more or less with the insurgents. That Suffolk had a few pieces of ordnance struck some fear, but had there been any determined attack Suffolk must have been annihilated and the way thrown open to London. But neither side wanted to fight. While the rebels hesitated, Suffolk used persuasion. They were to go home peaceably, and everything would be all right.

The King had sent a proclamation composed in that high style of which only a Tudor was capable. He managed to combine boasts as to how loving and merciful a lord he was with threats that he would burn, kill, and destroy all their belongings and their wives and children. As for the choosing of his advisers, Henry told them, "I have never read, heard nor known that princes' councillors and prelates should be appointed by rude and common people. How presumptuous, then, are ye, the rude commons of one shire, and that one of the most brute and beastly of the whole realm, and of least experience, to take upon you, contrary to God's law and man's law, to rule your prince, whom ye are bound to obey and serve, and for no worldly cause to withstand." He pointed out that the suppression of religious houses was under act of Parliament and asserted, "There be none houses suppressed where God was well served, but where most vice, mischief and abomination of living was used." [1] He did not condescend to answer the other points in their petition but urged them to lay aside their "ingratitude, unnaturalness and unkindness" toward him. They were to disband and to submit themselves to "such condign punishment as we and our nobles shall think

---

[1] The Lincolnshire men knew better. And they had recently learned how Cromwell had informed the Bishop of Lincoln that the Priory of Spalding in his diocese was in his "cure" and not the Bishop's. Longland was to see to it that the prior Cromwell had recently appointed should not be interfered with by the "busy fellows" of the town.

you worthy to suffer." But they could not have thought this would be much, as they had not actually used their arms against the King. A group of them had, indeed, killed the Chancellor of the diocese, and another group had killed Dr. Leigh's cook, a man who had made himself objectionable. While these murders should be punished, it would not be just to punish people who had merely done what every subject had a right to do—submit a petition. So the mob drifted away, and the King's officers went through the county, making about a hundred arrests. But nobody at this time was brought to trial. It was believed that all those taken into custody would be eventually released.

In this Lincolnshire was vastly mistaken. If there were no executions just then, the reason was that the government wished to avoid acerbating a far more dangerous rising that occurred immediately afterward. This was the true Pilgrimage of Grace, which was in Yorkshire and the adjoining counties. Had it only been synchronized with the Lincolnshire affair the demands for redress would have been irresistible. Even the North standing alone could have forced the King to change his course. There there existed organization; there leaders were discovered among the nobles, though most of these took the precaution of waiting to be threatened before they came forward; there the issues were defined more sharply and in greater detail. The Pilgrimage of Grace was ruined by two things operating together: one was the moderation of its leaders and their sanguine trust in the royal pledges; the other was the royal perfidy.

The North was more feudal in spirit than the South. It was there also that the great rebellion of 1569 occurred. The people of the northern shires were of a tougher fiber than those of the South. Moreover, they were almost wholly agricultural, all trade being centered in London and other seaports. Only by the commercial classes was Cromwell fairly well liked. Professor Merriman points out too that the reports of the monastic visitors in the South often indicate that the monks show themselves amenable to religious changes, whereas the reports from the monasteries of the North, where the monks always stood firm, had to fall back upon charges of immorality and unnatural vice. It is noteworthy that the districts where the risings occurred contained nearly a quarter of all the

168

houses affected by the law passed earlier that year; and it is strange indeed that where the religious were allegedly most vicious they were also most esteemed!

The Lincolnshire affair was about the most pitiful exhibition of ineptitude that can be imagined. Yet the Yorkshire rising (which, I repeat, was not really a rising but a demonstration, though in force) was, in the event, not much less inept. In both cases the same root trouble may be discerned: a reluctance to appear as rebels, a desire to state grievances moderately and without threats, and (worst of all) the belief that the royal word was to be trusted.

The initial mistake made in Yorkshire was that of giving the command of the Pilgrimage to a lawyer named Robert Aske who practiced in London and was only in Yorkshire by accident at the time. The lords and knights who served under him did so, one fears, because he could be made a convenient scapegoat in the event of anything going wrong. Most of the gentry did in fact get off on the plea that they had been forced to take the Pilgrims' oath. So, for that matter, had Aske himself been forced; though having once taken it and finding himself at the head of an army of 60,000 men, his vanity gloried in the title somebody gave him of "the Great Captain." Why such nobles as Lords Scrope, Darcy, Latimer (at that time husband of Catherine Parr), and Lumley were content to remain relatively in the background was not lost on the government. It was understood that their hearts were not really in this business.

On the other hand, several of the nobles leading the royal forces had been more than suspected of communication with Chapuys the previous year. It would not have taken very much for them to go over to the rebels, and, as Norfolk was to admit, at least half the men under him were disaffected. Cromwell was so relieved that the Earl of Shrewsbury was, at least for the moment, loyal to the King that on October 9 he wrote to him in a strain of hysterical gratitude and sought to keep his allegiance by all kinds of promises. "The demonstration," he wrote, "of your noble courage and truth hath so comforted me that whilst I live and if I might after my death I will and would honor you and your posterity as the man and most worthy earl that ever served a prince, and such a chieftain as is worth eternal glory." In the West such men as the Marquis of Exeter and Lord Montague were ostensibly raising forces for the

King but were probably only standing by to see which way the cat would jump. Their sympathies were certainly with the Pilgrims.

Pollard makes the suggestion that those on this Pilgrimage were "probably drawn from evicted tenants, deprived of their holdings by enclosures or the conversion of their land from tillage to pasture, men who had nothing to lose and everything to gain by a general turmoil." [2] If this was so, the eviction of tenants must have been on a much greater scale than anybody has supposed. While doubtless there were many men serving under Aske who had genuine economic grievances—for these were stressed—there can be no doubt that the main, though not the sole, cause of the Pilgrimage was religion, something made very sharp and concrete by the suppression of the monasteries.

Some historians—especially Catholic historians angry with Aske for the chance he threw away—have accused him of being a traitor to the movement he was leading. If any odium is to be distributed, it should be to some of the nobles and knights who used Aske as their front. Poor Aske was, indeed, vain, which is always a weakness that can be played upon; and his abilities, though considerable, were not of the kind most needed at that juncture. Had any peer put himself boldly forward as a leader, the Pilgrimage could not have failed. But none did, and English yeomen were a little confused at finding themselves under the command of a lawyer. Aske did impose discipline, so that there were none of the violent acts that had occurred in Lincolnshire. But as he was a lawyer, he wished to do everything with strict legality, and in Henry and Cromwell he encountered legalists who were adept at making the law cover their most atrocious deeds.

Cromwell did not of course himself take the field against the rebels; had he done so, they would have been roused to such a pitch of fury that they would have attacked at once. So he crept away into the shadows. Nor did the King take the field. Never once in all his long reign did this famous rider in the lists expose himself in battle. But there was no battle. Cromwell instructed the Earl of Shrewsbury and the Duke of Norfolk, whom he had to bring out

[2] *Henry VIII*, p. 352. The professor admits that his estimates have been challenged but says that his remark was intended to "guard against the theory that the grievances were entirely religious."

of retirement (regretfully and only because of necessity), to avoid fighting, if possible, and to rely instead on negotiation.

Henry wrote that Norfolk was to do nothing against the royal honor, but later he wrote to tell him "to esteem no promise" he had given nor to think that the King's "honor touched in the breach and violation of the same." Even more than this was done: Thomas Miller, Lancaster Herald, was sent north with Henry's answer to the Pilgrims' petition. As it was too truculent, Aske refused to allow him to read it, though the Herald begged permission for this on his knees—an act that later cost him his life. In vague and rather general terms, however, some of the Pilgrims' demands were granted. Henry did not abdicate as Head of the Church (for even that was not specifically called for), nor did he undertake to have the monasteries restored. Here he was on solid ground, for he could not undo Parliamentary statutes. But he passed in silence over what was asked as to the expulsion of Cromwell from the Council and the punishment of Cromwell, Layton, and Leigh. And he said nothing about the strict application of the enclosure laws. Actually he conceded nothing except that a free Parliament should be held at York and that Queen Jane should be crowned there. Also he extended a general pardon, and he invited Aske and Lord Darcy and Sir Robert Constable to go to see him, under safe escort, to discuss their grievances. Though Constable, and to some extent Darcy, were in favor of being on guard and even of pressing the military advantage they held, Aske persuaded them that they had already gained their main point. A parliament at York could be counted upon to repeal the laws to which they objected. The Pope's spiritual authority would be restored, and the seized monasteries—to which the Pilgrims had already sent back the ejected monks—would continue as before. And after a meeting that had been held at Doncaster between Aske and Norfolk, the Lancaster Herald was sent through the North to proclaim the royal pardon. In it Henry protested that he had "ever tendered them in all things rather like his natural children than his subjects." The lie worked; the Pilgrims dispersed.

At this point I might remind the reader that Cromwell was the first of the English Machiavellians. Those who know *The Prince* will remember how, in Chapter XIV, the Florentine writes, "It is necessary for a prince wishing to hold his own to know how to do wrong, and to make use of it or not according to his necessity. . . .

It will be found that something which looks like virtue, if followed, would be to his ruin; whilst something else, which looks like vice, yet followed brings him security and prosperity."

Still more explicit is Chapter XVIII, which seems to have provided the blueprint for dealing with the Pilgrimage of Grace. "Our experience has been that those princes who have done great things have held good faith of little account, and have known how to circumvent the intellect of man by craft, and in the end have overcome those who relied on their word." Again we read: "A wise lord cannot, nor ought he, to keep faith when such observance may be turned against him, and when the reasons that caused him to pledge it exist no longer. . . . Nor will there ever be wanting to a prince legitimate reasons to excuse this non-observance." Finally, this sentence might be quoted: "He who seeks to deceive will always find some one who allows himself to be deceived."

This some one was found in the guileless Aske. The Machiavellian maxims, as supplied by Cromwell, were used against him. Machiavelli said that a prince should try to seem just, religious, and merciful, and in his youth Henry had really possessed these qualities. But Cromwell was now able to impress upon his disillusioned mind: "I shall dare say this also, that to have and always to observe them is injurious; and that to appear to have them is useful: to appear merciful, humane, religious, upright, and to be so, but with a mind so framed that you should not require not to be so, you may be able and know how to change to the opposite." Henry, as always, was sure of his good conscience, so he could act on the maxim: "A prince cannot observe all those things for which men are esteemed, being often forced, in order to maintain the state, to act contrary to fidelity, friendship, humanity and religion." In short the Pilgrimage of Grace was dealt with in the best Machiavellian style.

Cromwell, though he had kept in the background, had not failed to send instructions to the royal officers. To the younger Sir Ralph Evers he wrote on November 10, "His Highness hath put everything now in such perfect order that if these rebels do continue any longer in their rebellion doubt not that you shall see them so subdued as their example shall be fearful whilst the world shall endure." To the same correspondent he said also, "Unless the commons would be soon pacified, there would be such a vengeance taken that the

172

whole world should speak thereof." And to the Commissioner at Doncaster he wrote in December, "Seeing that they have broken promise therein with his Grace, his Majesty shall not need but at his pleasure to keep promise in all things with them."

Fair promises in the end undid Aske. But the first method attempted was that of having him kidnapped or assassinated, the instrument chosen being a cousin of his who had a private quarrel with him. As that failed, Norfolk managed to get a message through to Darcy to see whether he would not deliver Aske up. Darcy's character had been misjudged; the tough old soldier declined to do so treacherous a deed. In his reply to Norfolk he wrote, "Alas, my Lord, that you, being a man of so great honor, should advise or choose me to betray any living man, Frenchman, Scot or even Turk. To win for me or for mine the best duke's lands that be in France, I would not do it for no living person." In saying farewell to the messenger, Darcy asked him to tell the King that he was doing the best service he had ever rendered him or his father and that if there was to be peace a speedy answer should be sent to the petition.

The messenger from Norfolk found himself in a room full of knights in armor. They crowded around him to ask the question in which they were most immediately interested, for the right answer on that point might be taken as assuring everything else they wanted: "Had Cromwell been put out of the Council?" Evasively the messenger returned that this or that nobleman was still with the King. At the mention of Henry's name there was a cheer, for they all asserted their perfect loyalty to him. But their question had not been answered: "But how of Cromwell? Has he been put from the Council or no?" When the messenger was obliged to say that Cromwell was still on the Council, he was plainly told, "Show the King and the lords that we will take no pardon till we have our will." It was the attitude they should have persisted in; nothing else was safe.

Their petition, in the drawing up of which Aske had the largest share, was long and detailed, running to twenty-four articles. Some of these called for the repeal of unpopular laws or the stricter enforcement of others. But the majority of the articles bore on religion. Not only was the reestablishment of the papal jurisdiction and the reinstatement of the monks called for, but Article XVIII

173

read: "That the privileges and rights of the Church be confirmed by act of Parliament; and priests not to suffer by the sword unless they be degraded. A man to be saved by his book; sanctuary to save a man for all cases in extreme need; and the Church for forty days, and further, according to the laws as they were used in the beginning of this King's reign." This meant that even the royal claims of 1515 were to be abandoned and the lost privileges of the Church of the Middle Ages given back. Over and over again in the articles we see the hatred felt for Cromwell and his agents; they are directly accused of being the propagators of heresy.

In London many members of the Council, greatly alarmed, recommended the solution of a parliament to adjust what needed adjustment, as much of this could be dealt with in no other way; at the same time they asked that the King should invite complaints against Cromwell and the other people mentioned, so that if the charges were substantiated the culprits might be proceeded against. But Henry had other plans. He sought by private letters to some of the peers to separate them from the movement by trying to make them feel that they were damaging their dignity by taking Aske as their captain. When he failed to detach them, he decided to work upon Aske by flattery.

Though Henry had conceded nothing except a pardon and a parliament at York, he made Aske feel when at last he got him to London that everything the Pilgrims demanded would be eventually granted. The King could be most charming and affable when he chose, and this was one of the appropriate moments. Cromwell was kept carefully out of sight, as the presence of that hated figure at Court would have made even the simple-minded Aske suspicious. At the King's request he wrote out an account of the rising, a document that later proved useful when the Pilgrims were prosecuted. Aske, completely taken in, returned to Yorkshire to advise his followers that they could safely disband, that their wishes were going to be met. He did not realize that Henry and Cromwell had already gained their own ends; all that remained to be done was for them to execute vengeance.

The Pilgrims of Grace had been the most orderly crowd that can be pictured. It is true that the Convocation of York had met and proceeded to undo, by way of anticipation, all the laws relating to religion, in which they may have exceeded their constitutional

174

right, although they acted according to constitutional forms. But in January a few groups of the men following Aske as soldiers got out of hand. As they had been so very well-behaved until then, I cannot help feeling that Cromwell, to whom the use of *agents provocateurs* was a familiar technique, had sent men to the North to instigate trouble. We have already noticed how he had learned from Machiavelli that when a prince wishes to discover reasons for not keeping his word he can always find them. It is of course also possible to create those reasons.

Apart from this possibility, provocation was given to the North by the fact that tax collectors, gathering the very taxes against which the petition had protested, began their work again. Also it was observed that Scarborough, one of the very few towns in Yorkshire held for the King, was having its fortifications strengthened. That naturally caused a doubt of the King's good faith. John Hallom, a well-to-do farmer, expressed what was in many minds when he said, "I fear me the gentlemen will deceive us the commons, and the King's Grace intends to perform none of our petitions." Hallom was probably only an incautious person; but the man with whom he operated, Sir Francis Bigod, must be suspected to have been worse. This for at least two reasons: he had been for a while in Cromwell's service, and he had professed "Gospel" principles until he had joined the Pilgrims. The possibility of a sincere change of heart cannot be altogether ruled out, but there must be doubt of his motives. The fact that he was executed proves nothing: in Elizabeth's reign several of the spies employed by Walsingham were sent to the scaffold, either because they knew too much, or because it was wished to prove that they had never been government agents.

The plan was that Hallom should seize Hull and Bigod Scarborough. That both attempts failed miserably was mainly due to the energy with which Aske, Lord Darcy, Sir Robert Constable, and Sir Robert Ellerker set out to repress this new rising which, to their minds, was the worst thing that could happen at that of all moments. Cromwell had already prepared the ground for the complete repudiation of all the royal guarantees by his letter written the previous month to the Commissioner at Doncaster, charging that on a minor point the Pilgrims had failed to live up to their undertakings with the Crown. Constable had been one of those in favor of vigorous action earlier, at the moment when all the cards were, militarily speaking, in the Pilgrims' hands; but that moment had been allowed to pass. Now it would be fatal to give the King and Cromwell a pretext for breaking solemnly made promises.

Full advantage was taken of the adventures of Bigod and Hallom, unauthorized though these were. The Pilgrims had scattered to their homes and in most instances knew nothing about what had happened until a body of the King's troopers marched up to their cottages, dragged them out of bed, and hanged them to the nearest tree under martial law. What had been one of the most formidable armies England had ever seen was by that time merely isolated units of sleepy, bewildered, and utterly helpless men.

How many men were actually executed can be only a matter of estimate. We know that in the towns big batches were strung up together. We also know that special instructions were issued that the monks who had dared to return to their suppressed monasteries were to be executed en masse. But the King stressed the need for having at least one execution in every village, however small, by way of example. No particular pains were taken to find the guilty; anybody would do, and, if it came to that, probably everybody was tinged with a certain amount of what could be considered guilt, as everybody had at least sympathized with the Pilgrims. The royal instructions made a great point of having those executed hanged in chains, so that their skeletons might dangle a long time. Norfolk had to write to Henry to explain that he could not find enough chains, so he had to fall back in some instances upon the hempen noose. This had to pass, but when Henry heard that women were creeping out at night to get the bodies of their men for burial, he was very angry and ordered that these women, when caught, should be hanged too. Several thousands of people must have been executed under martial law.

The nobles implicated were let off, except for Lord Darcy. He also had been pressed into leadership, perhaps not very unwillingly, but his real offense had been that he had refused to dishonor himself by handing Aske over to Norfolk. At his trial he said to Cromwell's face, "Cromwell, it is thou who art the very original and chief causer of this rebellion and mischief, and art likewise the apprehension of us that be noble men, and dost earnestly travail to bring us all to one end and to strike off our heads, and I trust that . . . though thou wouldst procure all the noblemen's heads within the realm to be stricken off, yet shall there one head remain that shall strike off thine head." On the commission of the peers that found him guilty were several men who were his close friends. Darcy was warning them against Cromwell, as well as warning Cromwell as to what he might expect in the end from his enemies among the nobility. But how little of the spirit of the traitor was in this man is apparent from what he said while awaiting execution: had he seen in the field the King riding toward him, he would have at once dismounted, and, holding his sword by the point, surrendered it into his Grace's hands. But then none of the Pilgrims had thought of rebelling against their King; the rebellion was merely against Cromwell and the other evil advisers of the King.

Darcy received a fair enough trial, in so far as any treason trial could be considered fair under the rules that prevailed. It was different with the lesser men, such as Aske and Constable, who were brought before juries. Their juries were not merely packed, but packed with a peculiar refinement: their relatives and friends had to sit in them, among them even Aske's brother. These dared do nothing else than bring in the verdict required by the prosecution.

Those put under arrest in Lincolnshire the previous autumn were not touched until the disturbances farther north were over, the reason being that severity would have had a bad effect just then. Nor were the Lincolnshire men treated in the same way as those of Yorkshire. The Lincolnshire fiasco was relatively lightly punished, only fifty men suffering there, a large number of them priests, and one of them, Dr. Mackerel, was not only an abbot but a suffragan bishop.[3] In this section—unlike Yorkshire—there was no perpetration of wholesale butchery. When Cromwell was able to crawl out into the light again, he reported to Sir Thomas Wyatt on July 8, 1537: "The traitors have been executed, the Lord Darcy at Tower Hill, the Lord Hussey at Lincoln, Aske hanged upon the dungeon of the castle of York, and Sir Robert Constable hanged at Hull. The residue were executed at Thylbourne. So far as we can perceive all the

[3] As the term will be unfamiliar to Americans, though it is still used in England by the Established Church, I explain that a suffragan bishop corresponds to our coadjutors or auxiliaries.

cankered hearts have been weeded away." [4] He was referring only to the principal leaders. The rank and file he does not deem worthy of mention, or even Lady Bulmer, who was burned.

Some of the great monasteries in the south and west of England had made voluntary contributions toward the maintenance in the field of the King's forces. These contributions may have been merely prudential, but they were just as likely to have been a means of protesting loyalty. For while there is no doubt that a great many people in England approved of what was asked in the Pilgrims' petition, of these a large proportion did not approve of anything like the appearance of an armed rising. Of the Pilgrims themselves, many had qualms of conscience about doing even as much as they did. It was this hesitancy that was their undoing, that and the pedantry and vanity of the well-meaning Aske.

Cromwell now had a pretext for proceeding against some of the large abbeys of the North, houses that had been exempted from the operation of the Act of Suppression. The Abbot of Barlings, Dr. Mackerel, had gone out with the Lincolnshire men, though only as the rest of the gentry had done, because he had been compelled to do so. There is no definite evidence that the Abbots of Fountains and Jervaulx and Whalley and Holm Cultram had done anything at all, though it is likely enough that they or some of the monks under them let it be known that they wished the Pilgrims well. That was enough to enable Cromwell—who had been created Baron Cromwell of Wimbledon on July 18, 1537, by way of Henry's defiant answer to those objecting to him—to devise a method of seizing these abbeys and a number of others, under attainder. In some instances the abbots were tried and hanged, and a bill of attainder against them passed at leisure afterward. In other instances, the threat of attainder was sufficient. The Abbot was told that he had a cankered heart and deserved hanging; he would however be spared if he either resigned in favor of somebody more amenable (who would be appointed by Cromwell) or surrendered his house to the

[4] Lord Hussey had taken no active part in the matter. But as a Lincolnshire magnate it was considered that he should have bestirred himself more in trying to persuade the men who had come out to go home. As one who had been an officer of the Princess Mary's household he was known to have sympathized with her cause, as he no doubt also sympathized with the Pilgrimage of Grace.

King. This was the beginning of the process of intimidation that soon took the place of the legal suppression of monasteries.

The method was most unjust but was not quite without precedent. Thus in 1529 Wolsey, after pleading guilty to having violated Praemunire and so having made himself subject to the forfeiture of his possessions, saw York House, the London palace belonging to the Archbishopric of York, taken over by the Crown. It was in vain he protested that York House did not belong to him. Neither was anything that belonged to an abbey the personal property of its abbot; it belonged to the whole community. This elementary fact was disregarded. If attainder or the threat of attainder was not more often used, this was because the knowledge that attainder could always be used was enough to bring about a terrified compliance.

It is possible (but by no means certain) that when the suppression started Henry intended only the reform of the monastic system. On the other hand the coldly realistic mind of Cromwell had always seen that this kind of "reform," once begun, would end in total suppression. He perceived that the process would be almost impossible to arrest in face of the greed of the King and the courtiers. While it is true that just before the fall of Anne Boleyn he was prepared to go as far as reconciliation with the Pope, as the price for cementing an alliance with the Emperor, he may have thought of this as only a temporary expedient. Apart from Henry's extravagant habits, if there came to be any war with France, a great deal of money would have to be found quickly. The hardheaded, round-headed Cromwell was aware that the limits of taxation had been almost reached; therefore the Crown would be forced to despoil the Church.

Cromwell had no ill will toward monks as such. But he did not think that they counted for much, for though some bishops took a fairly active part in politics, no abbot had been prominent for some time in that capacity, in spite of the fact that the abbots constituted thirty of the fifty spiritual peers.[5] Therefore the spirituality was al-

[5] It should be explained perhaps that by no means was every abbot entitled to a seat in the House of Lords. Those who were members were so by virtue of the magnitude of their manorial holdings. Few of these, however, bothered to attend the sessions of Parliament. And those who would have liked to attend were, during these crucial years, "excused," which meant, in effect, that they were ordered to stay away.

ways able to outvote the temporality, and if the abbots ever combined forces, the holdings they had and the large numbers of tenants and retainers upon whom they could draw would have made them extremely formidable. Therefore they had to be lulled as a group into a feeling of security while this and that religious house was uprooted, in each instance as though it were being dealt with as a quite exceptional case. Cromwell must have marveled at the ease with which he hoodwinked them.

He emerged from the crisis with greatly enhanced power and prestige. So also did the King, for though neither in Lincolnshire nor Yorkshire had there been anything but protestation of perfect loyalty toward Henry, he would have considered himself badly damaged had he been obliged to redeem his promises. As it was, he had a chance such as would not occur again for suppressing a rebellion with exemplary cruelty; by doing this he would forever remove rebellion from the range of future possibilities. To crown everything, he was now expecting an heir. The previous year he had been so despondent about this that he told Chapuys he was feeling old and doubted whether he would have any children by the Queen.

But on June 6, 1537, shortly after the last embers of the revolt had been trodden out, Cromwell was able to write to Wyatt to say that the Queen was quick with child. Henry was in high feather and with characteristic delicacy used to pat Jane's stomach in public and refer to the child who was there. On October 12 the Queen did bear a child, and it was a boy. The Tudor line was now assured, twenty-eight years after Henry's accession. God had kept him waiting but had at last rewarded him according to his deserts. When Jane died twelve days later, Henry grieved as much as was possible for one of his monstrous egotism. When he laid her to rest in the chapel of Windsor Castle, he arranged that he was to be buried beside her. And at their tomb Masses were to be said, "as long as the world shall last." He even founded the monastery of Bisham in Berkshire in December, with an abbot and thirteen monks, for this purpose. That is to say, he refounded what had formerly been a priory, adding to their members and revenues from smaller houses. It was surrendered back into the royal hands a year later.[6]

[6] The previous July he had refounded a convent at Stixwold in Lincolnshire—perhaps in mere whim, perhaps as a thank offering for his triumph

Cromwell had permitted the Duke of Norfolk, who had been forced into retirement for some time, to emerge from it, because his services as a commander, a double-dealer, and a hangman were indispensable. But after the collapse of the Pilgrimage, Cromwell saw to it that the Duke should find no employment at Court. He could not afford to run the risk of having the Duke lead an aristocratic reaction, which might be even more serious than the popular demonstration that had just broken down. Norfolk was therefore kept in the North at his work of "pacification" while Cromwell drew up plans for a more effective administration of the northern counties. Here almost all the Duke's recommendations were rejected. Norfolk was for putting the control of the reorganized Council of the Marches in the charge of the nobility; against which Cromwell successfully pressed the argument that the nobles had just shown they were not to be trusted.[7] Accordingly, under the new title of the Council of the North, its powers were somewhat extended, but instead of nobles it contained bureaucrats, men directly dependent upon Cromwell; and its president was a bishop, Tunstall of Durham, an orthodox man but also a firm supporter of the royal supremacy. As Cromwell was the King's Vicegerent in ecclesiastical matters, Tunstall was his subordinate. The Duke was completely defeated in his contest with his baseborn rival. He was kept in political obscurity and was consulted, if at all, only as a matter of form. Cromwell was more powerful than ever before; and he was hated more than ever before.

---

over the Pilgrimage of Grace, perhaps to show that he intended no general monastic suppression, but perhaps as an act of piety.

[7] The Marches were the borderlands between England and Scotland.

Chapter Eleven

THE LEGATE

Reginald Pole, the Cardinal-Legate appointed in 1537, had all the apparent qualifications. He was a Plantagenet, the grandson of the Duke of Clarence and the son of the Countess of Salisbury whom Henry used to describe as the saintliest woman in England. The King's cousin, he had what many considered a better claim to the throne than Henry himself. Moreover, he was learned and so pious and disinterested that he must be described as a dedicated man—one who, if not actually a saint, was on the road to becoming one. The Papacy came within his grasp, and he refused to close his hand on it. Similarly the Crown of England was his to take, as Mary's consort, at the beginning of her reign; that too he refused. Ability, charm, distinguished bearing, and courage—these were his and added to his prestige.

Unfortunately his genuine humility did not exclude vanity—a vanity in his erudition and his elaborate literary style. It was no great moral failing, but it helped to undo what otherwise he might have accomplished. In his correspondence with his royal cousin, Pole had a distressing way of showing off, perhaps not so much with the intention of glorifying himself as of impressing his arguments upon Henry. The King had asked him to be perfectly candid; so he was, in a Ciceronian Latin full of classical and Biblical tropes and allusions. With the best will in the world and with an affection that sought only to recall the King from the error of his ways, Pole dubbed him at one moment Nero, at another Satan. No other legate could conceivably have ventured upon this; but then no other legate would have had Pole's cousinly freedom.

It is, however, only fair to Paul III to say that he did not know of the letter—in bulk really a book—that Pole had addressed to the King in 1536. It is also necessary to say that Pole's appointment as legate came too late—just at the moment when the Pilgrimage of Grace was about to collapse. Not even the most tactful papal diplomat would have been of any use just then. Further it is only fair to the Pope to say that, though he was loudly accused of having instigated the rising, the proof of his innocence is that he did not appoint Pole until the appointment was useless. What Paul did know, of course, in a general way, was that England was seething with discontent and that a legate, appearing at the right moment, might strengthen a Catholic reaction. It was Pole who held him back. In this respect, as in his tactlessness (to call it by no worse a name), it was Pole who was mostly to blame. As events turned out, he was accused of being the archtraitor of his own day and, as such, made the subject of endless vilification in the pages of Froude.

Reginald Pole to the end retained both admiration and affection for Henry. And Henry, for his part, began with admiration and affection for Pole, though this, as in the case of all his friends who failed to give him complete approval, turned to bitter animosity. But it must be remembered that Henry supplied the funds for Reginald's education at Oxford, Padua, and Paris. Though it is true that this cost the Crown nothing, as Pole, while still a layman, was endowed with the Deanery of Exeter, it was the King who saw that he obtained this.

If I might make a complaint, it is that Reginald was too highly educated. In his youth he had been in contact with Sir Thomas More, the ripe and rounded scholar, full of homely wisdom and humor; later he fell in with Cardinal Bembo, whose literary taste was so delicate that he would not read St. Jerome's Vulgate for fear of contaminating his own exquisite Latinity. Though Pole is not to be blamed for this, it helps to explain his rather ineffectual career. He became a humanist of the Italian rather than the English type. While this no doubt had its advantages, it served to cut him off from a complete understanding of the English mind.

Queen Katherine had hoped that he would marry her daughter

Mary. She felt this would make up for the political murder by Henry VII of Reginald's young uncle, whom he never saw, the Earl of Warwick. But she also thought that such a marriage—that of a Plantagenet to a Tudor—would greatly strengthen Mary when she came to the throne. But Pole, though he would undoubtedly have acquiesced in the project, was devoid of ambition and so did nothing to further his cause, as he did nothing to further any cause from which he might extract benefit. He was anything in the world but a pretender to the English throne. He was simply a scholar, happy among his books but rather at a loss regarding political or dynastic issues. Even after he was made a cardinal, the possibility of his marrying Mary remained, for he was not at first (as was possible, according to the rules of those days) even in minor orders but had only the tonsure, though, as to that, even priestly vows of celibacy could have been dispensed under the circumstances.

He was in England in 1527 and again during 1530 and 1531, still on the most cordial terms with Henry. The King indeed offered him the archbishopric of York, as previously he might have had the See of Winchester, but of course Henry expected him to declare in favor of the divorce. Wishing to please Henry, of whom he was so fond, Pole prepared a written statement which he hoped would be acceptable and yet safeguard his conscience. But when he met the King by appointment at York House, he suddenly saw that his statement was one of a straddler and so spoke extemporaneously and from the heart. Henry's face flushed, and his hand slipped to his dagger, until, mastering himself, he stalked out of the room, slamming the door behind him. Not long after this Reginald, noting Cromwell's rise, decided that England was not a safe place for one of his opinions and so asked and received permission in January, 1532, to resume his studies at Padua.

Reginald Pole had come in contact with Thomas Cromwell fairly early. One of their first encounters needs to be recorded. It occurred, it would seem, in 1527, when Cromwell was still in Wolsey's service. Cromwell was then of little social and no official standing, but he had his forceful ability and the weight of his middle age, whereas Pole, in spite of his high lineage, was only a young student. One fancies a certain deference on his part, even a certain diffidence, before the knowledgeable Cromwell, for though Cromwell had read fewer books than Pole, he was obviously a practical man, a man of the world; as such Pole respected and listened to him.

It was on this occasion that Cromwell, smiling a bit loftily at some mention that Pole had made of Plato, dismissed that philosopher as a mere theorist and advised Pole to study instead writers who had a firsthand acquaintance with politics. He offered to lend him a book proving that what the politician should do was to penetrate the disguises thrown by monarchs over their real aims and to devise expedients by which those whom they served might gratify their inclinations and appetites without appearing to affront morality and religion. The book in question was Machiavelli's *The Prince*.[1]

Pole was greatly shocked, for he saw at once Cromwell was proposing principles that obliterated all differences between right and wrong. He must have shown that he did not wish to borrow the book that Cromwell desired to lend him, for it was never sent, and only some years later did Pole read Machiavelli. Then he recognized in *The Prince* the molder of Cromwell's political thought. Here was the perfect Machiavellian, with a perfect opportunity for putting the maxims into practice.

Henry continued to feel very kindly toward Reginald, even after he had not been able to extract from him the approval he wanted. The income from the Deanery of Exeter continued, for as a younger son of the Poles, Reginald had only a very slender income of his own. Perhaps the King hoped that this fact would be enough to prevent Reginald from going too far in opposition, and as he very much wanted to be able to say that his adhesion had been obtained, Reginald was invited to "declare his sentence" about the royal marriage "truly and plain without color or dark of dissimulation, which his Grace most princely abhorreth. He does not wish for a great volume or book, but the most effectual reasons plainly and briefly set forth."

Pole took the King at his word. Henry got perfect candor, but he also got, instead of the short statement asked for, a treatise that

---

[1] Paul Van Dyke in his *Renascence Portraits*, pp. 401–404, argues, not very convincingly, that the book that Cromwell offered to lend Pole was not *The Prince* but Castiglione's *The Courtier*. But this book would hardly answer Pole's description of it. All that can be said is that Cromwell was acquainted with Castiglione as well as with Machiavelli.

showed that Reginald had labored hard and long. But though the Latin had been polished until it had caught the authentic Ciceronian gleam, it was a style too high-pitched, self-conscious, overstrained. His *Pro Unitatis Ecclesiasticae Defensione* was much wider in scope than the statement asked for and by its violence seriously alarmed those few to whom the King gave it to be read. (Pole had undertaken that, so far as he was concerned, it should not be published; it was intended only for Henry's eye.)

Reginald's idea was the same as Katherine's, that Henry was at bottom well-intentioned but misled. Therefore, if only he were sternly told to do his duty, he would turn from his evil courses. It is an idea that animates many innocent and simple minds. Unfortunately the world is ruled by minds far from simple, and this was especially true of England in Cromwell's time. It was only to be expected that the *De Unitate*—to use its short title—was ineffective.

Henry, however, dissimulated his anger. When Lord Montague, Reginald's elder brother, having heard of the kind of plain speaking that the King had had to suffer, hurried to London to repudiate sharing such views, the King told him in what seemed to be a most magnanimous style, "I cannot be offended with so dutiful and affectionate a letter. I love him in spite of his obstinacy; and were he but of my opinion on this subject, I would like him better than any man in my kingdom." Reginald's mother was induced to write to him inviting him to England, assuring him that the King only wished to discuss in greater detail the points raised in his treatise, but at the same time managed to convey privately the alarm that all the family felt and so warned him to stay away.

Cardinal Contarini, who alone of all men, it would seem, had seen the manuscript before it was sent and had advised Pole that it was injudicious, told the Pope that Henry wanted Pole to visit him. "And will Reginald go?" asked Paul, to get the answer, "Not if he is wise." Three days later, on July 15, Pole replied to a letter the King had written him on June 30, saying he would have run through fire and water to answer the royal summons were it not that it would be contrary to God's will for him temerariously to cast his life away. There was, however, he said, nothing in what he had written that called for any explanation, for he had written so plainly that he could not possibly be misunderstood. He adds, "Never was a book written with more sharpness of words, nor again more fervor of love." He reminds the King that he had written at his express command and has been so forthright because nobody except one like himself, one in a safe place, ever is at liberty to tell a prince the whole truth.

The book arrived just after the execution of Anne Boleyn, something that gave Reginald high hopes. Now that God has rid Henry "of that domestical evil at home that was thought to be the cause of all your errors, and with her head, I trust, cut away all occasion of such offences as did separate you from the light of God," and moreover as God "hath given you one full of goodness to whom, I understand, your Grace is now married . . . wherefore, this is the time, Sir, to call to God that he will not suffer you to let pass this so noble an opportunity . . . that your ancient years now growing upon you, you may finish your time in all honor and joy."

The *De Unitate* was conveyed on May 27, 1536, by means of Bishop Tunstall, who was made the medium through whom much of the subsequent communications flowed. Pole wrote to this friend, "If God would give his Grace to taste but one tear of pure penance . . . all the pleasure and comfort that ever I had from childhood or the whole world would give were not to be compared with the sweetness thereof."

As though this book had not incensed the King enough, the Pope insisted that Pole accept a cardinalate. He had several times previously suggested this but each time had been held off because Reginald had explained that this would be to the undoing of his family, making him regarded in governmental circles in England as a declared enemy. Now on the very morning of the Consistory of December 26, 1536, the Pope ordered him to submit and sent a prelate with a barber to cut Pole's tonsure. Paul III had decided that the news from England about the Pilgrimage of Grace made it necessary to send a legate to the scene of action at once—and of course Pole was the obvious man to choose.

It was, however, just too late. Henry saw to it that he was not received in France as a papal legate, protesting that otherwise diplomatic complications would be created. For the same reason Pole was excluded from the Low Countries and had to find a rather ignominious refuge at Liége, to which neutral city he was obliged to go in disguise. Already the Pilgrimage of Grace was collapsing.

In the knowledge of this Cromwell wrote a coarsely abusive letter, to Michael Throgmorton, that friend and servant of Pole's who had recently been acting as his messenger in England. Cromwell had tried to detach him from Pole, and having failed in this, says in September, 1537, "I thought that the singular goodness of the King's Highness and the great and singular clemency showed to that detestable traitor, your master, in promising him not only forgiveness, but also forgettings of his most shameful ingratitude, unnaturalness, conspiracy against his honor, of whom he hath received no more but even as much and all that he hath; I thought I say, that either this princely goodness, might have brought that desperate rebel from his so sturdy malice, blindness and perversity, or else have encouraged you to be his Highness' true and faithful subject. But now I remember myself too late. I might better have judged that so dishonest a master could have but a servant as you are." Which long rigmarole means that Cromwell is enraged because Throgmorton had refused to make himself a party to Cromwell's plot of persuading Pole to entrust himself to Henry's hand.

He then passes to threats: "Pity it is that the folly of one brainsick Pole, or to say better, of one witless fool, should be the ruin of so great a family." That threat was not idle, as the event was to show. But not content with hinting very broadly that the whole Pole family in England would suffer, Cromwell hints also at assassination: "Hath he not just cause to fear lest every honest man should offer himself to revenge this so enormous unkindness?" Nor will he be safe, even if he returns to Italy: "There may be found ways enough [there] to rid a traitrous subject. Surely let him not think, but where justice can take no place by process of law at home, sometimes she may be enforced to seek a new means abroad."

Pole realized that Cromwell would stick at nothing. The only reason the repeated attempts at abduction or assassination were not successful was that Pole took the precaution, after this, of always having a bodyguard. After demands for extradition had failed—only resulting in Pole's being told that his presence was an embarrassment and that he had better move elsewhere—his kidnaping was planned. Offers, however, were first made to the Regent of the Low Countries of payment for 4,000 soldiers for ten months and 50,000 crowns besides. They were tempting but so dishonorable that they had to be refused. Cromwell had written to Gardiner and Bryan on April 25, 1537, at a time, it should be noted, when he was still trying to lure Pole to come to England of his own accord: "Forasmuch as we would be very glad to have the same Pole by some means trussed up and conveyed to Calais, we desire and pray you to consult and devise between you thereupon." Gardiner could have had no sympathy with such plans, but they were in accord with the mind of the Vicar of Hell, so Bryan made arrangements with Sir Thomas Palmer—whom we have seen figuring in the Rich perjury against Sir Thomas More and who at this time held the office of Porter of Calais—to go to Flanders, on the pretext of buying a horse, with half a dozen men for Pole's abduction. On May 6 Cromwell was informed that the party was setting out the next day. They did not succeed, perhaps because Cromwell wrote on May 18 to say that, although the King was not prepared to advance money for this bit of business, anyone who carried it through could count on a handsome reward.

A little later a Welshman named Vaughan (who had to clear out of England because of manslaughter) proposed to undertake what Cromwell wanted. He contrived to insinuate himself into the Cardinal's household but was won over by Pole's affability and may have also been stricken in conscience. The Cardinal, without giving any indication of suspicion about Vaughan's errand, reminded him that they both had Welsh ancestry and offered to employ him later in Italy. Vaughan must have seen from the expression in Pole's face that his project had been discovered and guarded against; at any rate, he was gone by the fall of night.

By this time it was evident that Pole's Legateship was altogether useless. He had not undertaken it in much hope and warned the Pope that Henry would probably do what in fact he did do: that is, make lavish promises and then, as soon as it was safe to do so, break them and exact heavy punishment. Hoping against hope, he stayed on awhile, doing nothing to foment further rebellion (for which, indeed, there would have been no chance) but being on hand should any unforeseen emergency arise.

Badly as the Pope may have misjudged the situation, Cromwell, for his part, bungled even more badly in his efforts to get hold of Cardinal Pole. It will be remembered that abduction plots had been made in May and that in September Cromwell in his rage showed his hand openly when writing to Throgmorton, so it was all too plain what fate awaited Pole should he go to England. Nevertheless, in this later month he sent lengthy instructions to Dr. Nicholas Wilson (who had been imprisoned in the Tower in 1534 for refusing the Act of Supremacy but subsequently released) and to Dr. Heath, who was to be Archbishop of York and Chancellor under Queen Mary, that they were to seek a meeting with Pole and assure him "that his Majesty will yet take him to mercy and besides put him in the state of an honest man if he will return home." Such assurances were utterly insincere, for the only terms upon which Pole could have made his peace with Henry were those of abject submission. On such terms his life would no doubt have been spared, as the adhesion of a cardinal-legate was worth obtaining. It is worth noting, however, that Heath and Wilson were told, most unhandsomely, to address him by no other name than that of "Mr. Pole." Pole, though he was unworldly, was nevertheless not a fool and so refused to be trapped.

Meanwhile Pole had been getting the reproaches of his kinsfolk and friends. Lord Montague had written, "Learning you may well have, but doubtless no prudence or pity, but showeth yourself to run from one mischief to another." That had some point, for the Poles were in great danger; but Bishop Tunstall and Stokesley wrote a joint letter that was wide of the mark when they told him, "For the vain glory of a red hat you have made yourself the instrument of his malice, who would stir up rebellion in the realm." To which Pole could only answer with perfect honesty that, if only Henry would reenter the Roman obedience, he himself would gladly resign the cardinalate and become a hermit.

The upshot of all this should have been foreseen. The Pope had not fomented rebellion in England, though that "most pestilent idol"—otherwise "the cankered and venomous serpent, Paul, Bishop of Rome"—was accused of having done so. For that matter, no rebellion had occurred, merely an orderly protest and a petition to the Crown, which Henry's subjects had every right to make. But even about this the Holy See had not been informed in advance—for the movement was wholly spontaneous. Therefore no advantage could be taken of it. And when Pole was sent on his second legateship to the Emperor, Charles would not act. The only result was the destruction of the Pole family. Paul had been warned that this would happen but had disregarded the warnings, forcing the legateship on a most unwilling man. Afterward the Pope was so overwhelmed by what had occurred that for several weeks after Pole's return he could not look him in the face.

What was done had, as part of its intention, the wounding of Pole's affectionate heart. And the worst stroke, still held in reserve, that against the Cardinal's mother, was not delivered until shortly after Cromwell himself had disappeared, though it was he who engineered the whole matter. In part, however, the destruction of the Poles was by way of getting rid of all possible royal claimants. That is why Henry Courtenay, the Marquis of Exeter, was also eliminated. He too was a Plantagenet and, as such, of far better blood than the usurping Tudors.

A plot had to be manufactured against them. But the evidence gathered was so weak that Cromwell was afraid that if they were tried the peers might refuse to find them guilty in the face of the defense these men could make. He therefore used another device. Attainder itself had often been used before but hitherto usually as a means of getting Parliament to confirm the sentence delivered by a court of justice or a panel of peers. The new method was so novel that Cromwell felt obliged to consult the judges as to the legality of what he had in mind. He asked whether if a man should be condemned to death under the act of attainder in Parliament, would it be possible to appeal against it? The judges showed that they did not much like the procedure but answered that Parliament, being omnicompetent, an attainder could not be reversed in a court of law but only by Parliament itself.

As usual, the blow fell without warning. Until the moment of their arrest the traitors remained to all appearances in the royal favor. Lord Montague had taken part in the baptism of Prince Edward on October 15, 1537, and in 1535 had—surely most reluctantly—been on the commission that found Sir Thomas More guilty of treason. As for Exeter, he had served (though, it was alleged, with insufficient energy) in command of those being recruited in the West for the King's forces at the time of the Pilgrimage of Grace. Their names were, indeed, among those upon whom Chapuys had been counting in 1534 and 1535, but as to this Cromwell (whatever his suspicions may have been) knew nothing definite, for it was not brought up against them when they were arrested. The most that could be charged were some harmless criticisms and petulant remarks. It was forcing the issue unduly hard when their crimes were made to consist of such things as writing to Cardinal Pole (the brother of the one man and the friend of the other), deploring the plunder of the monasteries, and expressing the pious hope that "the world would amend some day." Jerome Ragland, a former servant of the Poles, testified that Lord Montague had said that "in times past the King's words had been believed, but nowadays they be used [to deceive]. Wherefore if the commons do rise again they will trust no fair promises nor words." Then, too, the accused possessed and admired the writings of Sir Thomas More —all of which, by the way, had been published with Henry's knowledge and approval.[2] In these More had been most careful to avoid touching on the Pope's authority.

The great bulk of this evidence was extracted from the Poles' younger brother, Sir Geoffrey, who, to save his life, turned state's witness. But even he could contribute nothing that could be fairly construed as proof of treason, though he was aware that it was more than sufficient for Cromwell's purpose. In his misery at what he was doing he twice tried to commit suicide, and when he was at last released, he managed to make his way to the Continent, where though he received forgiveness at the feet of his brother, Cardinal Reginald, he lived the rest of his days in the greatest dejection and shame.

Against the Countess of Salisbury was produced the only tangible piece of evidence. But though tangible, it is highly questionable whether it meant anything like what Cromwell said it did when he produced it in Parliament. The evidence was a garment found in the house of the Countess; on it was embroidered the emblem of the five Wounds. This emblem had indeed been taken by the Pilgrims of Grace, but, as it was one in common use, to implicate Lady Salisbury in this rising was rather farfetched. Another supposedly damning point was that this emblem was encircled with pansies and marigolds. Cromwell explained that the marigolds stood for Mary and the pansies for Reginald Pole. No doubt Pole's mother had at one time hoped (as had Mary's mother) that a marriage between these two would be possible. It is hard to see how this constituted treason.

The act of attainder was of a most sweeping character, con-

[2] The only exceptions were the works More produced in the Tower. These remained in manuscript until 1557.

demning not only a number of living persons but some already executed, such as Lords Darcy and Hussey. Among the living people condemned were William Peto, the Observant friar whom Henry himself had permitted to leave England in 1532, Michael Throgmorton, and of course Cardinal Pole. The chief of those among the living who were attainted were Montague and his mother, Exeter and his wife, Sir Edward Neville, and some canons of Chichester. The Marchioness of Exeter was eventually released, but Lady Salisbury was kept in the Tower, to be dealt with on a later occasion.

With them were imprisoned two young boys: one of them, Edward Courtenay, was Exeter's son, and the other Montague's son—both of them detained merely because of their Plantagenet blood. Of these Courtenay was not released until Mary came to the throne, when she might have married him had he not indulged in dissolute habits as soon as he was out of prison. The other boy could not be found at the time; nor is there any record as to what happened to him. He may have died in the Tower, but the probability is that he was murdered there: Henry had a fiercer grudge against him than against young Courtenay. With this wholesale eradication of two royal or semiroyal families Cromwell gave fresh proof that his monarchical ideal was the sultanate.

Cromwell, as he could not bring Cardinal Pole to England, continued to dog his footsteps with hired assassins, in true totalitarian style, as did Henry after Cromwell's death. They might have saved themselves the bother. So far from being dangerous, he was rather ineffectual. By nature he was a scholar living in an ivory tower. But he was forced, against all his inclinations, to accept a legateship that brought him into collision with Cromwell, the most formidable antagonist that can be imagined, one devoid of scruples and with all the machinery of politics at his command. Under normal circumstances Pole might have made a better showing, but he came upon the scene too late. This was due to his personal modesty, his fears for his family, and his wish not to affront a King whom, in spite of everything, he loved to the end. Had it not been for these personal factors, Paul III would have appointed him legate sooner than he did; then the history of England would almost certainly have taken a very different course.

Chapter Twelve

THE ADMINISTRATOR

Professor Merriman remarks of Thomas Cromwell, "It was not alone in Parliament, Convocation or Privy Council that he reigned supreme; on every department of the government service the stamp of his individual genius remains indelibly fixed. The permanence of his work was largely due to the way in which he clinched every reform which he introduced." The praise is just, apart from the Cromwellian foreign policy, for there he lacked the Wolseian sleight of hand, and if his destruction of the monasteries and the ties with Christendom be excepted, for these, at least in my opinion, were enormous disasters. But in order to avoid confusion, these exceptions are dealt with separately, and here Cromwell will be shown only as the administrator of internal affairs. Here he was at his best or at least his most efficient. Though no aspect of his work can be said to be free from tyranny or corruption, at least it must be admitted that he gave England an orderly government and kept steadily before him the necessity for peace.

In many ways his policy was a return to that of Henry VII. With a king like Henry VIII on his hands, it was of course not possible to build up a financial reserve. In several other important points Cromwell's mind would have accorded better with that of the first Tudor than with the second. His commercial policy was one of these; under the businessman Cromwell, trade was promoted, whereas during the early years of the reign insufficient attention had been

194

paid to the matter. And partly as a concomitant of this but also because of the fear of war in 1539, English shipping was encouraged
and increased. The King got the credit for this, but it was really
Cromwell's. And as long as he was in power, peace was pursued,
—this, in spite of the fact that much of England's foreign policy—
whether initiated by Cromwell or forced upon him by Henry—was
likely to bring on war. During the first years of Cromwell's administration there was, it is true, no money available for expensive military action on the Continent. But the suppression of the larger monasteries during his last years gave ample funds for this, and yet
Cromwell refrained from war. It is due to him that so much as even
half the immense monastic loot was applied to national defenses instead of being completely swallowed up by the King's personal
extravagance.

Greatly superior to Cromwell though Wolsey was in foreign
affairs, Cromwell's superiority to Wolsey was at least as marked
when we look at affairs at home. Cavendish, it is true, does say "that
in my judgment I never saw this realm in better obedience and quiet
than it was in the time of [the Cardinal's] authority, nor justice better administered," and he was in the position of comparing both
administrations. From his own point of view—which stresses justice
and bears in mind that there was no rebellion under Wolsey—he is
right. But Wolsey was always too busy with what was happening
abroad to give much attention to what was happening at home. Fortunately for him, things could, in his time, more or less run themselves in England. Under Cromwell, when England was passing
through a period of revolution, unremitting attention had to be given
to domestic details. And it must be said that no detail was too small
to escape Cromwell's scrutiny. He had to show a prodigious capacity
for work and a prodigious intellectual alertness.

The central point in Cromwell's policy—as has been said already
and as will have to be said again—was that of making the English
monarchy unassailable and absolute. In this the breach with Rome
was hardly more than an incident but was in Cromwell's judgment
necessary in order to deliver all authority into the King's hands.
The spoliation of the monasteries was another incident, one whose
purpose was to give the Crown the economic security without which
political authority would have failed. But another element that has
been sometimes overlooked or not given its due weight was his

195

grand design of forming the whole British Isles into a single entity.

The suzerainty of the English Crown over Scotland had often been asserted, but no king had ever been able to maintain it successfully. So Cromwell was careful not to make an effort in that direction which he believed would fail. Without ruling it out of his general scheme, he was of the opinion that the time for aggressive action against Scotland was not ripe. Moreover he was again of Henry VII's opinion, when he married his daughter Margaret to James IV of Scotland, that even if from this union came a king of Scotland who would be heir to the English throne, the preponderant strength of England would be more than sufficient to turn him into an English king. Accordingly Cromwell cultivated young James V, trying indeed to detach him from the Roman obedience and get him to seize the Scottish monasteries but being invariably conciliatory toward him. Had Charles V invaded England, with however small a force in 1534, 1535, or 1536, and had James moved at the same time, nothing could have saved Henry. The fact that Henry reversed his policy after Cromwell's death, though without any solid gain, proves that the Scottish policy prevailing until then was that of the King's minister and not of the King.

It is true that the border was, at best, in a state of precarious peace. But raids were one thing and full-scale military operations another. Even raids were discouraged after the reorganization of the government of the North following the Pilgrimage of Grace. The letter that Cromwell wrote to the Earl of Northumberland in December, 1532, represents Henry's mind rather than his own, for though Cromwell at this date already had very considerable power, he did not enjoy anything like the plenitude he afterward obtained. So Cromwell sends the Earl the King's congratulations and his own for the recent raid: "Wishing to God that your Lordship did know and hear as I do how lovingly and acceptably the King's Highness doth regard and take the same, which undoubtedly would double the hardiness and courage of any man living to do his Grace service." After he had more fully rounded out his internal policy, Cromwell preferred, as regards Scotland, services of a less bellicose character.

Two years later, at a moment when relations with the Emperor were more than usually bad, Cromwell made an effort to draw Sir Adam Otterburn, a Scottish envoy recently arrived in London, over to the antipapal side, proposing "certain dishonorable and heretical articles." These were received by Otterburn with such horror that they were withdrawn in a hurry. And though later Cromwell tried hard along the same lines, sending his friend Sir Ralph Sadler to James V, he did not have any better luck. Under Cardinal Beaton, Scotland remained at once Catholic and an ally of France. If the Emperor or Francis had attacked, either jointly or together in 1539, as seemed likely, Scotland would have attacked too. That there was no war during Cromwell's regime must in large part be set down to his skillful management of the Scots King.

It was quite other with regard to the Welsh and the Irish, as these had no allies, except for the Irish hopes that perhaps Spain might do something for them. They never realized that for Charles to send even a small force to their unhappy country would be more trouble than he would consider it worth. He could at best merely annoy Henry from that quarter, whereas the same number of men landed in England before or during the Pilgrimage of Grace would have toppled Henry from his throne, unless he completely reversed all that he had done. Even in 1539, after the series of executions that followed what is called the Exeter conspiracy, enough disaffected elements remained to have ensured the success of a rising should help be given from the Continent.

We may, however, leave Ireland until later and glance at Cromwell's one great success in the program he had for bringing all the British Isles under one head. Wales was a small country and a weak one. It had its sentimental attachments to the house of Tudor, as it was from Wales that the Tudors had come, one among a hundred petty chieftains. Now the time had arrived, Henry announced under the unsentimental Cromwell's advice, for showing his fatherly affection toward a race for whom he had a special favor by reducing them to a compliance with English laws alien to their character.

In this it need not be denied that Henry and Cromwell had some right on their side. Wales had been for a long time a principality, ruled, in theory, by the King of England's eldest son. Actually it was hardly ruled at all, except in its own rather mysterious way, until Cromwell took the matter in hand. He intended to bring it under direct English control, though at first he was not able to effect the amalgamation under which Wales came under English law and sent representatives to the English Parliament. There had been many

complaints (some no doubt justified) about the "manifold rob-
beries, murders, thefts, trespasses, riots, routs, embraceries, mainte-
nances, oppressions, ruptures of the peace, and many other malefacts
which be there daily practiced, perpetrated and done." So now the
authority of the President of the Council of the Marches was extended, the main reason being, as Chapuys thought, that Wales,
along with Cornwall, had been thought of as a suitable landing place
for a Spanish army. The Imperial Ambassador naturally hoped to
turn the discontent there to his own use.

Rowland Lee, who had served with Cromwell under Wolsey
and was appointed Bishop of Coventry and Lichfield in 1534, was
at the same time made President of the Council of the Marches. He
was the man who had married Henry to Anne Boleyn (unless that
was, as some say, Dr. George Browne); but cleric though he was,
he showed himself to be precisely the kind of administrator Cromwell wanted. His hand fell heavily on evildoers or those whom he
regarded as such; and in a couple of years 5,000 Welsh were hanged,
and their resistance, which had never been very formidable, was
entirely broken.

Part of Wales had already been divided into shires; now all of it
was, and these were further subdivided for the administration of
justice. In the law courts only English was to be used, which must
have made it hard for most of the accused people to defend themselves; in fact, the existence of the Welsh language was refused
any kind of legal recognition. In 1536 the Act of Union between
England and Wales was passed, after which Wales was hardly more
than a geographical term.

Though a commission was appointed to inquire into local Welsh
customs and laws and the retention of some of these was permitted,
most of the results were obnoxious to the people, though they never
dared anything like rebellion against the ruthless and efficient Bishop
Lee. Yet, while one cannot but deplore the methods used, Cromwell's Welsh policy was statesmanlike and in the upshot for the
benefit of the Welsh, however many of them first had to dangle in
a noose. The plan or something like it should have been carried out
long before this but had been impossible to think of during the Wars
of the Roses. Then the first Tudor had been too grateful to the large
Welsh contingent that formed the main part of his army at Bosworth
to disturb them; and Henry VIII, until the arrival of a period when

he could give some thought to something besides his futile French wars and then his divorce and the breach with Rome, had no time to give to the Welsh problem. But with the arrival of the immensely capable Cromwell, the absorption of Wales at last became possible. The great achievement was carried out with astonishing rapidity, and it has remained, in its essential features, permanent. If any Welsh nationalists exist today, they are national only in the sense of wishing to preserve, through such institutions as the eisteddfod, their indigenous culture. In spite of Cromwell's laws, they triumphed at this point; and they are alone among the Celtic races of what I hope an Irishman will pardon me for still calling, for the sake of convenience, the British Isles, in holding on to their Celtic language for general use.

But if Cromwell was successful in the case of Wales, in the case of Ireland, while he obtained what seemed, at the time, a very large measure of success, this proved in the long run to be a complete failure. For it was he who initiated that policy of oppression which carried down, though with diminishing ferocity, to living memories has been the greatest blot on the fame of England. Yet it must be conceded that Cromwell's was at least a real policy, whereas, since the late twelfth century, when Henry II received Ireland as a papal fief entrusted to his charge, no English king had known what to do with the country. It added nothing to English strength, and so far from being a profit it was rather a drain. While at no moment a national danger, at any moment it might become one and therefore had to be held. This meant, however, that it was held with a minimum of military power, the English rule extending hardly beyond the "Pale" around Dublin, though a right to govern the whole of Ireland was asserted.

So far from there being any incompatibility between the two races, one of the difficulties of administration was that the Anglo-Normans sent over by the King of England always tended to be absorbed quickly by the circumambient Irishry. This has sometimes been described as a form of "going native"; the mild Irish climate softened the sturdy Englishmen! The explanation is rather that the English officials and soldiers were charmed by their Irish neighbors, taking wives from among them, adopting the Irish dress, the Irish tribal customs, and even the Gaelic tongue. This tongue had the advantage at that time of a more advanced literary development than

English. But whatever the reason, the fact is that the Englishman in Ireland did not remain an Englishman long. Or if he himself remained one, his children were always completely Irish.

Here of course were the true elements of the Irish problem, had anyone been acute enough to recognize that fact. The chieftains— whether of the old Irish stock or of the more recently imported Englishry—ran things, each in his own territory, in the Irish way, and yet the "lordship" of Ireland claimed by the King of England received a kind of acceptance even by the clans or tribes (the words are not quite accurate but will have to serve) who lived outside the Pale. The policy—if such it can be called—of allowing nature to take its own course might in the end have accomplished much, especially had it been intelligently directed. It would certainly have spared Ireland much suffering and England much shame. It did not seem tolerable to the efficient Cromwell.

It should be remembered, as a kind of extenuation, that during the reign of Henry VII Ireland had shown itself a strong Yorkist center. The young men who were Pretenders—one who claimed to be one of the two princes murdered in the Tower by the usurping Richard III and the other to be the Earl of Warwick, the nephew of Edward IV—were received with enthusiasm in Ireland. In each instance the authenticity of their claims was admitted not because of any proof but because of a wish to believe. But this extenuation had little validity in Cromwell's time. No Yorkist party existed. And the Plantagenets were all dead, except for the aged Countess of Salisbury, Cardinal Pole, and two young boys safe in custody. The worst that might be expected were little local disturbances, though these of course were used to justify the idea that Ireland was a turbulent country always likely to give trouble.

What really lay at the root of the Cromwellian policy was that Henry, after the schism with Rome, insisted the Irish should renounce the jurisdiction of the Holy See. Nor can it be said that the official classes in Ireland or even the higher clergy showed much inclination to oppose this. It can be understood why the Irish or Anglo-Irish chieftains were willing to accept their share of the loot of such monasteries as Henry could reach: these were men who had, in many instances, received titles of nobility from the English Crown and owed some fealty to the English King, intermittently as they paid it. What is hard to understand is why the two archbishops and

200

the eight bishops who met at the summons of Cromwell's old friend George Browne, since 1536 the Archbishop of Dublin, were willing to take the Oath of Supremacy. If this be explained on the ground that they were for the most part Englishmen or owed their episcopal nominations to Henry, there is another fact to be met: the oath was eventually taken by twenty-two out of thirty Irish bishops, and, as among these were several men who had been appointed by the Pope in disregard of Henry's wishes, it must be obvious that they were not especially papal in their convictions. Either that, or they were more timorous than experience shows Irishmen to be.

But whatever their chieftains or their higher clergy might do, the mass of the Irishry remained loyal to the Holy See. Indeed, what had begun to happen was a revelation to Irishmen of their own principles. Until then they had been a cluster of disunited, and often warring, units; now they began to feel themselves a nation, with their political ideas still rather undefined but with a growing consciousness of their Irish culture and their Irish genius. After centuries of easygoing living with the English officials, whose nominal rule had been hitherto good-humoredly accepted in theory, the Irish suddenly discovered an antagonism toward them. Archbishop Browne retaliated by showing his contempt for Irish traditions in a startling way: he burned Ireland's most sacred relic, the staff of St. Patrick, in a Dublin street.

By that time the Irish were cowed or were supposed to be cowed. What had been regarded as the only serious outbreak against English authority had been suppressed between 1534 and 1536, in the usual style, by perfidy. The rebellion was led by a dashing but not very judicious young man, popularly known as "Silken Thomas." He was of the Fitzgerald family, who had the title of Kildare. (The Norman origin is self-evident, as is that of the Butlers with their title of Ormonde.) Further inland were other great families, more purely Irish, but the Fitzgeralds and Butlers were within the Pale or not so far outside it as to be unamenable to English influence.

Partly by way of placating these Anglo Irish magnates and of flattering them, but partly also to effect economies in an Irish administration that was ruinously expensive, the office of deputy had been given to the head of the Fitzgeralds, the Earl of Kildare. Then in 1534 he was summoned to England (he supposed it was merely in the ordinary course of official business) and on arrival was put into the Tower, though with no specific charges laid against him, except that it could almost always be charged that a deputy had been negligent in the performance of his duties. This detention may have been at the instigation of his rivals, the Butlers, but it was sheer Machiavellianism that prompted the announcement (not officially given out, to be sure, but as a report officially encouraged) that Kildare had been executed.

What happened played straight into the hands of Cromwell, already meditating a new policy for Ireland. Kildare's son, Silken Thomas, who, had his father really been dead, would have been the new Earl, raised a rebellion against Henry. He marched into Dublin; he seized John Allen, the Archbishop, as he was on the point of escaping, and assassinated him; and as Ireland was a papal fief, Silken Thomas declared himself the supporter of the papal power there. In the expectation of carrying out his not very well-developed designs, he offered the Earl of Ormonde half of Ireland as his share when the English had been ejected. Ormonde declined this, out of jealousy or caution, and another instance of factional rivalry ruined the Irish cause.

The fortress of Maynooth, which had been considered impregnable, was unable to hold out against artillery, and Silken Thomas surrendered to his uncle, the new deputy, Sir Leonard Grey, on the understanding that his life should be spared.[1] Though that pledge was kept for the moment, it was only because it was not thought advisable to execute him so long as other rebels remained at large who might be induced to submit if assured of the King's clemency. But the five uncles of the young Earl (he really was that by now, as his father had died in the Tower) were scooped up, all by treachery —three of them at a dinner to which the English authorities had invited them. Then, when all the leading Geraldines were safely within his hands, Cromwell proceeded to deal with them. They were now condemned to death, and, though at least Silken Thomas, being an Earl, should have had the grace of the block, he and all his uncles suffered at Tyburn.

There is in Ireland a favorite imprecation, "the Curse of Crom-

[1] Grey's case is typical. He was an Englishman, one of the sons of the first Marquis of Dorset, which made him an uncle of Lady Jane Grey and a connection by marriage of King Henry. He was married to an Irish wife. In 1541 he was beheaded on a charge of having favored the Geraldines.

well." Oliver Cromwell, the great-great-grandnephew of Thomas, is thought of, then, as personally responsible for massacres and other atrocities. But Thomas Cromwell, perhaps because he worked as Henry's agent and merely started something that nobody imagined would be carried so far, is often forgotten. Yet he was the initiator of repressive measures in Ireland. The best that one can say for him here is that he believed a little severity applied at this moment would solve all problems. And this might have been a solution had not Cromwell, by driving in the dividing wedge of religion, made reconciliation between England and Ireland impossible.

Cromwell's policy toward Ireland was, as at so many other points, in direct opposition to that advocated by the Duke of Norfolk. The Duke was not a notably humane man, so if he argued, as he did, in the Council for a continuation of the old easygoing method of maintaining a hold on Ireland, this was because he believed it would be more effective and cheaper than Cromwell's drastic ideas. He had served for a while, shortly before he came to his dukedom, as Lord Lieutenant of that country, about which he considered he knew a good deal. What he feared was the sucking down of English armies and English gold into the Irish bogs. But the policy of Cromwell prevailed; Ireland was to be bludgeoned into submission as Wales had been. This policy seemed at first to be almost as successful as the similar harsh methods of dealing with Wales. If in the end it failed, this was because it neglected to take into account what Cromwell did not consider worth a practical man's consideration; it failed because the Irish were loyal to the Holy See.

We have, as it happens, more letters from Cromwell regarding the administration of Calais than the other matters mentioned. This was not because Calais was more important in itself, though its importance to Tudor England can hardly be overestimated. When Cromwell was at the head of affairs, the charge of this gateway into France was committed to Arthur Plantagenet, a natural son of Edward IV, not by the famous Jane Shore but by another of the royal mistresses. He was given the title of Viscount Lisle in 1523 and had associated with him at Calais, toward the end of his regime, John Dudley, who was made Viscount Lisle when Arthur Plantagenet died.

The letters to him are of especial interest as revealing how no detail was too small for Cromwell's attention. For instance, we find

203

him writing to Lisle on February 8, 1535, telling him to appoint one Ralph Hare to the next vacant position at eightpence a day, and on the following May 21 he expresses astonishment at Lisle's delay in giving Thomas Apponwell a place in the garrison. In general, however, it must be said that Cromwell deals with weightier matters than these. He has to send Lisle rebukes frequently for his negligence or his extravagant scale of living. As the minister was obviously deeply concerned about this Continental outpost, one wonders why he allowed a man of such meager ability to remain there as long as he did.

Religious matters receive Cromwell's close attention. Thus he writes to Lisle on July 17, 1537, ordering him to send two priests, named William Minstreley and William Richardson, as prisoners to England, as they are suspected of papistical tendencies.[2] At the same time Lisle gets a rebuke that must have made him quail: "His Grace cannot a little marvel to hear of the papistical faction that is maintained in that town and by you chiefly that be of his Grace's Council." A week later Lisle is warned against being lax with regard to "superstitious old observances and rites." Nevertheless Cromwell reassures him, "Whatsoever be written in the same, my Lord, think none otherwise that I remain still your perfect and sincere friend."

The accusation that the Governor of Calais had been protecting papistical priests may account for his looking the other way when he heard about priests of heretical tendencies in the territory under his jurisdiction. For on May 6, 1538, Lisle is reproved for not sending information about the "sacramentaries" there. It was all a bit confusing because eight days later Lisle received—along with further instructions about laying by the heels those who had spoken disrespectfully of the Sacrament of the Altar—an order to pull down the statue of "Our Lady of the Wall," as apparently "many abuses and fond superstitions were maintained by the same."

In all this Cromwell was being devious. For, after telling Lisle on July 16, 1538, "I perceive that in the same King's town of Calais there is some infection of certain persons denying the Holy Sacrament of Christ's blessed Body and Blood, of such opinions as commonly they call sacramentaries" and ordering the Governor, "not only to cause them to be punished to the example of all others, but also provide that no such errors pernicious be spread abroad but

[2] See footnote on p. 211.

utterly suppressed, banished and extincted," we find Cromwell on May 27 of the following year instructing Lisle that about these matters he should be "discreet and charitable." More specifically Cromwell says, "Mine opinion is that you shall by all means devise how with charity and mild handling of things to quench this slanderous bent as much as you may, ever exhorting men discreetly and without rigor and extreme dealing to know and serve God truly and their prince and Sovereign Lord with all humility and obedience." The letter continues in the same vein; Cromwell, without daring to say so openly, broadly hints that heresy might be winked at. It was a very dangerous game for him to play. He played it only because he was at that moment trying to come to an understanding with the Lutheran princes of Germany, about which more will be told in a later chapter.

Cromwell soon perceived his danger and, when he did, at once took an opposite course. The reason was that the Six Articles were being debated in Parliament and were—Cromwell could not but sense—about to become law. They affirmed transubstantiation and rejected Communion in both kinds. They said further that priests by the law of God might not marry, that vows of chastity were to be observed, that private Masses might be celebrated, and that auricular confession was not merely expedient but necessary. Henry ignored the fact that clerical celibacy was merely a disciplinary law of the Church; he declared it part of God's law. This ferocious "Whip of Six Strings" for the suppression of erroneous doctrines obliged Cromwell to write to Lord Lisle again on June 8 about an Adam Damplip who had been preaching by permission of the Commissary of Calais "most detestable and cankered heresy" on the subject of transubstantiation. Accordingly, Lisle, who two weeks before, had been told that the matter was of slight importance, was ordered to send the two priests to London for punishment.

Religion, however, was only one of a hundred details that Cromwell had to watch with a vigilant eye. Even in a letter dated January 21, 1540, at a time when Cromwell, though he did not know it, was tottering to his fall, he still showed himself the careful administrator, reprimanding even the son of a king, as he considers that the occasion called for it. Lisle is warned to make sure of the defenses and the provisioning of the town and the alertness of its garrison, especially the officers. Though Cromwell says he does not anticipate any immediate danger, instructions are sent that all carts and wagons coming into Calais should be carefully searched, as those carrying straw, or hay, or wood might have men hidden in them. A Trojan Horse method of attack was always a possibility.

Dover was less important than Calais, but it was highly fortified as the main guard set over the Channel. Thomas Wingfield, its Comptroller, was reproached on December 6, 1536, for his inefficiency and wastefulness. "It appeareth right well," Cromwell tells him severely, "how little ye regard his Grace's charges and how much you set by your own profit (if spoil may be called profit) and by the setting forth to the King's charge of those that it liketh you with the King's purse to maintain when at the last order taken for discharge of some part of the workmen ye have kept in a great many men as clerks and such other that be very chargeable to the King's Majesty." (Evidently Wingfield had been using a good deal of public money for the support of his own lavish household. As he was merely rebuked and not instantly removed from office, we must assume that such was the usual practice.) Wingfield is told: "You should for your part have been the King's housewife and especially have looked to his Grace's profit. And you have devised upon nothing more than how to keep his Grace in great charge to a little purpose." Corrupt though Cromwell was, he was, unlike Wingfield, a most efficient administrator.

Finally, it should be briefly indicated how the Cromwellian administration operated. So far from disliking and fearing Parliament, as Wolsey had done, or attempting to govern without it, Cromwell summoned it more frequently than ever before and kept it in almost constant session. But he discovered how to control Parliament, first by packing it with enough of his own creatures to assure that all he wished be given statutory effect and then by working on individual members by intimidation, persuasion, and flattery. The function of Parliament, according to his ideas, was to register the King's will; but the real instrument of administration was the Council.

Cromwell was in effect the Council, dictating its decisions and subjecting all those who might be described as ministers (though the modern conception of ministers, each responsible for his own department, had not emerged) to his own autocratic control. And in the end he contrived to give the Council, under parliamentary statute, the right to legislate by proclamation. This meant, in prac-

206

tice, that Cromwell himself did the legislating, though of course always subject to the will of the Crown. Again one discovers absolutism, totalitarianism in its earliest form.

Cromwell delegated very little, and those to whom any little bit of authority was delegated had to report regularly to him. The system would of course be unworkable in even a small modern state, because of the complexity of its machinery; nor would it have worked even in Cromwell's England had there not been at the head of everything a man of extraordinary ability and industry. He was stocky and burly, and he usually enjoyed excellent health; he could therefore assume any weight put upon him, and he wished to carry everything himself. The other members of the Council were assembled hardly more than *pro forma*. Those who might have had some influence—men like the Duke of Norfolk and Bishop Gardiner—were kept employed at a distance or were not employed at all.

There does not seem to have been any special vanity in this. Cromwell soberly assessed himself as the one man in England capable of managing affairs. He was devoted to the purpose of making the King all-powerful; the nobles of England could not be trusted to carry out this concept, to which in fact most of them were opposed. They could not but remember the time when theirs was the preponderant power in politics or the time when they made and unmade kings. So in the coarse hands of the plebeian all the reins of government were retained. He was the efficient man, the practical man, and he intended to rule—thereby preparing his own destruction.

Cromwell's good points, almost as much as his bad points, increased the number of his enemies. He was looked upon merely as a glorified official, and nobles and bishops resented his dictation. Norfolk's animosity was aroused by the fact that in nearly every instance when their views differed, those of Cromwell prevailed. But in addition, his interest in, familiarity with, and promotion of commerce made him despised by aristocrats. Even his peace policy seemed inglorious to nobles whose knowledge was limited to the art of war. Yet disastrous as was much that Cromwell did in its immediate or ultimate effects, wicked and cruel as he often was, his efforts to build up the nation through a peaceful commerce were beneficent. Whatever else may be said about him, Thomas Cromwell must be admitted to have been one of the most remarkable administrators that the world has ever seen.

Chapter Thirteen

THE TERROR

ℐMMENSE AS was Cromwell's administrative capacity, he owed a large part of his success to the fact that he governed under terror. I do not of course imply that any people—perhaps least of all the English—can be well governed under such a system. The free assent of the governed is always necessary to good government, if it is to be permanent. But during periods of revolution—and Cromwell was nothing if not a revolutionary—it may be maintained that only terror is a sufficient force to bring about social and other changes. He provided a spectacle from which I would like to avert my horrified eyes. Everybody cringed to the upstart—nobles and bishops alike—knowing well that he had his own secret police and that on the basis of their accusations bills of attainder could be pushed through Parliament against the highest in the land.

The terror began in full force in 1535, with the executions of the Carthusians and Fisher and More. If it mounted to the height of frenzy after the failure—or rather the betrayal—of the Pilgrimage of Grace, we must ascribe this to Henry rather than to Cromwell. For though Cromwell thoroughly approved of the wholesale hangings—especially as the Pilgrimage had put him in the extremity of danger—it was in dispassionate judgment rather than rage that he decided this opportunity for exemplary punishment should not be lost. In the same way he saw an opportunity for forcing the great northern abbeys to surrender under the threat of attainder. On this point Merriman makes a curious comment, as historians do who attempt a defense of the indefensible. "It is but justice," he writes, "to Cromwell's agents to say that their methods of intimidation were so highly effectual that attainder was the exception and surrender the rule." In other words it is but just to Cromwell to say that he was known to be a man who would stick at nothing!

Cromwell, after using this means of suppressing a group of northern abbeys—those that might be more or less plausibly accused of implication in the Pilgrimage of Grace—desisted from further suppressions for a while. By way of masking what was in his mind, he sent a circular letter to the rest of the larger monasteries. In this he first assures them that they have no need to fear they will be suppressed; if they have heard anything to the contrary, this is a malicious slander. He goes on, "Whereas certain governors and companies of a few religious houses have lately made free and voluntary surrenders into his Grace's hands, his Grace's Highness hath commanded me for your reposes, quiets, and for the causes specified on his Grace's behalf to advertise you that unless there had been overtures made of the said houses, his Grace would never have received the same." As the monks so addressed must have got wind of how "voluntary" such surrenders had been, these assurances could hardly have greatly contributed to their peace of mind. Still more disturbing must have been the following passage: "His Majesty intendeth not in any wise to trouble you or to devise for the suppression of any religious house that be exempt, except they shall either desire with one whole consent to resist and forsake the same, or else misuse themselves contrary to their allegiance. In which case they shall deserve the loss of much more than their houses and possessions, that is the loss of their lives. Wherefore in this you may repose yourselves." The whole idea of this circular was to lull the remaining monks to sleep until Cromwell was ready to deal with them. Otherwise they might hide some of their monastic treasures, which in fact some of them did.

In spite of all Cromwell's exhibitions of duplicity and greed, of his fawning flattery until he had gained his end, and of his brutality and cruelty when he was sure of his ground, he did occasionally exercise mildness and clemency. When on February 15, 1540, he wrote to an unidentified peer on behalf of a Richard Smith, who was the parson of Langham in the county of Pembroke, no great mercy, to be sure, was shown; for the directions are that Parson Smith is to be kept in prison until he had cleared himself of speaking against the King. The supposition, however, seems to be that the parson will be able to clear himself, so that the noble lord no doubt took the hint and dropped the proceedings. About the same time (November, 1539) Cromwell writes to the Bishop of Lincoln, asking that the parish priest of Horncastle be relieved of excommunication: "I with diligence examining the said matter and perceiving the same more to proceed of simplicity and ignorance than of malice or arrogancy." In somewhat similar cases I have suggested what must almost always be suspected of Cromwell—the taking of a bribe. But these men would not have been in a position to raise any large sum, and though of course it is not impossible that they had wealthy friends, I fall back upon the supposition that whims of mercy now and then overcame him.

Yet in granting so much, it must also be said that they were only whims and that he usually acted with implacable severity. There is the case about which he wrote at length to Henry on May 14, 1539, when an Irish monk and friar had been caught in a French ship blown ashore at South Shields. Cromwell said that they carried letters to the Pope and also to Cardinal Pole. He has therefore engaged men who knew both Gaelic and Latin to question them. He appeared to think that they had increased their guilt by having on them, among other missives, a letter from the Abbot of Melrose to a friend in Rome, asking that no special privileges or dispensations obtained there should take effect in Scotland without the license of King James.[1] Cromwell adds, "I trust our duty shall be so well employed to your Grace's service, that you shall have good cause of contentment at the least to take our doings in good part." What those doings were comes out in another letter in which he says that the following day he intends to take these men to the Tower and put the monk on the rack, so that "by torment [he be] compelled to speak the truth." One gathers that Cromwell intended to supervise this little operation himself, and it is reasonably certain that this was by no means the first time he had done so.

[1] This last piece of information should have pleased Henry and may have been sent to him only by way of general information, as perhaps indicating a change in Scottish religious policy. At all events it involved no treason to Henry.

Torture was used freely in those days, though legally its use was supposed to be restricted. Cromwell was not the kind of man to be too scrupulous about such niceties. For instance, he ordered Sir Gilbert Talbot and Sir John Russell on September 7, 1536, to examine the Vicar of Crowle in Worcestershire, "using all the ways ye can possibly devise to fish out of him whether he hath had communication with any other person or whether he know any man minded or disposed if he might get such opportunity to such purpose, not sparing for the knowledge thereof to pinch him with pains to the declaration of it in case good advertisement will not serve to the same." The passage casts a good deal of light on Cromwell's disregard of strict legality. It also reveals that he took it upon himself to direct judicial decisions, though he was not a judge, still less a judge hearing a case in court.

Such instances could be multiplied. To take only two more—for the record is sickening—he issued in December, 1539, instructions to the Earl of Southampton that two priests he had in custody might be executed, "if the laws and justice will condemn them both, and if not, then to proceed to the execution of Richardson and to award such punishment to the other for concealment as your wisdom shall think expedient for the example of both." [2] The implication is plain: if the law could be stretched, both men were to be hanged; if that seemed too much, at least Richardson should die. As a matter of historical fact, both men were executed on April 10, 1540.

Finally, we might take Cromwell's letter of September 21, 1538, to Lord Hungerford regarding the "cankered malice" of one Richard Henley—seemingly a Carthusian—ordering "that at the next coming in that country of the justices of assise ye cause him to be indicted and further process to be made against him, so that he may to the terrible example of like presumptuous and traitrous persons be punished according to his demerits as law right and justice do require." This duty was probably pressed all the more firmly upon Hungerford because he was suspected of papist sympathies. He was in the end attainted of treason, along with a chaplain of his named William Bird, who had said to a relative summoned to serve with the royal army sent against the Pilgrimage of Grace, "I am

[2] This was the same man about whom instructions were sent for his arrest to Lord Lisle in 1537. His crime was that of observing the Feast of St. Thomas of Canterbury.

sorry therefore. Seest thou not how the King plucketh down abbeys and images every day?" It was Lord Hungerford's fate to be executed the same day as Cromwell.

Cromwell, as has been noted, spared the friars in 1536, though he had exacted a strict oath from them. But if they were allowed to possess their priories for the time being this—as has already been pointed out—was because their houses were of no value except for the purpose for which they were built and because the friars very rarely had any manorial estates. This fact, however, when their suppression was decided upon, meant that the friars were handled even more roughly than the more richly endowed monks. A monastic pension presupposed a property against whose revenues this could be charged. This being so, the friars were simply turned adrift with a few shillings and a suit of secular clothes for each man.

Their plight was all the harder because they, unlike the monks, found it hard to obtain employment as secular priests. For this they needed what was called a capacity, that is, a signed certificate that they might accept a benefice, if one was offered. It is somewhat to the credit of Cromwell that, on at least one occasion, he saw to it that such certificates were obtained. For on April 25, 1539, he issued one house of friars capacities under his personal signature, being careful to note on it that this document was issued "freely without requiring anything for the same." [3] A group of seven, individually named, benefited from this, though whether it actually obtained them any ecclesiastical appointment is unknown. But at least it shows unwonted good will on Cromwell's part.

Most of the friars had got out of England by the time their houses were suppressed, many of them assisted by friends (some of them in the government service) to make good their escape. It cannot be said, however, that the record of faithfulness on the part of the friars was very high, except in the case of the Observants, though they may have been no worse in this respect than the monks, taken as a whole. Heroism on account of religion—heroism in any form—was not conspicuous in England at this time. On the other hand, there was no desire to make martyrs wholesale—there never is among administrators possessed of even the glimmerings of sanity—so that there may have been a number of men, about whom we know nothing, who

[3] But this speaks volumes, suggesting that often some payment was demanded for a capacity.

would have accepted death had they been subjected to the test.

Heroism at least appears in the case of John Forest. He had been Queen Katherine's confessor and a friend of Henry's, who paid him special attentions, such as sending him dishes from his own table (whose acceptance would hardly seem to be in consonance with the strict Franciscan rule he professed). Moreover, though he was imprisoned in 1534 he was later released and allowed to stay at large. It was expected that he would show his gratitude by adhesion to Henry's cause. When he failed to give this in ample enough fashion, he was arrested again in 1538. Four years before this Queen Katherine had written to tell him that she did not doubt his willingness to die for Christ, and now he showed that he was willing to do precisely that.

He was found guilty of both treason and heresy. His heresy could only have been that of repudiating—in the face of the Gospel—the doctrine that the King held both the spiritual and temporal swords. But his treason under the existing laws was unquestionable. He was therefore singled out to expiate both crimes, though it is clear that a word of his, even at the last moment, would have saved him.

Hugh Latimer, appointed to the Bishopric of Worcester in 1535, was invited to preach at his execution and accepted with alacrity. He had thought John Forest too leniently treated in prison and had written to Cromwell, "Some think he is rather comforted in his way than discouraged; some think he is allowed to hear Mass and also to receive the Sacrament; which, if it be so, is enough to confirm him in his obstinacy." Latimer himself had enough obstinacy or honesty to resign his bishopric in 1539 because of the Six Articles, but on that date in May, he was of that now considerable group of the "new men" among the bishops that Cromwell and Cranmer were building up against the day the King died or could be won over to their side.

Cromwell wished to make John Forest's martyrdom a very special occasion. So did Latimer, for in replying to Cromwell's invitation he wrote, "If it be your pleasure, as it is, that I shall play the fool after my customable manner when Forest shall suffer, I would wish that my stage stood near unto Forest, for I would endeavor myself so to content the people that I might also convert Forest, God so helping, or rather, altogether working. Wherefore, I would that he shall hear what I shall say—*si forte*—if he would yet with his heart return to his abjuration, I would wish his pardon. Such is my foolishness."

213

Special preparations had to be made at Smithfield. The eloquent bishop was the most popular orator of the time, with a style combining pungency, grace, force, and racy humor. Hardly a great man, Latimer was at least a great character; and I find it an attractive trait in him that he so breezily admits in his letter to Cromwell that in his sermons he played the fool. For Forest a special gallows had to be erected, one from which he could be slung over the fire with chains fastened to his waist and armpits. Only chains would do, as the fire would have quickly burned through the ropes. For the hanging there was a noose round his neck, but this was only symbolical; it was not pulled taut; the essence of his punishment was that he should endure a slow fire; his pain was intended to be greater than that of those who died at the stake.

A big crowd was present, graced by many notables, including the rich Sir Richard Gresham, the Lord Mayor and a notable speculator in monastic lands. He was accompanied by his aldermen. The Dukes of Norfolk and Suffolk were there also, and the Lord Admiral, and of course Cromwell himself. Before them Latimer orated, perhaps in the "passionate language of passionate conviction" (to use Froude's phrase) but with all the tricks an experienced showman knows how to employ. He ended with a question to the friar: What state did he wish to die in? Forest answered, according to Stow, "If an angel should come down from heaven and teach him any other doctrine than he had seen and believed from his youth he would not now believe him. And if his body was cut joint from joint, or member after member burnt, hanged, or what pain soever might be done to his body, he would never turn from his old profession." Still more effective was his rejoinder that "the bishop seven years before would not have dared to make such a sermon for his life." Everybody there was well aware that in 1532 Latimer had made a recantation of heretical opinions; those who were of the Court knew that shortly before the schism he had preached before the King in defense of the Papacy. Just what were the real convictions of this charming but unstable man must remain a mystery. The explanation may be that he mistook his feelings for settled beliefs. But he had by degrees worked himself into an advanced position, and he continued to advance so far that by Mary's time he had reached a position from which, in spite of all his tacks and veers, he could not very well change. Then he went to the stake, still acting a part but acting that part magnificently.

This burning is only one incident in the Cromwellian terror. Other incidents have already been recorded, and others will follow; and they create, even after four centuries, an impression of inextinguishable horror. What we have to try and understand is the heavy feeling of dread that hung over everybody in what had been, not many years before, a happy country. The skies hung low and leaden; the air was thick, an atmosphere in which it was very difficult to breathe. But perhaps the worst part of the terror was that under which the second and final dissolution of monasteries was made, for that was a slow fire, like the one which consumed Friar Forest.

Of the 376 houses that fell within the scope of the law of 1536, 123 had been respited or rather refounded with a guarantee that they should remain forever. These might still be suppressed under the pretext that their reestablishment was only conditional and that they had been found to be still full of "vicious, carnal and abominable living." But in addition there were the abbeys which the act had praised for their virtue, the "great and solemn houses where, thanks be to God" religion was well observed. There was no legal process under which they could be proceeded against. Though after the Pilgrimage of Grace a number of the northern abbeys had been suppressed under attainder, this procedure could not be carried on indefinitely and would have been absurd in the case of the religious houses of the South and West, many of which had made handsome contributions toward the expenses of maintaining the royal army. A new method had to be found.

It was not really a new method but the one whose technique Cromwell had mastered under Wolsey—that of persuading monastic houses to make a free and voluntary surrender. Unless they did that, the King, with his high-minded respect for law and order, could not accept what they offered. He was not a thief to seize what did not belong to him; but he was always willing to accept a gift. The monks, however, were made to understand what would happen to them if the gift was withheld. They also were made to understand that the King would be generous toward them if they were generous toward him.

If an abbot was thought to be of the kind that would cause trouble, Cromwell, by virtue of his powers as Vicegerent, could force his resignation and then, under the same powers, appoint a new abbot. This also was a technique used by Wolsey. Instead of the assembled monks electing a new superior, the election was promitted. These promissions were incidentally a valuable source of revenue to Cromwell, for his appointments went to the man who could pay most.

Then the process was to arrange the terms of submission. Though it is not easy to imagine that the victory often went to the abbot, as against the hard-faced, tight-lipped agents of Cromwell, clerics are sometimes very shrewd bargainers; the men of the other world in some instances know a surprising amount about this world. One must use imagination in writing history, and under the pile of official papers one now and then glimpses a suave monk fully the match of those he confronted. How else are we to account for the enormous pensions frequently paid to surrendering abbots? To the Abbot of Kenilworth went one hundred pounds sterling a year, guaranteed in a letter from Cromwell to Sir Richard Rich, dated May 5, 1538. (That Rich was at Kenilworth suggests the Abbot was a hard nut to crack.) Similarly the Abbot of Wigmore was assigned eighty pounds sterling a year on April 3, 1539. While these pensions were considerably above the average, some abbots got three times that amount. And one superior of a convent of nuns—that of Ambresbury—received one hundred pounds sterling a year. This meant that such people were endowed as handsomely as most peers of the realm.[4] In some ways this is the most shocking aspect of the matter. The superiors were regarded as the owners of the houses they surrendered; their abbeys were regarded as domains ruled by feudal lords. Though the signatures of their subjects were asked by way of confirmation, this was not looked upon as essential. Those who did sign received only enough to keep body and soul together, usually six

[4] This was after Margaret Bonnerman, the Prioress of Ambresbury, had announced, "If the King's Highness command me to go from this house I will gladly go, though I beg my bread; and as for pension, I care for none." She resigned, getting no pension, but her successor, appointed by Cromwell, received a handsome reward for her compliance. It should be said again that these figures should be multiplied by twenty-five to arrive at their modern values.

pounds sterling a year for a monk and four pounds sterling a year for a nun, often less.

Only rarely were the abbey buildings spared. When this happened, as in the case of Peterborough and Gloucester, the abbeys were turned into cathedrals. But sometimes, as at Romsey, the local community bought the abbey church to establish a parish. The normal procedure was to strip the church roof of its lead, as this was valuable. It was torn off and melted, with the carved choir stalls and rood screens providing fuel for huge caldrons. After that the walls and windows offered little resistance to the elements. In a short space of time there was nothing left but a ruin.

Now and then some part of the abbey could be remodeled as a residence for the use of the new proprietor, but more often not. Nor were other suggestions always practicable, as when Sir Arthur Darcy, who had been at the suppression of Jervaulx, wrote to Cromwell that the place was very suitable for the breeding of horses, "for surely the breed of Jervaulx for horses was the tried breed of the north." He thought it might be as well to transfer the royal stud there from Thornbury, the great estate confiscated from the Duke of Buckingham in 1521.

An effort was commonly made to use the stone of the buildings as a quarry, officials being appointed to sell it. But this as a rule did not prove very satisfactory; it was hard to estimate just how much stone was there, and the officials were notoriously dishonest. Accordingly the shells of the structures came to be abandoned, and any local man who needed masonry just loaded his cart. Even tombs, many of them wonderful works of art, were seldom respected. And mock auctions were held, at which it was possible to pick up a pair of brass pots for fourpence, an alabaster altar for a few shillings, and a whole library for a couple of pounds. The despoilers rarely had to sing even that merry little song for what they acquired; they simply purloined anything that took their fancy. And the junk dealers followed the commissioners around and did a most profitable business.

By the time the commissioners were ready to depart not only had the lead gone from the roofs but the bells had been melted down to be used in the manufacture of guns. Doors and casements and gutters and hinges were ripped away, and a good deal was winked at when local people came and helped themselves. These people had usually been on terms of friendship with the ejected monks or nuns but per-

217

haps for that reason thought that they now had the best title to what their friends had possessed. They were not interfered with, so long as they did not go too far, out of fear of making the spoliation still more unpopular. The poor of the neighborhood felt that they were partially reimbursing themselves for all kinds of benefits, now lost, that they had been accustomed to receive from the religious.

The immediate result of the upheaval was the impoverishment of large sections of the people. The ultimate result, however, was deeper and more extended. Though it would be excessive to say that capitalism was the child of the Protestant Reformation—for its beginnings were much earlier than this—capitalism, in the form we know it, which is industrialism, was stamped into shape in England. And though this could not have come about without England's rich natural resources, the exploitation of those resources would not have been possible had not a new concentration of wealth occurred.

Even had the spoliation of the monasteries not been the immensely immoral act that it was—naked theft carried through by systematized defamation, fraud, and cruelty—it would still have been an economic disaster. Had the Crown managed to conserve the whole wealth (as was originally intended), there would still have been a crime and a disaster even greater. Cromwell's design was, as we have seen, to establish an absolute monarchy, endowed to its plenitude. What actually eventuated was something very different. The administration discovered that, under the pressure of the "new men"—some in the Council and others in Parliament—many of the estates reserved as Crown lands had to be parted with, given away as placating presents, or sold. Henry had to derive dubious consolation from Cromwell's argument that the more influential people were implicated the more would it be to the interests of such people to uphold what was being done. Up to a certain point this argument was sound; at any rate it was usually possible to persuade the beefy Henry to accept ideas that relieved him of further thought. Quietly, with his lips hardly moving, Cromwell would throw out his reasonable suggestions. That they were so reasonable may have stored up in Henry almost as great a fund of resentment as he came to have against Anne Boleyn. The heavy-footed terrorist treads on delicate ice; Cromwell's success largely contributed to his undoing as soon as all the loot had been gathered in.

There is this much to be said for Cromwell. In 1539 England was in danger of war; but when had it not been since Henry had quarreled with the Papacy? Then militia musters were held, and about half of the money obtained from monastic rents or the sales of monastic estates was used to build up fortifications on the coast that Henry should never have allowed to fall into disrepair. This restoration should be credited to the practical Cromwell; Henry himself had always been inclined to let such things drift. Though some of Henry's defenders have been disposed to attribute to him a conviction of the impregnability of England and to disparage Cromwell for being so nervous, the truth is that there *was* no impregnability. If England remained safe during 1539, it was because of Cromwell's vigilance. It was due to his foresight that a much larger part of the monastic proceeds was not squandered. But as there would have been no danger of war at all had it not been for Henry's violence and Cromwell's cunning, whatever credit is given must be qualified.

One of the strangest facts about this vandalism is that it was carried out by Cromwell, a connoisseur of literature and the arts, with the hearty approval of Henry who was, in however limited a way, a creative artist, being a poet, a composer of music, and an architect. It was from the King's own designs that York House was remodeled as Whitehall Palace. He also was the director in the building of Nonesuch and the supervisor of the alterations made at Hampton Court and Greenwich. Yet this talented architect obviously cared more for hard cash than beauty, for he permitted the destruction of the most beautiful things that England contained. That he well understood what he was doing is shown by the commission he gave John Leland to make an extended tour through England, so as to preserve in his *Itineraries* a picture of a monastic England that Henry himself was obliterating. Had his professed plans been carried out, the monasteries could have been transformed into schools and colleges and hospitals. As it was, he left his country a legacy of ruins.

It was not only the monks who were despoiled but the common people of England. Up to this time the poorest and most ignorant of Englishmen could look admiringly not only upon some of the most perfect specimens of architecture the world has ever seen but also upon countless masterpieces of craftsmanship. Those who were themselves craftsmen could learn much from the study of wood carvings, the brasses, the glorious tombs, and the stained glass, of which the monastic churches were full. Some of the specimens of goldwork and silverwork were preserved but locked up in the collections of rich men. Most of the Church plate was simply melted down, and of this, as of the wonderful illuminated manuscript books of the monks' libraries, only a very little has survived. If Henry and Cromwell had artistic tastes (as we know they had), it is evident that these weighed as nothing when set against the appetite for gain. In that both men were completely ruthless.

The seizure of the great abbeys—for that is what it was, in spite of the pretense about voluntary surrenders—was not legalized until almost completed. Then on April 28, 1539, an act was passed declaring that "whereas sundry abbots, priors, abbesses and prioresses and other ecclesiastical governors . . . have of their own free and voluntary minds, good wills and assents, without constraint, co-action or compulsion of any manner of persons . . . given and granted . . . all their said monasteries to our sovereign lord, be it enacted that all such monasteries are dissolved . . . and all their property vested in the King." The same would apply to any religious houses, not yet surrendered, that would be surrendered in the future.

Such an act, which cloaked theft with hypocrisy, could of course be passed only by a completely subservient Parliament. And Parliament was so subservient because it was packed. That this was so appears in many places, though we do not often have as clear an indication of the technique used as in the now famous Canterbury election of 1536. But it is a safe inference that what was done at Canterbury occurred in many other places and that by 1539 Cromwell had improved upon his earlier methods. Indeed, he himself told the King with smug satisfaction that there never was so tractable a Parliament as this last one. In 1536, however, to go back to that year, the Sheriff of Canterbury, John Hobbs, summoned, as was his duty, the electors to choose two members of Parliament, whereupon John Starky and Christopher Levyns were elected. Later that same day a letter arrived from Cromwell and Audley directing that Robert Derknall and John Bridges "should fulfill the said rooms." When the Sheriff wrote to Cromwell explaining that his letter had reached him too late and asking that what had been done should be allowed to stand, the Mayor of Canterbury was peremptorily ordered to disregard the election. Cromwell chose to ignore the fact of his belated letter and charged the election officials with "little or nothing regarding but rather condemning" the royal wishes, saying that they had acted "of their own wills and minds contrary to the King's pleasure and commandment in that behalf." The King, they were told, marveled at their temerity; they were ordered to proceed to elect those nominated by the Crown and to inform Cromwell "if any person will obstinately gainsay the same." None of course did; the implied threat struck such terror that the first election was quashed and the royal nominees—who were Cromwell's nominees—were sent to Parliament. It was by means of this kind that the tractability of Parliament was obtained.

The financial returns—even when we add the proceeds of both monastic spoliations together—were much less than they should have been. Cromwell was to be accused in 1540, in the bill of attainder passed against him, of being responsible for having allowed this wealth to slip through the King's fingers. The charge was unjust, for though there had already been a good deal of selling of monastic estates at ridiculous prices or of giving them away outright, the great wave of forced selling occurred after that astute businessman had gone.[5] The truth is that Henry's personal extravagance was to blame. This had been manifested from the time he came to the throne, but it greatly increased as soon as he had so much additional wealth at his disposal. It is still something of a puzzle to know where the loot of the monasteries vanished, so that Lingard can speak of "some invisible abyss." Part of the explanation is that Cromwell and his agents—but mainly Cromwell—were busy abstracting this or that little thing from the glittering mound of treasure in the confident expectation that its absence would not be noticed, and the bribes they accepted left that much less for the royal coffers. The main loss, however, came from the giving away of manors to influential politicians, or officials, or favorites, or, when

[5] Thus Cromwell's nephew Richard obtained Romsey Abbey for something under £5,000, whereas it had a revenue of £1,700 a year. This means that he got for less than three years' purchase what would have been cheap had it been sold for twenty times its yearly rentals. And Thomas Cromwell—no doubt thinking he was very restrained—sold Launde Priory to himself for less than four times what its yearly revenue brought in.

there was no actual giving, from allowing such people to obtain estates by exchange or purchase often much to the disadvantage of the Crown.

How small was the King's actual profit is shown by the fact that from Michaelmas, 1536, to the end of Henry's life—a little more than ten years—the revenues derived averaged only £37,000 a year and in no single year more than £45,000, whereas the true value of these estates was several times that amount. But to this figure must be added the sum of £855,751.18.5 brought in by the sale of lands. It was a huge figure, but it should have been twice as much. Even when we add to this the amount of about £80,000 in gold and silver plate and an unspecified quantity of precious stones, Henry did not receive much more than, roughly, £110,000 a year.

The accrued profits diminish still further when we remember that they were as large as they were only because they included the plunder of a number of immensely rich shrines. These sometimes had endowments for the support of their custodians, but their principal wealth consisted of gold and silver decorations (promptly melted down as bullion) and of gems which the King retained or gave away. The bullion naturally served for the coinage, and with so much hard cash available Henry spent it freely. The chief of these shrines were those of St. Thomas at Canterbury, St. Cuthbert at Durham, St. Swithun at Winchester, and that of Our Lady of Walsingham.

The shrine of St. Thomas was despoiled on the pretext that St. Thomas had been a traitor to King Henry II. The others were looted on the plea that they were the cause of popular superstition; therefore their eradication was to the glory of God. It is hard to discover on what ground the four hospitals of London were taken over by the King, except that they had large endowments. Henry, it is true, restored the buildings of St. Bartholomew's Hospital (but not until he was on his deathbed), and even then he did not restore all that hospital's revenues. There came a time when Henry, pressed by the exigencies of the wars he indulged in after Cromwell had gone, confiscated many of the funds of the chantries, which provided for the saying of the Masses for deceased members of a guild, or other association. Even university endowments only just escaped. Nevertheless, Cromwell, while looting the nation and hoodwinking the

King, did at least fulfill his promise to make him rich and powerful. The power of the Crown for the time being remained, but much of the wealth poured away down a rathole.

Among the last abbeys to be "surrendered" were St. Augustine's at Canterbury, and those at St. Albans, Beaulieu, Buckfast, Croyland, Evesham, Milton, Rievaulx, Sherborne, and at Woburn, where the Abbot and two of his monks were hanged on an oak tree still standing. Waltham, a foundation made by the Saxon King Harold, was almost the last to go and may be counted the last of the very great abbeys; but the seizure of Whitby, with its memories of St. Hilda and Caedmon, actually concluded the process, and this happened on December 14, 1540, after Cromwell was dead.

There were three great abbeys that for a short while managed to resist all threats and blandishments, though in each instance at the cost of the Abbot's life. These abbeys were Colchester, Reading, and Glastonbury. The last named of these, according to tradition, had been founded by Joseph of Arimathea, the man who gave the tomb he had prepared for himself for the burial of Christ. He is supposed to have planted from the crown of thorns a rosebush which flowers every Christmas. Arthur and Queen Guinevere were said to have been buried there, and, however this may be, the abbey church contained the tombs of a number of famous people, all of which have been obliterated. One would have supposed that a place so sacred in England's history—or, if you like, its mythology—would have been treated with due respect. The very least that Henry should have done was to have preserved it as a national museum.

Cromwell did not wait for the conviction of the three abbots before taking possession of their monasteries. That in itself makes clear that their condemnation had been decided upon in advance, but this is made even more evident by his "Remembrances." Among these we find: "*Item* to see that the evidence be well sorted and the indictments well drawn against the said abbots and their accomplices. *Item* the Abbot of Reading to be sent down and tried and executed at Reading with his complices. *Item* the Abbot of Glaston to be tried at Glaston, and also executed there with his complices." [6] As usual Cromwell was in charge of the affair.

[6] Mr. Pickthorn has made a disingenuous attempt to explain away these remembrances. Not to go into the matter again, I refer the reader to my

It is enough to take the case of the last Abbot of Glastonbury, Richard Whiting. He was old and ill but summoned to London. There Cromwell charged him with having in his monastery a book against the King's divorce, some papal dispensations, and a life of St. Thomas of Canterbury. At his trial it was also alleged (what is likely enough) that he had hidden some of the valuables of the monastery, something that was regarded as a felony—the robbing of his own house—though it must be remembered that no voluntary surrender had occurred and that therefore, under the most rigorous interpretation of the law, these still belonged to the abbey and were the Abbot's to dispose of as he thought best.[7] His real offense was that, being at the head of a community with a yearly income of £3,000, or £75,000 in modern values, he had dared to gainsay Cromwell and the King.

Abbot Whiting, after being examined in London, imagined that his answers had been satisfactory, as he was told that he might return to Glastonbury. Cromwell appointed one of his agents, a man named Pollard, to accompany him. At a certain stage during the journey to the West, the Abbot's suspicions were aroused; so he said, "Mr. Pollard, if you be to me a companion, I pray you wash with me and sit down; but if you be my keeper and I your prisoner, tell me plainly." Upon this Pollard protested that he was his companion "in respect of the reverence he bore his age and virtues, and that he was appointed by those in authority to bear him company of worship's sake, and therefore might not forsake him till he did see him safe in Glastonbury."

Having arrived there, the Abbot was put on trial before Lord Russell, one of the timeserving politicians of the period—a man who lived to join the Lady Jane Grey conspiracy but afterward rendered service to Queen Mary. He ended as Earl of Bedford, and it is from him that the Dukes of Bedford are descended. According to Cromwell's instructions, he sentenced Whiting to death. The Abbot's execution, in company with two of his monks, took place on November 15, 1539, when they were dragged to the top of Tor Hill, facing

footnote on p. 102. As early as 1534 we find Cromwell predetermining verdicts.

[7] We may go further. It was Cromwell's practice to treat the abbeys as though they were the personal possessions of their abbots. But as it is impossible for a man to rob himself! . . .

the abbey, and there given the barbarous death of traitors. They had been so injudicious as to make a test case of the law and to create difficulties about a voluntary surrender. As the Abbot of Reading suffered the same fate on the same day and the Abbot of Colchester soon afterward, all possibility of opposing Cromwell's will was broken. Our horror is only slightly mitigated by our knowledge that for Cromwell himself the sands were already running out and that he was destined to go a few months later to the scaffold.

Chapter Fourteen

THE VICEGERENT

Henry INTENDED to be the Head of the Church and Defender of the Faith in a real sense. The bishops were not only to be appointed by him (that had been the case for a long time) but directly dependent upon him. Because he intended to keep the Church orthodox—and believed that orthodoxy not only in England but everywhere had as one of its main articles subjection to the prince—he reserved to himself the right to decide what was and what was not sound doctrine.

His versatility had always included a taste for theology, and he had shown himself a good amateur theologian in his treatise against Luther, which when presented in Rome was somewhat fulsomely pronounced a "golden book." To produce it, he must have done some hard work, though he used the stock arguments and cited only such authors as were likely to be represented in the compendiums of the time. Later, while retaining his theological tastes, he did not bother himself very much with reading, in spite of the fact that he gathered a rather good theological library. His method of keeping himself posted was to give new books, whether Catholic or Protestant, to one or another of his chaplains and bishops to read. From this reader he obtained the gist of the argument and an opinion of its validity, after which he got somebody else of another school of thought to do the same thing. Henry's powerful memory retained what he heard, and in this rather lazy way he kept abreast of the theological discussions of the time.

226

His piety was of a genuine, if a somewhat formal, sort. He continued as of old to hear two Masses a day, with a High Mass on holy days and Sundays. Sometimes in an excess of devotion he heard five Masses. When at the end of his life he became fantastically obese and the sore on his leg more and more painful, it was suggested that he receive Holy Communion in his chair. This concession he refused, saying that he would like to be not only on the ground but under the ground if thereby he could do honor to the Sacrament of the Altar. Even what were only the disciplinary laws of the Church—such as celibacy and the Friday abstinence—he wished to enforce as though they were laws of God and in 1539 actually hanged a man for eating meat on a fast day. On May 15 of that same year a man named John Worth could write to Lord Lisle, "On Good Friday last the King crept to the cross from the chapel door devoutly and served the priest to Mass that same day, his own person kneeling on his Grace's knees."

But though the Defender of the Faith intended to keep England Catholic, only by fits and starts did he make much effort to defend orthodoxy. As for the details of administration, these were things that he could not be bothered with, though of course here, as in internal administration and foreign affairs, he remained in general control. It was convenient to delegate his authority to Cromwell, so far as this meant the working of the machine. But it was the King who, whenever there was any question, dictated the doctrine that was to be believed.

Cromwell as Henry's Vicegerent personally presided over Convocation or, when he was unable to be there, sent a man to represent him, being always careful that this should be a layman. He intended to emphasize that the Church was now subject to the royal power. Bishops had to take out licenses from Cromwell for the exercise of their episcopal functions, and by degrees he contrived to get seven men of very doubtful orthodoxy raised to the episcopate, at the same time keeping the men who were orthodox employed at a distance, so that they would not have the ear of the King. Thus Bonner was nearly all the time from 1536 to 1540 away on foreign embassies, as was Gardiner; and Tunstall was kept busy as President of the Council of the North.

The appointment of Thomas Cromwell as the King's Vicar-General would be inexplicable were it not for the fact he was given his office because of his skill and experience in monastic suppressions. For though he kept up the externals of religious practice, he was a practical atheist in the sense of counting religion of no importance except as it could contribute to some political end. In this field he was completely amoral, making no distinction between right or wrong but considering only what was useful.

Cromwell worked as a rule in close accord with Cranmer. The Archbishop of Canterbury was very serviceable to him, as Cromwell was in some ways serviceable to the Archbishop. Cranmer honestly believed that the so-called "new learning" was the true learning and lost no opportunity to push the Church in England a little nearer to what we now understand as Protestantism. Cromwell, for ends of his own, entered into a kind of partnership in Cranmer's scheme. Indeed, without Cromwell, Cranmer could have accomplished very little. But though they managed several times to befool a king who was all too ready to allow subordinates to deal with what he should have made his own business, they both had to be careful not to go too far. Cromwell, rather pathetically, had to tell the German Lutherans who came to London in 1538 in the hope of coming to an understanding with Henry that he could have no religious opinions except those held by the King. As for Cranmer, while now and then venturing to insinuate heresy in official statements of doctrine, he always made it clear to Henry that he held his opinions with a light hand and was ready to abandon them under correction. To him obedience to the prince was the first of religious duties. Whatever the prince commanded, that the subject should instantly perform. Even though the King should order something that seemed to be contrary to Christian belief, he should still be obeyed, as the responsibility fell on the prince, who would one day have to answer to God. The subject, on the other hand, would have to answer to God for any failure to obey the prince. Cromwell, without concerning himself with theories of this sort, found them useful; and in his estimation it was only the useful that mattered.

Henry of course never attempted to exercise any of the functions of a priest, though it would seem that Cranmer would have upheld him even there had the King taken it into his head to do so. At any rate Cranmer wrote: "To be a bishop or priest needeth no consecration, by the Scripture; for the election or appointing thereto is sufficient. If it so fortuned that all the bishops and priests of a region

228

were dead, and that the Word of God should remain there un-preached, the King of that region should make bishops and priests to supply the same." As a Catholic Henry could hardly have agreed, but to him as King the view was flattering.

Cranmer and his opinions have to be mentioned because the Archbishop was a kind of theological adviser to Cromwell, a man quite ignorant of such matters. Yet though the injunctions the Vice-gerent issued to the clergy in August, 1536, bear some indication of having been examined by a theologian, for the most part they are concerned with practicalities, such as Cromwell was capable of dealing with alone. The first thing priests must bear in mind is to obey the statutes made "for the abolishing and extirpation of the Bishop of Rome's pretensed power and jurisdiction within this realm"; they were to preach about this at least once every quarter, declaring "that the King's power within his dominion the greatest potentate or power under God, to whom all men within the same dominion by God's commandment owe most loyalty and obedi-ence, afore and above all other powers and potentates on earth." The Creed, the Paternoster, and the Ten Commandments were to be taught to the people in their mother tongue. Children should be brought up either to learning or some honest occupation or farm labor lest they should later take to stealing, as had happened to so many sturdy beggars. The priests should "diligently provide that the sacraments and sacramentals be duly and reverently ministered in their parishes," and if they were obliged to be absent from their benefices they were to find "a good, learned and expert curate" to take their place; . . . "And always let them see that they nor their vicars do seek more their own profit than the profit of the souls they have under their cure or the glory of God." In order to encourage learning it was ordained that every beneficed priest who had an income of one hundred pounds sterling a year was to "give competent exhibition [otherwise, a scholarship] to a student at one of the universities or at a grammar school, with an additional scholar for each additional one hundred pounds sterling he had. The superstitious use of relics and images was condemned, es-pecially all attempts to make profit from them; so also were pil-grimages frowned upon "as though it were proper or peculiar to that saint to give this commodity or that. . . . But they shall ex-hort as well their parishioners as other pilgrims that they do rather apply themselves to the keeping of God's commandments and fulfilling of His works of charity. And persuade them that it doth conduce more towards their souls' health if they do give to the poor and needy [what] they thought to bestow on the said images or relics."

Except for the order to preach against the Pope, there is nothing that can be seriously objected to in this. Neither the invocation of saints nor the veneration of images nor the going on pilgrimages were forbidden; it was only superstition that was disapproved of. The admonition about the beneficed clergy supplying scholarships to students was well-intentioned, though probably not carried out to any great extent. So also with regard to the injunction that clerics were not to frequent taverns, except in case of necessity, or sit playing cards all day: that had been said over and over again by various Convocations with slight effect. Finally the clergy were to contribute a fifth part of their income toward the repair of their churches, when repairs had to be made; they were to expound to their flocks the recently promulgated Ten Articles; and they were to announce "the abrogation of certain superfluous holy days."

The last item was very unpopular, yet had some reason in it, though it was a matter for the hierarchy, not for the lay dictator to the Church. There was nothing but hypocrisy, however, when Cromwell wrote: "The goods of the Church are called the goods of the poor, and in these days nothing is less seen than the poor to be sustained with the same." The admonition comes with the worst possible grace from one who officially describes himself as "the Vicegerent to and for and concerning all [the King's] jurisdiction ecclesiastical within this realm"; for at that moment he had already started to despoil the poor by suppressing the monasteries, a fact vigorously pointed out during the rising that occurred a couple of months later.

These injunctions followed closely after the drawing up of the Ten Articles, which Cromwell had to issue in the King's name, though he could have had no part in the framing of them. They came after a conference at Wittenberg between English and Lutheran theologians which had failed to reach any accord. Yet the Lutherans, with the approval of Melanchthon and of Luther too, made many significant concessions but not enough to suit the orthodox

Henry. Though much of the Wittenberg terminology was retained in the Ten Articles, they were, so far as they go, sufficiently Catholic. It is true that they indicate only three sacraments, but these three are defined as "necessary to salvation," and are Baptism, Penance, and the Eucharist. Holy Orders, Matrimony, Confirmation, and Extreme Unction are not "necessary" in quite the same sense. Those mentioned are expounded in a perfectly Catholic way, and the following year in the so-called "Bishops' Book"—which was really the King's Book, though a work published in 1543 was popularly known under that title—the four sacraments that had not been dealt with by the Ten Articles are included and given a full and accurate definition. If they do not appear in the Ten Articles, this was probably due not so much to Cranmer's desire to lead England on the road toward Lutheranism—though that desire operated—as to Cromwell's purpose to avoid offending the German allies he had begun to seek after the King rejected the alliance his minister proposed with the Emperor.

Cromwell, like Henry himself, was not above using heretics when it suited his purpose, even while protesting his orthodoxy. Tyndale would have been so used had he not made himself obnoxious to the King by refusing to admit that he was in the right about his marriage to Katherine of Aragon. Cromwell burned his fingers so badly in this case that in May, 1531, he had to write hastily to his friend Stephen Vaughan at Antwerp telling him to cease advocating Tyndale's cause and to try to detach the priest John Frith (who suffered at Smithfield a couple of years later) from Tyndale. Switching at a moment's notice, Cromwell wrote to Vaughan that Tyndale "showeth himself in mine opinion rather to be replete with venomous envy, rancor and malice than with any good learning, virtue, knowledge, or discretion." Yet a notorious heretic, Robert Barnes, was one of the commissioners sent to Wittenberg, and he was employed later in the negotiations leading to the Cleves marriage, after which Cromwell gave him a good benefice. Here, as will be seen a little later, he overshot the mark, for this contributed to Cromwell's downfall and also resulted in Barnes's death at the stake.

This sort of double-dealing was something at which the King was adept, and in it Cromwell was often only Henry's instrument, one who could be repudiated if necessary. Henry sometimes, it would seem, permitted him to encourage heretics for no other purpose than that of annoying the ecclesiastical authorities and of throwing up a kind of smoke screen behind which he himself could be up to some little trick. But Cromwell sometimes acted on his own initiative, and his methods are revealed by a letter written by him on January 7, 1538, to an unidentified bishop advising him—and here I do some italicizing—that in preaching "the people may be taught the truth, and yet not charged *at the beginning* with over many novelties, the publication whereof, *unless the same be tempered and qualified with much wisdom* do rather breed contention, division and contrariety in opinion in the unlearned multitude." In other words the "advanced" sort of doctrine should be advocated only cautiously, but so long as it is done discreetly "the people may be taught the truth." The year before Cranmer had complained to Cromwell that the Court, under the influence of Jane Seymour, ate fish on Fridays and observed the holy days that had officially been abolished. "My Lord," he said, "if in the Court you do keep such holy days and fasting days as be abrogated, when shall we persuade the people from keeping them?" This was something that Cranmer would never have dared to say to Henry, with whom he had to be most obsequious. But largely because of this side of his character, the Archbishop was able to exercise a pervasive influence, preparing the country for the changes he foresaw would come after the King's death. In so far as this accorded with Cromwell's political designs, he unobtrusively backed up Cranmer's gentle and persistent pressure.

Leaving until later the more important aspects of Cromwell's work as Vicegerent (though not forgetting that he was appointed as such in order to deal with the monasteries), some of the minor details of his administrative methods in this field of his activity might be glanced at. One of his first acts was his peremptory ordering of John Webley, the Prior of Dudley, on February 10, 1535, to appear before him to answer certain unspecified charges. The Prior is told: "The King's pleasure and commandment is that ye shall immediately upon the sight hereof, all delays and excuses set apart, personally repair unto me wheresoever it shall chance me to be, without failing, as you will answer to his Grace at your extreme peril." Possibly this had something to do with the Oath of Supremacy, which had gone into force on the first of this month. As we hear no more about the matter, Webley may be supposed to have done what was required of him, though, as we have seen, there is reason to suppose that a good many people suffered death of whom no record has been kept.

In September of the same year he writes to the Prioress of Wilton desiring her "to be good lady and friend to my loving friend William Neville about the farm of Chalke." [1] He lets her have a veiled threat but also a promise that, if she does what he wants, "I will not forget sembly to requite." It is interesting to note that this letter was addressed from Wolf Hall, the house of Sir John Seymour. At this time Henry's infatuation with Jane Seymour began.

The Prioress of Wilton, like so many other religious superiors, looked upon Cromwell as a friend to whom she could appeal at need or at least as one who, if he chose, could control his agents. A man named Christopher Willoughby had been put in charge of the community, as it lacked an abbess: "And because that we differ [upon] such matters as he would that we consent to, the which as we suppose and think are not lawful, nor yet profitable to our house, he does sore and grievously threaten us." The appeal of course went unregarded. Willoughby had been sent to Wilton to make life so miserable for the nuns that they would the more willingly surrender to the King. One may surmise that the Cecily Willoughby appointed abbess shortly afterward to give regularity to the surrender must have been this man's sister or cousin.

Cromwell, however, could make concessions—usually for a consideration. Thus we find him writing in 1535 to an unnamed abbot, telling him that, because of his willing mind, he may visit the manors belonging to the abbey, so long as he does this in such a way that it will not be talked of too much and thereby create a precedent that Cromwell wished to avoid. The practice had already begun of keeping all monks cooped up in their houses, so that they could not attend to the business connected with their estates, which in consequence would become neglected and later provide the color needed for the accusation soon to be made in Parliament that monastic holdings were being mismanaged.

It will have been already noticed that Cromwell took it upon

[1] Merriman in his heading of this letter, describes her as the Abbess, but it would seem from what follows that no new abbess had been elected since the death of Isabel Jordan.

233

himself to control even such details of his ecclesiastical office as one would have supposed would be left to bishops. Thus we find him writing in 1537 "in my right hearty manner" to Dr. Sandwich of Canterbury College, Oxford, appointing him to preach at Paul's Cross on the twelfth Sunday after Trinity Sunday, August 19, "to open the word of God, at the said day, as I may thereby take occasion to think the report made of you [that is, of Dr. Sandwich's sound antipapalism] to be true."

Similarly we find Cromwell ignoring the jurisdiction of the Bishop of St. Asaph, when he wrote on October 19, 1538, to Sir William Sulyard, Justice of Flint, and Roger Brereton, Sheriff of the same county, ordering them to send the two men who were each claiming the parsonage of Whitford to London, so that he might decide between them. On the other hand, the Vicegerent did sometimes delegate his authority or allow an ordinary to exercise his rights, as when he wrote at the beginning of 1540 to Robert Holgate, the Bishop of Llandaff, who had succeeded Tunstall as President of the Council of the North, instructing him that he should decide the dispute between Thomas Grayme and John Blacket over the Vicarage of Iderton in Northumberland. This, however, was an exceptional case. Even while riding to his fall, we find him writing to Roger Brereton saying that the King was highly displeased that his scholar, Hugh Whitford, was disturbed in the possession of his parsonage. And on May 31, only a few days before his own arrest, he wrote to the Bishop of Salisbury, desiring him to admit a certain priest to the living of Hilperton in Wiltshire, to which he had been appointed by Cromwell's friend John Walgrave.

These things are of slight importance except to show how Cromwell in ecclesiastical as well as secular concerns allowed nothing to escape his careful scrutiny. Some of these little incidents—like others previously cited—indicate that he was misusing his authority, as when he demanded from this or that head of a religious house that a friend of his be given a lease of a farm. But it is clear that he always expected to be obeyed. And one cannot but suspect that, at least in some of these instances and in those when he demanded that a bishop should appoint a particular person to a benefice, this was because a private transaction to the profit of the Vicegerent of the Head of the Church had occurred.

Whether or not there was any venality in these particular cases (and with regard to Cromwell, such a suspicion is inevitable), he and Cranmer, operating together certainly were very disingenuous in the publication of the first printed version of the Scriptures that was allowed to be circulated in the English vernacular. It is not too much to say that here they deliberately hoodwinked the King.

First it should be said that there was no objection to an English translation of the Bible, provided that this was made by a competent scholar and used with discretion. Wycliffe, who died in 1384, had made a translation of the Scriptures, but this insinuated his heresies, which is a sufficient reason for believing that what is exhibited at the British Museum as a copy of Wycliffe's Bible is not his at all, as it is free from heresy. But that Wycliffe's was by no means the first translation is made clear by the fact that the Synod of Oxford in 1281 prohibited the circulation of unauthorized versions, showing that at least one of this sort had already appeared. The Constitutions of Arundel in 1408 were of course directed against the Wycliffite translation, but the Constitutions at the same time indicated that an orthodox translation would be acceptable.

Such translations had been made, though of course only in laboriously handwritten books, for we find Sir Thomas More writing, "I myself have seen and can show you Bibles, fair and old, written in English, which have been known and seen by the bishop of the diocese, and left in the hands of laymen and women, whom he knew to be good Catholic people and who used the books with devotion and soberness." But such manuscripts were prohibitively expensive. So while the essential content of the Bible was contained in Catholic doctrine, accepted by everybody, and the Bible stories seen in innumerable pictorial representations in the churches, a printed English translation was needed, as was fully recognized by the English hierarchy.

The difficulty was to find somebody competent for the task. The Bible is an obscure book, full of apparent contradictions and of texts so mysterious as to be susceptible of widely varying interpretations. Therefore the English bishops were a little afraid that, during troubled times, its publication might be inopportune; at any rate all the more care had, for this reason, to be exercised. This was why Cranmer hoped that an English Bible—and he had in mind something rather different from what the orthodox bishops desired—

235

would further the cause he had at heart. It was made possible only because of the cooperation of Cromwell.

The Tyndale translation was unacceptable as it stood, for though it was, in its way, a magnificent performance, it translated a number of key words in a definitely Lutheran sense, and it incorporated a good many of the notes Luther had printed in his German translation.

Cromwell was for it, as he hoped it would show the German Lutherans, whom he was courting for political purposes, that he was on their side. Cranmer was for it, because Tyndale's version, if published in England, would help to draw the country away from orthodoxy. Yet neither man dared bring out this version, for not only would Henry have smelled its heresy but he had a personal objection to Tyndale because of his refusal to accept the royal view of the Katherine of Aragon divorce.

A way was found out of this difficulty. The Tyndale translation (completed by Miles Coverdale) might be introduced in disguise. Accordingly it was stripped of its notes and toned down in its text and published as the work of a Thomas Matthew who did not exist. Its reviser was John Rogers, a notorious heretic, who was at this time the pastor of the Protestant congregation at Wittenberg. As such its circulation in England was officially approved by Cromwell and Cranmer, and the unsuspecting Henry was taken in.

Cromwell did even more. In June, 1538, he sent a circular letter to the bishops in which, after complaining that his Injunctions to the Clergy of 1536 had been very imperfectly observed, he gave an order that was designed to make sure that the Bible he authorized would receive the widest possible circulation. He wrote, "His Grace's pleasure and high commandment is that you with no less circumspection and diligence cause the Bible in English to be laid forth openly in your own houses and that the same be in like manner openly laid forth in every parish church at the charge and costs of the parsons and vicars, that every man having free access to it by the reading of the same may both be the more apt to understand the declaration of it at the preacher's mouth, and also the more able to teach and instruct his wife, children and family at home."

The same point was stressed in Cromwell's Injunctions to the Clergy of that year. In it he again attacks the Pope and orders that priests hearing confession should demand from their penitents the recital of the Creed and Paternoster in English and bar those who failed to pass this test from Holy Communion. As for the Bible, the cost of purchase was to be borne half by the priest and half by his parishioners. He added: "You shall discourage no man privily or apertly from the reading or hearing of the said Bible but shall expressly stir and exhort every person to read the same, which is the lively word of God, that every christen person is bound to believe, embrace and follow, if they wish to be saved."

Cromwell does, however, offer the admonition (probably at the King's insistence) that the readers of the Bible were to "use an honest sobriety in the inquisition of the true sense of the same, and to refer the explication of obscure places to men of higher judgment in Scripture." Indeed, this admonition was soon given statutory force, though not until 1542, after Cromwell had departed this life. The possession of the Bible was to be limited to the higher ranks of society, which might be supposed to be the best educated; but of course the law was quite ineffectual in controlling the heretical tendencies promoted by immature people, who, not comprehending the true import of what they read, gave it an eccentric interpretation. The King admitted this in his last speech to Parliament at the end of 1545, when he said, "I am very sorry to know how unreverendly that precious jewel the Word of God is disputed, rhymed, sung, and jangled in every alehouse and tavern."

Protests were soon made by orthodox ecclesiastics about the Bible introduced by Cromwell and Cranmer, so that it had to be revised further. This edition was known as the Bishops' Bible. Yet Cromwell was not prevented from having a new edition of Rogers made by Richard Taverner, a lawyer and a good Greek scholar. But he was a heretic, and his Bible had an introduction that denied a sacerdotal priesthood and reduced the sacraments to mere external signs. It was to contribute to Cromwell's downfall (though Cranmer was more guilty than Cromwell himself), and it revealed how set were these two men—though for differing reasons—upon inserting the disrupting wedge of heresy into the orthodoxy King Henry wished to maintain.

Pious as were Cromwell's words in his Injunctions and letters, he was still thinking of an alliance with the Lutheran princes of Germany against the Emperor. He had played with this idea off and on since 1535, but in 1539 the only political support he could hope to obtain was in that quarter. It was with this in mind that a new conference was held with the Lutheran divines, this time in London; but as at Wittenberg no agreement could be reached because of the King's obstinacy. Nevertheless Cranmer's object was in part achieved: a section of the English people drifted toward Protestantism. But Cromwell, whose eyes were fixed solely upon a political object, failed completely. He did, as we shall see, bring about the Cleves marriage, but after his fall there was no further dickering with the German princes; it was clearly recognized that there was no possibility of an alliance with them.

Yet Henry's insistence upon sound doctrine was made apparent by the promulgation in 1539 of the Six Articles. These were not passed without some opposition on the part of the "advanced" men and resulted in the resignation of two bishops, Latimer and Shaxton. Cranmer was, as usual, as compliant as even Henry could wish. When the so-called King's Book had been published in 1537, he had written to Henry, "All Christian princes have committed to them immediately of God the whole cure of their subjects, as well as by the administration of God's word for the cure of souls, as concerning the administration of political and civil governance." On this principle he accepted, on the surface, the distinctive Catholic doctrines he secretly disliked. So now in 1539, while he ventured some criticisms of the draft of the Six Articles that had been sent to him, he let the King know that he always deferred to the royal Pope. Nothing could touch a man who could write as Cranmer did to the King: "This is mine opinion and sentences at present, which nevertheless I do not temerariously define, but refer the judgment thereof wholly unto your Majesty."

Nevertheless he came very close to getting himself into serious trouble with his enemies on the Council, who were closely watching for him to make a false move. His annotated draft of the Six Articles was being carried to the King by Ralph Morice, his secretary, in a boat on the Thames. But a bear belonging to the Lady Mary was swimming in the river and capsized the boat, so that the manuscript fell into the hands of the bearkeeper, who, like all those attached to Mary's household, was a strong Catholic. When he saw what Cranmer had written, he refused to surrender the manuscript, intending to present this damning proof of the Archbishop's heresy to the Council. But Morice forewarned Cromwell, so that when the man appeared, Cromwell saw him privately and threatened him so dreadfully that he lost courage and handed the incriminating document to the Lord Privy Seal. Had Cranmer fallen at that time, Cromwell would probably have fallen with him. It must be said, however, that Henry was perfectly well aware that the Primate was a heretic at heart; this, in the King's eyes, was completely offset by Cranmer's perfect willingness to profess officially whatever was asked.

It has been sometimes suggested that the Six Articles were issued with the intention of placating Charles V and Francis I, from whom Henry had cause to fear a concerted attack that year. And that may well have been a subsidiary motive. But the whole course of events since 1536 indicated that Henry was determined to insist on a stricter orthodoxy, in which he must be counted perfectly sincere whatever other considerations weighed with him.

When the Six Articles were introduced into Parliament in 1539, several bishops of the new school spoke in the House of Lords in favor of the marriage of priests. Cranmer understandably did so, for he was already surreptitiously married. Shaxton, Latimer, Hilsey, and Barlow held with him, and Cranmer and Barlow argued in favor of Communion under both species. But regarding celibacy, none of the temporal peers gave the bishops of the "new learning" any support. On the contrary, one of them wrote, "We of the temporality have been all of one opinion." And the Articles were very popular with the mass of the people, who took it as a sign that the tide had turned—this though the King was at some pains to let it be known that he was as antipapal as ever.

The penalties imposed by the Six Articles were so ferocious that they came to be spoken of as the Whip of Six Strings. For anyone who spoke against transubstantiation, the penalty was death, and no chance of abjuration was given, as had formerly been the case. As for the other five articles, for the first offense the heretic was liable to be punished with imprisonment at the King's pleasure, and for the second offense he was put to death. It was even enacted that persons who refused to confess at the usual times or to receive the Sacrament were to be treated as felons.

We do not hear of anybody suffering on this account or of any priest being condemned on account of a secret marriage or be-

239

cause of breaking his vow of chastity. But there was great con-
sternation, and Cranmer hurriedly packed off Mrs. Cranmer to
Nuremberg. The statute was in fact too strict to enforce, and those
who were responsible for its enforcement (in particular, Cromwell)
saw to it that it usually remained a dead letter. Yet there were a
few victims, among them a boy of eighteen named Richard Mekins,
who was quite willing to recant (and with seeming sincerity) but
whose abjuration was not accepted. From time to time during the
rest of the reign there were others who suffered, but almost all of
them were, like Mekins, deniers of the doctrine of transubstantiation. In the last months of Henry's reign Anne Askew went to
the stake after having been so horribly tortured that she had to be
carried to Smithfield in a chair. Shaxton was accused with her, but
by that time the application of the law had been mitigated, so that
he was allowed to abjure. He demonstrated his orthodoxy by
preaching at Anne Askew's auto-da-fé, much to that truculent
lady's disgust.

That Henry's orthodoxy was not something paraded for political
reasons is shown by the famous trial of the Protestant martyr, John
Nicholson, in the autumn of 1538, before the passage of the Six
Articles and at a time when Henry's relations with the Emperor
and Francis were reasonably good. About this Cromwell wrote at
length on November 28 of that year to Sir Thomas Wyatt, the
English Ambassador to Charles's Court. He had, needless to say,
the expectation that his letter would be shown to the Emperor to
prove how very orthodox Henry was. One passage reads: "It was
a wonder to see how princely and with how excellent gravity and
inestimable majesty his Highness excercised there the very office of
a supreme head of the Church of England; how benignly his Grace
assayed to convert the miserable man; how strong and manifest
the reasons his Highness alleged against him. I wished the princes
and potentates of Christendom to have [had] a meet place to see
it. Undoubtedly they would have marvelled at his Majesty's most
high wisdom and judgment and reputed him none otherwise after
the same than in manner the mirror and light of all other kings and
princes in Christendom. The same was openly done with great
solemnity, whereby I doubt not but that some of your friends that
have good leisure shall by their letters advertise you of the whole
discourse thereof." This last was a delicate touch; Cromwell wished

240

to appear casual and offhand lest by saying too much he should be suspected by Charles of trying to prove what in fact he did want to prove. In the Emperor's dominions things of this sort were in charge of the Inquisition.

Cromwell probably did admire the way the King conducted the affair, for Henry had a majestic presence and could speak with almost overpowering force. But Cromwell's own orthodoxy was merely "official" as was the orthodoxy of several of those who had conducted the preliminary examination of the accused man. Among those who extracted poor Nicholson's views about the Eucharist were Cranmer, Shaxton, and Barnes, all of whom held opinions in private hardly distinguishable from his own. They would have condemned him, just as Cranmer was largely responsible for the burning of John Frith in 1533, had not Nicholson appealed to the King.

Upon this a wonderful show was staged in Westminster Hall on May 16. Henry sat on his throne, clothed from head to foot in white, and gave almost an entire day to the affair. Nicholson let it out that he had sometimes used the alias of Lambert, which prejudiced the King against him at once, as Henry, being the very soul of candor, abhorred anything that savored even faintly of deceit.

In spite of this the man got a fair trial. For seven bishops, including Cranmer, were put up in turn to show Nicholson how badly he had been misled; and Henry paraded his own theological learning. In face of all this Nicholson got confused but would not recant. In the end he threw himself on the King's mercy and got the sentence, "Then thou must die." And die he did four days later.

Nicholson was a brave and sincere man and as such must be respected, though Cromwell describes him to Wyatt as "a miserable heretic sacramentary." But so, as Cromwell must have known, were Cranmer and Barnes and Shaxton. At least Cromwell had no share in putting to death a man whose doom Cranmer should have shared. Official though Cromwell's orthodoxy was, in so far as he had any convictions, they appear to have been of a Catholic strain. The blame that attaches to him is that of utilizing in turn orthodoxy and heresy, neither of which he considered very important, except as something that might be useful to his political plans. Even so, he left Westminster Hall that day in May with a better conscience than that of the Archbishop of Canterbury.

Chapter Fifteen

THE BLUNDER

ODIOUS AS were some of the features of Cromwell's domestic policy—odious in fact as was almost all of it, with the exception of his promotion of trade, and that benefited only the small commercial class—it was at least apparently successful. Wales, little liking it, was brought into the English political system; Ireland came closer to being subjugated than it had been before; and the monasteries were suppressed. What the mass of the people happened to think was regarded as of no consequence, and since the savage repression of their protest in 1536 this was no longer expressed. What the higher ecclesiastics and the officials, and especially the nobles, thought mattered a good deal more than Cromwell realized but was disregarded. Cromwell, having proved his value to the King, had a position that seemed to be stronger than ever before.

It was rather different, however, when it came to his handling of foreign affairs. Though Henry usually allowed himself to be persuaded by his minister, he often had doubts and reservations, and sometimes he peremptorily rejected Cromwell's advice. It must be remembered that the King had been trained by Wolsey—a virtuoso in foreign politics—and that he had more experience in this department than Cromwell. His mind ran along Wolseian lines. He wished to maintain the balance of power in Europe or, as he put it, be the "mediator for the peace and happiness of Christendom," which fine phrase meant that no chance should be lost of embroiling Charles and Francis with one another. But there was now an important difference: whereas Wolsey had always kept in mind the interests of the Pope, in his capacity as secular monarch, Henry, after his breach with the Holy See, would have been glad to infuriate him. Nevertheless the policy of playing off the Emperor and the King of France against one another remained his settled principle, even when circumstances momentarily obliged him to depart from it.

We have seen how immediately after Katherine's death early in 1536 the Emperor made advances to Henry, if only in the hope of detaching him from Francis, and that those advances were rebuffed. Cromwell, who was an imperialist, considered that a tragic mistake had been made but was obliged to fall in with Henry's wishes. But as Francis was an ally never quite trusted by Henry and as there was a tendency for him to draw closer to Charles, Cromwell, in the hope of safeguarding England, sent his friend Stephen Vaughan to Germany to try and come to an understanding with the Elector of Saxony, the Duke of Brunswick-Lüneburg, and the Landgrave of Hesse. But as they were members of that alliance of German Protestant princes and cities called the Smalkaldic League and demanded Henry's acceptance of the Lutheran manifesto, the Augsburg Confession, with which Henry would have nothing to do, the negotiations broke down, though in 1536 the Lutheran divines at the conference of Wittenberg were prepared to make considerable concessions. Nor did anything come of the mission of Christopher Mundt to the Duke of Bavaria, who, though a Catholic, was an enemy of Charles. The overtures to the German Protestant princes were several times renewed but without success. Yet Cromwell continued to believe that England would have to obtain its allies somewhere in Germany.

He had toyed with this idea first as early as 1533, as at that time the chance he would have liked to take early in 1536 of returning to the traditional alliance with the Emperor had not occurred. All that eventuated then was an alliance of little or no value with Lübeck. This came about almost by accident when in the August of that year some ships of Lübeck anchored in Rye Harbor, where their crews were arrested as pirates. However, their leader, Marc Meyer, had a scheme to present to Henry, and he was listened to.

Lübeck, which had recently come under the government of an adventurer named Jürgen Wullenweber, was trying to effect a confederation of Protestant cities on the Baltic, and the Crown of Denmark was, so they believed, at their disposal. This they offered to Henry, saying that if he did not find it convenient to accept it he might nominate some German princeling, who would be a kind of vassal to himself. Marc Meyer sailed home with an English knighthood, and the following February an envoy arrived in England from Lübeck. In August a treaty was signed under which the Lübeckers engaged themselves to provide Henry with twelve ships of war to help him gain the throne of Denmark, should he want it, and (unlike the rest of the Lutherans) undertook to uphold Henry in his marriage to Anne Boleyn. In return Henry made Lübeck a loan of fifty thousand gulden for its Danish campaign.

The treaty remained inoperative, except for the loan (which was eventually repaid); Christian of Holstein, though his claims were contested by Wullenweber, became King of Denmark. In the end Lübeck split into factions, and Wullenweber was overthrown and executed. Though in February, 1536, Henry made a treaty with King Christian, from whom he obtained promises of support, no advantage was gained except the dubious one of having annoyed the Emperor still further.

About the same time Francis, prompted by Charles, sent an embassy to England, under the Admiral Chabot de Brion, to propose that Mary be married to either the Duke of Angoulême or the Dauphin. Nothing came of this because it would have involved a declaration of Mary's legitimacy (with the further admission that Henry's first marriage was valid), which of course was what Charles had been aiming at. Henry's refusal served only to make Francis feel that he had been rudely repulsed.

A year and a half later, after the death of Jane Seymour, when Henry was again in the marriage market, the Emperor offered him the hand of the sixteen-year-old widow, the Duchess of Milan. This time the proposal was entertained, at any rate to the extent of Cromwell's instructing Philip Hoby to arrange for Hans Holbein to paint her portrait, so that Henry could see what she looked like. Hoby was also provided by Cromwell with a speech that he was to deliver to the Duchess, in which she was to be told: "For the great good reports of my Lord of your virtues and goodly qualities and mine own view and experience of the same, considering the King's Majesty is widower and without a wife, would to God it would please his Majesty to advance your Grace to the honor of Queen of England, considering your virtuous qualities are a great deal more indeed than ever was notified, and for a great confirmation of amity and love to continue between the Emperor's Majesty and the King's Highness."

The portrait was painted and the speech delivered, but when it came to the point, the negotiations broke down because Charles wished Mary to marry Don Louys, the Infante of Portugal, at the same time. But again the question of Mary's legitimacy came up, and, even apart from that, Henry was reluctant to have so close an alliance with Charles as might have committed him to a defense of Portugal and to side with the Emperor in the dispute over the duchy of Milan. Henry's envoys were instructed to make difficulties and to insist on terms that he knew Charles could not accept.

At this time Henry was, as usual, trying to play Charles and Francis off against one another. Yet he was upon the whole inclined to marry a French princess in the expectation of weakening the bond between France and Scotland. With this in mind he asked Francis to give him Madame de Longueville (Mary of Guise) on the plea that, as he was a big-built man, he needed a substantially built bride—but really because the lady had been promised to James V of Scotland. Francis declined because he wished to retain the Scottish alliance. Upon this Henry considered other French ladies of high rank, among them Louisa of Lorraine (the Duchess of Longueville's sister) and Mary of Bourbon, the sister of Anthony of Navarre. Francis sent him their portraits when these were asked for, but Henry's further demand, that he should be allowed to see them in person either in England or at Calais, was refused, Francis saying that they were not to be trotted out like hackneys for sale.

A year later Francis and Charles had patched up their differences, and at the Treaty of Toledo, signed on January 12, 1539, the two monarchs bound themselves not to make any alliance, whether political or matrimonial, without the other's consent. Henry was now forced to admit that Cromwell's scheme of finding an ally in Germany had to be fallen back upon. An idea of negotiating a league with the Dukes of Urbino, Ferrara, and Mantua, though

Cromwell wrote about it at great length on January 21, 1539, to his emissary, Edmund Harvell, was taken up only to be dropped. Henry would have been able to do nothing for the Dukes, nor they for him, unless perhaps weaken the Papacy under its political aspects.

Nothing was hoped for from the idea of this league because in the same month Cromwell wrote to Christopher Mundt to open negotiations for marriages between the Princess Mary and the Duke of Cleves and between Henry and the Duchess Anne, his sister. It was the measure of Cromwell's difficulties that he could think of nothing better than a matrimonial alliance with Cleves, a not very important German dukedom. But he hoped through this to come to terms with the Smalkaldic League, for though a religious understanding with the Lutheran princes could not be reached, a purely political alliance, he thought, might yet prove feasible. As for Henry, one of the arguments used to persuade him was that he might be able to convert the Lutherans—not of course to the extent of inducing them to return to the Roman obedience but to renounce their doctrinal errors.

Doctrinal error was being much discussed in England at this time. Stephen Gardiner had just returned from his embassy in France, and the Duke of Norfolk was permitted to emerge from his retreat at Kenninghall. They were needed to give their weight to the passage of the Six Articles, which were presented to the House of Lords by the Duke and not Cromwell. But though Cromwell knew these men to be his bitter enemies, he felt himself safe, all the more so because he was on the point of effecting the Cleves alliance. For their part his enemies felt that this might give them the chance they were looking for. Cromwell had staked everything upon the Cleves marriage, but they had been too long in politics not to know how evanescent were alliances, even when cemented by marriage, and that the interests of Charles and Francis were too opposed to keep them long together.

Cromwell was thinking of Cleves only as a last resource. After writing to Christopher Mundt on March 10, 1539, sending him instructions about the Cleves negotiations, only twelve days later he wrote to the same agent directing him to make another attempt with the Landgrave of Hesse and the Elector of Saxony. He was to urge all princes who favored the Gospel and evangelical truth

246

to stand together, adding, "Truth it is that the bruit has been very sore that the Emperor would convert his strength and power against the King's Majesty, and also the French King, at the Bishop of Rome's intercession, for none other cause than misprising and avoiding of his abuses and maintaining of the word of God." But in order to scare the Germans, Mundt was to tell them that the Emperor was intending to start "first against the princes of Almayn." It did no good; the German princes had long since ascertained that Henry's religion differed in no respect from that of the Pope, except in the matter of union with him. As for the danger to the princes of the Smalkaldic League, they had no fear of that: Charles was not in a position to start full-scale war against them, and if he did, Francis would find this a golden opportunity for joining with them to ruin his ally.

These German allies would have been valuable to Henry just then, could they have been secured. But even had he been willing to accept their doctrinal demands or able to secure a merely political accord, he would of course have sought reconciliation with both Charles and Francis at the earliest possible moment and then, as of old, have played his game of fomenting dissensions between them while pretending to be the bosom friend of each. There was no chance of that at the moment: they had combined against him and might strike at any time. Cromwell managed to persuade Henry that his immediate danger was too pressing to permit delay: an ally had to be found at once, and the Duke of Cleves was the only possible ally left.

The arrangement was feasible only because the Duke had not as yet declared himself a Protestant, though he already inclined in that direction and had friendly contacts with the Smalkaldic League. Writing to Henry on March 18, Cromwell was able to tell him that the Duke of Saxony had promised to promote the marriage but adds that the German painter Lucas Cranach was ill and so could not make a portrait of Anne of Cleves. He assures the King, however: "Every man praiseth the beauty of the same lady as well for the face as for the body above all other ladies excellent. One among other purposes said that she excelleth as far the Duchess [of Milan] as the golden sun excelleth the silver moon."

This was excessive praise, as Henry probably suspected. The marriage was primarily a political one, but Henry wished to make sure that Anne had at least passable good looks, so Holbein was commissioned to paint her portrait. This painting is still in existence and certainly does not represent Anne as any beauty; though, if it comes to that, she was not much inferior in this respect to the rest of Henry's wives, even Anne Boleyn and Catherine Howard. If she was actually worse-looking than her portrait, this can only have been because Cromwell ordered Holbein (that careful and accurate delineator) to flatter her in his canvas. She was, however, tall and portly, and as Henry had specified his need for a big woman when asking Francis for the hand of the Duchess de Longueville, he ought to have been satisfied.

Moreover, Nicholas Wotton, who had been sent to Cleves, reported on May 3 that Anne was "of lowly and gentle conditions. . . . She occupieth her time most with the needle. . . . She can read and write [German] but of French or Latin or other languages she knoweth none, nor yet she cannot sing or play any instrument." As this did not sound very exciting, Wotton tactfully added, "They take it here in Germany for a rebuke and an occasion of lightness that great ladies should be learned or have any knowledge of music." It cannot be said that Henry was not fully informed as to what kind of a bride he was going to get. In spite of this he persisted, for only in this way could he make the needed alliance with Cleves.

The whole affair had to be handled with the utmost discretion. Cromwell was most careful not to make any matrimonial offer directly to the Duke, for though this was not exactly a misalliance, it hardly consorted with Henry's dignity as a king to ask outright for the sister of one of the Emperor's vassals. Accordingly he instructed Mundt to confer with Dr. Franz Burkhardt, the Vice-Chancellor of Saxony, and to get him to give them "a prick to stir them to offer her, as the noblest and highest honor that could come into the noble house of Cleves, if they could bring it to pass." He knew how skittish Henry was, how touchy about what he considered his due; and Cromwell was determined not to allow this marriage project to fall through on that account.

It must be emphasized that the whole idea was Cromwell's; that Henry had accepted it with a reluctance as a *pis-aller;* and that even for Cromwell it represented only the partial success of the policy he had been advocating, off and on, for several years. For all these reasons Cromwell must have understood that he was incurring considerable risks. The alliance had to be proved valuable, or he would be discredited. Nevertheless he accepted those risks as unavoidable, hoping for the best. He felt that it was less dangerous to take the hazard than not, for he was in mortal fear of concerted action against Henry by Charles and Francis.

The King sent 400 gentlemen, headed by the Earl of Southampton, to escort his promised bride to England, and there were many lifted eyebrows when they saw what she was like. She was a nice, kind, sensible, simple woman, but they not only saw she was plain but discovered that she was devoid of accomplishments. Southampton, knowing how bored Henry would be in the society of a woman with whom he could hardly exchange a word, did his best while they were waiting at Calais for the weather to clear by teaching her to play cards. It was not much, but it was something. He also tried to improve the situation by writing to Henry praising Anne's looks. After all, if everybody did this, the King might be brought to believe that she was not so bad-looking. It was notorious that he was not much of a connoisseur in such matters.

Henry had been a widower for over two years, all of which time he had been scouring Europe for a wife through whom he would gain political advantage. But he had been influenced by the accounts that had reached him of Anne's charms, so that now that she was arriving, the forty-nine-year-old King was all impatience. Instead of waiting for her in London, he hurried down to Rochester to meet her. To his first meeting he went in disguise, which was a reversion to the days of his golden youth, when he frequently arrived in this style at parties, ostensibly unexpected. Then Queen Katherine had always pretended to be astonished when his identity was revealed.

He found Anne at a bearbaiting, evidently enjoying the spectacle. But from the instant that Henry's eyes fell on her he was dismayed, "marvellously astonished." He felt a strong repugnance toward her, and, after a few moments during which hardly a word was spoken, he left. To Sir Anthony Browne, his Master of the Horse, he complained, "Say what they will, she is nothing so fair as she has been reported." He had suddenly found that his taste was not for big women, especially when they were dressed in the unbecoming German style. Dress was something that might be improved later, but Henry never recovered from the bad initial impression Anne had made.

This meeting was on New Year's Day, 1540, and the marriage was to be celebrated five days later. Something must be done and at once. Therefore, such members of the Council as were there were summoned for consultation. It was quickly made clear to the King that to jilt Anne almost on the altar steps would be a deadly affront to her brother and also to the Elector of Saxony, as he had furthered the marriage. It would, in fact, be taken as an insult by all the German princes. Henry's political position would be worse than ever if he sent her home, for he would have a new set of enemies.

The King could not but recognize that hard fact. But could not some impediment to marriage be discovered, something that would enable him to protest to the Duke of Cleves that he desired nothing more on earth than to marry his sister but was debarred from doing so? Inquiries were made, and it was learned that twelve years previously, and from time to time since then, there had been talk of her marrying the son of the Duke of Lorraine. Henry sighed with relief; as there was a precontract, marriage was impossible. Unfortunately it was shown that all this had been merely a plan for bringing pressure to bear on the Emperor and had never been seriously intended. And the prospective bridegroom, to clear up the question, had signed a paper that set Anne free. Henry could only ask miserably, "Is there then no remedy, but I must needs, against my will, put my neck into the yoke?" As there was no way out, he married her, saying glumly to Cromwell on the wedding morning, "My Lord, were it not to satisfy the world and my realm, I would not do what I must do this day for any earthly thing." And the morning after the wedding he confided, "Surely, my Lord, I liked her not well before, but now I like her much worse." He even went, if Cromwell is to be believed, into very intimate details.

Cromwell was disappointed that things had turned out like this, but he did not realize how desperate his own position was. He flattered himself that he had brought about what would prove a useful alliance between England and Cleves. Though the duchy was not very powerful, it was at least capable, in the event of the Emperor's attacking Henry, of giving help on the flank and perhaps of aligning some of the other German princes. Or rather the fact that Cleves was known to be capable of this would, Cromwell was confident, be enough to prevent the much harassed Emperor from engaging in war. As for Anne herself, Henry might come by degrees to discover her good qualities: her cheerful good nature was in her favor, and as a good *Hausfrau* she could do much for the comfort of a man who had always been accustomed to having a woman around. Even if a sufficient liking for her did not come into being, Henry could always find a mistress, though to do him justice, we do not hear of any mistresses after 1535.

There could have been very slight expectation of Anne's bearing him a child, however glad he would have been to have had another son—or even another daughter, as both Mary and Elizabeth were now bastardized. Henry was prematurely old, and though three years before he had begotten a son by Jane Seymour, there is reason to believe that, even before that, his potency had begun to diminish. It is therefore not at all improbable on the face of it that with a bride so distasteful as Anne he had never consummated his marriage.

He began to be exercised (or was pretending to be) about the supposititious precontract between Anne and the Duke of Lorraine's son. He was saying, "I have done as much to move the consent of my heart and mind as ever man did, but the obstacle will not out of my mind." This very broad hint that the King's conscience was troubling him and that there were grounds for a declaration of nullity was not taken. Cromwell had committed himself to the Cleves alliance and still hoped by means of it to obtain other allies in Germany, or even to bring Henry to see that he should, as a matter of political necessity, accept the demands of the Smalkaldic League and declare himself a Protestant. He went on hoping that somehow everything would turn out well.

Cromwell should have realized his extreme peril when on June 7 Wriothesley had a conversation with him. Then Wriothesley told him, "The King loves not the Queen, nor ever has from the beginning; insomuch as I think assuredly she is yet as good a maid as when she came to England." But when Wriothesley went on, "For God's sake devise how his Grace may be relieved one way or the other!" Cromwell merely returned, "But what and how?" It was an answer which when carried back to the King infuriated him. Cromwell was the man most fully informed as to Henry's marital relations; he was therefore the man who was in the best position to help him to a divorce. Cromwell was shrugging off Henry's troubles as though they did not matter compared to the political game he was playing. It was not without significance that he fell three days after this talk with Wriothesley.

Yet he might have been saved had he managed to effect another German alliance by a marriage between Mary and Philip of Bavaria. Here was something much more to Henry's taste, as Philip was a Catholic. Cromwell was in charge of an affair which was conducted with the utmost secrecy, even going with the Duke to see the Princess. He wanted to effect an alliance, and it was of no consequence to him whether it was with a Catholic or a Protestant prince. In fact, the Lutheran princes were by now virtually written off as hopeless. But while Philip was willing enough to marry Mary, he made the familiar demand that Mary's legitimacy be recognized; and as that involved a number of other things the most that the German Duke could promise was that he would go through with the project provided that it met with the approval of his family. As that was not forthcoming, the marriage fell through. And yet it was a far less dangerous scheme than committing Henry to the Smalkaldic League, for it would not have put him into permanent opposition to the Emperor. If it failed, the fault once again was Henry's stubbornness—this time not in defense of orthodoxy but in his repudiation of the Pope.

It soon became evident that Cromwell had blundered not only in foisting upon Henry an undesired wife but had made a political blunder as well. The alliance between Charles and Francis began to crumble almost as soon as constructed, the Emperor breaking his promises to Francis the moment he left his country. In particular he refused to give up Milan to the French King. And Henry, seizing his chance, did all he could to widen the breach between them, professing friendship for Francis while letting Charles know that he preferred an alliance with him above one with the Duke of Cleves. On April 10 Marillac, the French Ambassador, wrote to his King saying that he believed Cromwell was likely to fall, adding, "If he remains in his former credit and authority, it will only be because he is very assiduous in affairs." Yet the very next day Cromwell appeared to have falsified Marillac's predictions, for he was created Earl of Essex and Great Chamberlain.

A man whom Cromwell would very much have liked to arrest, but dared not, was Stephen Gardiner. Instead Gardiner, long an enemy—a man whom Cromwell had alternately roughly ordered about and then attempted to mollify with soothing words and heart-rending complaints that he could not understand why the Bishop of Winchester was so opposed to him—was among those chiefly instrumental in bringing him down. He was able to do so only because Cromwell made a third blunder.

It happened this way. Cromwell had used Robert Barnes, the ex-Augustinian Prior of Cambridge, on various diplomatic missions, most recently in the Cleves negotiations, a circumstance that did not help either man. That Cromwell now made him a prebendary might have been overlooked, though that Barnes entertained heretical opinions was, to say the least, generally suspected. Henry did not particularly mind this—as witness his protection of Cranmer—so long as a complete official acceptance was accorded what had come to be called "the King's doctrine." Cromwell, however, as a pre-liminary to Gardiner's overthrow, had put Barnes up to preach at Paul's Cross on the first Sunday in Lent, February 15, two weeks after the Bishop had preached from the same pulpit. There Barnes attacked Gardiner, and in very insulting terms. Gardiner was incensed and complained to the King, demanding an examination before impartial judges. Upon this, Barnes found it advisable to admit himself in the wrong and to ask Gardiner's pardon. He was ordered to preach again and make a public recantation during Holy Week, which he did, but in so unsatisfactory a fashion that he, along with two other heretical priests named Garret and Jerome, who also had been ordered to make recanting sermons, were committed to the Tower, from which they emerged only to be burned at Smithfield. Meanwhile, on March 20, Cromwell and Gardiner dined together and had a talk lasting four hours, in which it was supposed that they had composed their quarrel.

This was not the case. Gardiner's resentment was still keen, and he was watching for a chance to drag Cromwell down. The same thing was true of the Duke of Norfolk and in fact of all the nobility and all the hierarchy, except for a handful of the "advanced" men.

In many instances the animosity was far more rancorous than even that felt for Wolsey; but some of those who joined Cromwell's enemies did so mainly in order to save their own skins. He had packed the House of Commons more carefully than ever and had written to Henry in 1539 that he had never had so tractable a Parliament. And the Speaker, Sir Richard Rich, was a creature of Cromwell's. The same was true of Audley and Wriothesley. Yet these men, when the time came, voted his attainder, with not a single voice raised in Parliament in his defense.

Cromwell had always known that he was unpopular. He had made himself unpopular even when in Wolsey's service. Further unpopularity came when it dawned on the people that it was he who had contrived, when Wolsey had failed, the divorce of the beloved Queen Katherine. This unpopularity was greatly added to when he began to despoil the monasteries: the Pilgrimage of Grace was primarily a demand for his execution; and since that time he had swept away all the great abbeys, so that monasticism was now extinct in England. But he was disliked also by the bishops whom he, a layman sprung from nowhere, had ruled with an iron hand. Finally, the nobles hated him, for though he had treated them with outward respect, he had seen to it that none of them had any influence with the King, as was especially true of the Duke of Norfolk. This would have been galling had it been suffered from a man of high rank; it was intolerable when suffered from one who, though he had received first a barony and just recently an earldom, was, as none of the nobility forgot, a baseborn fellow. Perhaps most of all they hated him for having obliged them to vote for the death of so many men of their own order—in most instances friends or connections by marriage—such as Lords Darcy, Hussey, Montague, and Exeter; nor could they forgive him for having sent Sir Thomas More and the venerated Bishop Fisher to the block. Though these particular offenses could not be charged against him, as the King was implicated in the judicial murders, the offenses, however, made the peers determined to destroy him before he could destroy them.

Cromwell's motive in decimating the peerage was well-understood. He had left the "new men" alone, for these were the ones with whom he worked. Yet this did not prevent their going over to his enemies—the Seymours joining with their rivals, the Howards. It was believed that in these executions he was actuated by a desire to

254

eradicate the ancient families, as they might be an impediment to his plans. They did not forget the time when the great nobles looked upon the Crown as something that they could bestow at will upon their own nominee. But of course Cromwell did not forget this either, and he was determined to make it forever impossible. Because he was sincere in his conviction that the monarchy should be transformed into an autocracy, operating under constitutional forms, this made him all the more feared and therefore all the more hated.

Up to a certain point Henry was pleased when his officials were unpopular. It showed, so he considered, that they were working in his interests, and it certainly made them all the more dependent directly on himself. But there was no cohesion among the bureaucrats, each member of which worked for his own advancement, envious of the men above him. Among the nobles there were rivalries, but they stood together where important matters were concerned. Such was not the case among the officials, chief of whom was Cromwell, for he, in spite of his titles and authority, was looked upon as belonging to the bureaucrats.

Another reason which probably operated—though it was one that could not be acknowledged—was that Cromwell had not ceased his moneylending activities but rather had extended them, because of greater opportunities. This put many important people in his power, even when they were not already in his power because of the information his secret service could supply. It made all such people anxious to get rid of him. With his fall and his death, debts would be canceled; many dangers would be removed. It is very perilous for a man to make himself powerful, unless he can also make himself invulnerable.

Invulnerable he had been for nearly ten years. But now his unpopularity had far passed the degree that Henry considered desirable. He was becoming an embarrassment. As Archbishop David Mathew writes in the chapter on Cromwell he contributed to *The Great Tudors*, "Most despotic sovereigns are prepared to learn that they have been ill-served by their closest intimates and, if suspicion is an almost inevitable concomitant of tyranny, the vein of naive suspiciousness in the King's character would be the natural reaction of a buoyant temperament seldom thwarted and rarely openly opposed."

Henry had never really liked Cromwell. William Paulet, who be-

255

came a marquis during Edward's reign, told the other courtiers, "As for my Lord Privy Seal, I would not be in his case for all that he hath, for the King beknaveth him twice a week, and sometimes knocketh him well about the pate; and yet when he hath been well pummelled about the head and shaken up, as it were a dog, he will come out into the great chamber shaking of the bush with as merry a countenance as though he might rule all the roast." Cromwell had cheerfully accepted all the royal insults; so long as he was allowed to retain power, he was willing to receive rough treatment at the King's hands. He regarded himself as indispensable, correctly gauging his own ability and sure that the complete devotion he had shown to Henry's interests could not but be recognized.

What he did not gauge at all correctly was the extent of the animosity of the nobility, and, despising priests as he did, he underestimated what a man like Bishop Gardiner might be able to do. He counted upon the King's backing, and he also may have counted upon the protection of a House of Commons, so many of whose members had been hand-picked by himself. He failed to realize that, when it came to the point, they would do exactly as the King wished.

His worst error of judgment concerned the King. For all Cromwell's keen knowledge of character, especially on its seamy sides, he had not fully fathomed Henry's infinite craftiness or his capacity for secretly storing up a fund of resentment, hiding this behind a smiling face until the moment had come for him to strike. Finally, he imagined that the King would be grateful to him. With what dispatch the monastic institution had been rooted out and with what immense profit to the royal treasury! Furthermore, during the last months of his tenure of office he had suppressed the forty-three immensely wealthy commanderies of the Knights of St. John of Jerusalem. It was an international order of chivalry, with its Grand Master holding his headquarters at Malta since the capture of Rhodes by the Turks. Some of the English knights abroad had acknowledged Henry's claim to be Head of the Church in England. This had resulted in their imprisonment, and the insult (as Henry regarded it) gave Cromwell a pretext for dissolving the order and taking over its possessions. Their Prior, Sir William Weston, who had distinguished himself at the siege of Rhodes, was handsomely pensioned but died of a broken heart on the very day of his order's suppression. As though this were not enough, Cromwell, by adroit management, induced Parliament to pass new and heavy taxes. These last two pieces of Cromwell's work brought in £3,000,000, far more than had been obtained by the seizure of the monasteries. Henry should indeed have been grateful.

Unluckily for Cromwell, his King was incapable of feeling gratitude. His minister had been too successful; there was now nothing more that he could do. The earldom he received in April may have been a reward; it may also have been a means for Henry to conceal his intentions until he was ready to pack Cromwell off to the Tower. More probably Henry was wavering in mind, as was habitual with him. At the last moment something might have happened to save Cromwell or at least to give him a further respite.

Early in April something did in fact happen that seemed to have justified Cromwell's policy regarding Cleves. News arrived that Francis was fortifying Ardres on the border of the bit of land England held around Calais, and when an explanation was demanded, Francis replied that he did not see why he might not build fortifications there, just as Henry had done at Calais and nearby Guines. The words were not said haughtily but were quite enough to cause grave misgivings in England. For Cromwell, however, the news was a relief; if Francis really meditated an attack on Calais, the Cleves alliance would be valuable.[1]

Cromwell's relief did not last long; Francis took no further belligerent action. Instead, word reached London from the Netherlands that the Emperor was demanding the surrender of Gelderland by the Duke of Cleves, and it seemed more than likely that he purposed to annex it forcibly. Then England, according to the terms of its treaty, would have been called upon to defend the Duke of Cleves; and a war with the Emperor would have almost certainly been the signal for Francis to attack Calais, if not to invade England. It was now abundantly clear that the Cleves alliance was a distinct disadvantage to Henry.

On May 11 Cromwell wrote at the King's instance a letter to

[1] On p. 206 we have seen how Cromwell instructed the Governor of Calais on January 20 to be on guard against a French Trojan Horse attack on Calais. It is possible that he wrote as he did more with the intention of scaring Henry than of warning Lord Lisle. In view of Henry's distaste for Anne he had to do everything possible to make him believe in the usefulness of the Cleves alliance.

Richard Pate, the new Ambassador to Charles, a letter that must have been very hard for him to compose. It is true that this only hinted at the abandonment of the Cleves alliance, but by way of friendly gesture to the Emperor he was informed that two men who had rebelled against him in Flanders had taken refuge in Calais. Charles was asked what he would like to have done with these men: "If he wish they might be delivered; you may of yourself say that you know right well that the King's Majesty will extend no such favors to traitors, but if the same be demanded he will gladly do therein as his leagues and amity doth require." This offer to give the men up, even before their extradition had been asked for, was intended to demonstrate Henry's good will; it was also an assurance that, if the Emperor intended to take military action against the Duke of Cleves, the King of England would leave him to his fate.

The previous month something had happened that Cromwell might well have regarded as ominous but perhaps discounted: it was suggested in the Council that Tunstall—the most orthodox of English bishops—should be appointed the King's Vicegerent. As Cromwell had completed his work of monastic suppression, it may be that he thought it of no special significance to turn over to an ecclesiastic what remained in the way of minor routine. In any event nothing was done about this. Instead Cromwell's confidence was restored when a couple of days later Sir Ralph Sadler and Wriothesley were made secretaries of state. As Cromwell was created Earl of Essex at the same time, he felt that he had little to worry about.

At all events he acted as though he counted himself not only safe but as having obtained augmented authority. For in May he sent Bishop Sampson to the Tower, and with him Dr. Nicholas Wilson. These were men who were considered, if not precisely papalist, as having secret inclinations in that direction. Cromwell even permitted himself to say that there were five other bishops who should be sent to join them. This caused a good deal of panic among the hierarchy, and this was increased by the introduction on May 29 of a new treason bill. On June 1 the attainder of three Catholic priests, including Abell, who had been in the Tower for six years, and Featherstone, who had been the Lady Mary's tutor, and of a third man named Powell, was passed by Parliament. On top of this a report was circulated that Dr. Barnes was to be released and Latimer restored to his bishopric.

Whether or not Cromwell's destruction had been decided upon at the time he was given his earldom, the increased arrogance that this induced in him and the fear that he was creating made his enemies perceive that they would have to act at once. The political situation, in which the Cleves alliance was shown to be without value, was the deciding factor; had it not been for this, Cromwell would probably have remained impregnable. The popular belief, however, was that the King's exasperation over his marriage brought Cromwell down.

Such was hardly the case. That marriage could have been dissolved by divorce, and Cromwell was the King's best witness here. If he did not choose to give his evidence at that time, it must have been because he still clung to the belief that the Cleves alliance would be a means of reaching an eventual accord with the princes of the Smalkaldic League. In March two envoys from Saxony wrote home that Henry had expressed hopes of coming to a religious understanding with them. At any rate, they said, Cromwell was virtually King, and as such he was preventing the operation of the Six Articles and working hard in the Gospel cause.

No doubt Henry did say something like this to the Saxon envoys: he was a consummate dissimulator. But of course in March it was not so apparent as it became by the beginning of June that the Cleves alliance would have to be repudiated as worthless. Cromwell's enemies had at last been able to prove to the King's satisfaction that this was so and therefore were permitted to take their revenge.

I have said that the popular notion that Cromwell fell because of the King's disgust with Anne is fallacious. But by this I do not mean that it had nothing to do with the matter. It had a good deal to do with it, but had it been the sole factor or even the main factor, Cromwell would have emerged safely. More specifically, had the political situation been in June what it was in January or even April —with Henry in need of the help of the Duke of Cleves against the possibility of attack from the Emperor—Cromwell's policy would have justified itself. Henry would in that event have put up with Anne, however ruefully, for the sake of the Cleves alliance. On the other hand, it is equally likely that Henry would have condoned Cromwell's lack of political success had he been pleased with his new wife. In other words, either thing, considered separately, might have been pardoned; together they were unpardonable. And Henry, as was his way, made his personal disappointment the paramount element in the case. It surely cannot be without significance that Cromwell's arrest occurred just three days after his conversation with Wriothesley. On that day, had he but realized it, he was being given his last chance.

Henry never got rid of one wife before he had another ready to take her place. Already Gardiner had seen to it that the King should meet Catherine Howard, a niece of the Duke of Norfolk's, at his house. Henry was attracted by her but seems as yet to have done nothing that would make anybody suppose that he was thinking of marrying her, which was perhaps why Cromwell was unaware of the matter. She was, in the eyes of Cromwell's enemies, an eminently suitable candidate, for through her Norfolk would reestablish himself, and through her, too, so Gardiner hoped, there would be a Catholic reaction. Apart from all this, it was necessary to stir up the King's emotions in order to bring him into action. Having seen Catherine, Henry was all the more infuriated with Cromwell for having saddled him with Anne.

It was on June 10 that the blow fell, at a moment when Cromwell was least expecting it, so secretly had everything been arranged. That morning he had attended a sitting of the House of Lords and in the afternoon went to Westminster Palace where the Privy Council was meeting. There, as soon as the clock struck three, the Duke of Norfolk rose in his place saying, "My Lord of Essex, I arrest you of high treason."

These were not empty words, for as Norfolk spoke the Lieutenant of the Tower and a couple of guards, who had been posted outside, waiting for the triple stroke of the clock, strode into the council chamber. Cromwell, seeing them, in a rage tore off his cap and threw it on the floor shouting, "This then is my guerdon for the service I have done! On your consciences, I ask you, am I a traitor?" But the hard faces of the Councilors told him that shouting did no good, so he said in quieter tones, "If the King my master believes so ill of me, let him make quick work." Cromwell was well aware that the game was up, that though Henry was usually slow in making up his mind he was utterly ruthless once he had reached a decision. And he knew perfectly well what could be charged against him; for much flimsier reasons he himself had sent many men to the scaffold.

Norfolk, to whose patronage Cromwell had owed his seat in the

Parliament of 1529 but who had long been his enemy, tore the St. George from his neck. William Fitzwilliam, the Earl of Southampton, and Lord High Admiral, a man whom he had thought his friend, removed his Order of the Garter. Other friends of his were there—Audley, the Chancellor, Wriothesley, himself to be an Earl of Southampton, Sir Ralph Sadler, and Sir Richard Rich, all of them men whose careers he had made possible—and looked on in silence.

Quickly he was led to a door in the palace that opened on the river. There a barge was waiting for him, and he was taken at once to the Tower. So secretly had everything been planned that the people of London got no inkling of what had happened until an hour or two later when they saw Sir Thomas Cheney, who was Treasurer of the Household, entering Cromwell's house to seize his papers and effects.

The papers showed only what was already known but were of course useful as positive proof of this: Cromwell had been surreptitiously favoring heretics. He could be prosecuted under the Six Articles. Strictly enforced, as they rarely had been (for Cromwell had largely nullified them), they permitted no abjuration. But as for his personal effects, these were less than had been expected, though they were large enough. Money to the amount of seven thousand pounds sterling was found in his coffers and somewhat more than that in plate, precious stones, and rich furnishings.[2] Translated into modern values and put in dollars, these alone made Cromwell a millionaire. The hoard was carried into the royal treasury, an indication that it would never be returned and that Cromwell's fate was already settled. But to the loot of that day must be added the many monastic estates that had come to him, on most of which he had done extensive building or remodeling. All his possessions under the law against treason would pass to the Crown.

Cranmer was thoroughly frightened at the way the wheel had suddenly come full cycle. He was now in greater danger than he had been even at the time of the fall of Anne Boleyn, for he did not know what might be discovered of his dealings with Cromwell or what might not be made of them. One thing is sure: if Cromwell was a heretic, much more so was Cranmer. There was, how-

[2] A good many ecclesiastical treasures were found, which Cromwell retained not only for their value but because they appealed to him as a connoisseur of *objets de vertu*.

ever, this important difference: Cranmer had been very cautious and had kept his opinions to himself, or, when he timidly ventured to hint at them, he always made it clear that he was prepared to disavow them the instant the King expressed his disagreement. Cromwell, on the other hand, had committed overt acts: such were his protection of heretics and his policy directed toward an alliance with the Lutheran princes of Germany. This Cleves project of his had been no more than a preliminary move in that direction.

In his alarm Cranmer wrote to the King on June 14 a letter much along the same lines as the one he had written when he heard of Anne Boleyn's arrest. "I heard yesterday in your Grace's Council," he said, "that the Earl of Essex is a traitor; yet who can be more sorrowful and amazed that he should be a traitor against your Majesty—he who loved your Majesty, as I ever thought, no less than God—he who studied always to set forwards whatever was your Majesty's will and pleasure—he that was such a servant, in my judgment, in wisdom, diligence, faithfulness and experience as no prince in this realm ever had—he that was so vigilant to preserve your Majesty from all treasons, that few could be so secretly conceived but he detected the same in the beginning! I loved him as my friend, for so I took him to be; but I chiefly loved him for the love which I thought I saw him bear ever towards your Grace, singularly shown above all others." If Cranmer had stopped at that point, his letter might be regarded as what some have called it, a courageous defense of Cromwell. Even so, it would have been more handsome to have written "has been arrested as a traitor" instead of "is a traitor." And Cranmer's "courage" was a desperate defense of himself rather than a defense of Cromwell. But the Archbishop went a little further and knocked down all that he had said: "But now, if he be a traitor, I am sorry that I ever loved or trusted him; and I am very glad that his treason is discovered in time; but yet again, I am sorrowful, for who shall your Grace trust hereafter, if you may not trust him? Alas! I lament your Grace's chance therein. I wot not whom your Grace may trust." [3] This last bit was intended to sow the seeds of suspicion in the King's mind regarding those now in the ascendant—in particular, Bishop Gardiner, for there was very

[3] It might be noticed that Cranmer was most careful not to touch on the charge of heresy brought against Cromwell—for self-evident reasons. He confines himself to Cromwell's alleged treason.

bad feeling between him and Cranmer. But the main point is: "I am glad that his treason is discovered in time."

Cromwell had made a novel use of attainder. Before his time attainder came after trial and convictions before a court of justice and was used to implicate the whole country in what was done. But Cromwell had found a way of condemning men to death without a judicial hearing, merely by act of Parliament. They then were given no chance to defend themselves or even to know what it was of which they were accused. This method was now used against himself.

In Cromwell's case it would not do to make his offense that of persuading the King into what had turned out to be an unlucky marriage and a useless political alliance. Nor could he be charged with the destruction of a number of nobles, for in this matter Henry was as guilty as Cromwell himself. Instead he was charged, very truly, of having sent many people (obscure people were meant) to their death for a word lightly spoken, for about these cases Henry knew nothing. It was also possible to bring against him that he had done all he could to make the laws against heresy of little effect. Only a little while before, when speaking to Burkhardt, who had come to England with Anne of Cleves, Cromwell had said that he must hold to the same belief as the King in religion, even though it cost him his life. But this statement indicates that his beliefs were merely official and that, if he were free to do so, he would steer a different course. It was toward this that he had been stealthily creeping—and not so very stealthily either, as was shown in the Barnes affair and the imprisonment of Sampson and Wilson.

Henry, magnificent liar though he often was, did not depart very far from the truth when he let Marrilac, the French Ambassador, know on the day of Cromwell's arrest that while he was seeking "by all possible means to lead back religion to the way of truth, Cromwell, as attached to the German Lutherans, had always favored the doctors who preached such erroneous opinions, and hindered those who preached the contrary." It was, however, a palpable lie that was written to Sir John Wallop, the Ambassador in France, that Cromwell had said that "if the King and all his realm would turn and vary from his opinions, he would fight in the field in his own person, with his sword in his hand against him and all other; adding that if he lived a year or two, he trusted to bring things to that frame, that it should not lie in the King's power to prevent it; binding his words with such oaths, and making such gesture and demonstration with his arms, that it might well appear that he had no less fixed in his heart than was uttered with his mouth." Wallop could not have been taken in by this fantastic nonsense, though of course he did what was expected of him and related the story at the French Court; but in the popular mind Cromwell was associated with Protestantism and hated by the general public accordingly. This view, from the Protestant side, was also expressed by John Foxe in his *The Book of Martyrs,* in which Cromwell figures as "a mighty pillar set up in the Church of God" and, because of his destruction of the monasteries, as "the subverter of the synagogue of Anti-christ."

Cromwell was condemned as both traitor and heretic. But he was not heretical in his opinions though, with purely political objects in mind, he had often protected heretics and was willing to work actively with them. However heavily one may discount the pious words in some of his early letters as merely a protective coloring, when one remembers his will of 1529, with its provision of money for Masses for the repose of his soul, it is impossible to believe that, at that time, he was without religious sentiments and convictions, superficial though these may have been. Later he laid all this aside, quite deliberately, and when he thought of religion at all, it was only as to how he might make use of it in what he considered much more important plans. His overt acts nevertheless were damning, and from these it was conveniently inferred that his connection with heretics proved that he held heretical opinions.

As for the charge of treason, no statesman—and I suppose one must allow that Cromwell was a statesman of the first rank—ever served his King more devotedly. Moreover, he offered this service with complete inner conviction. Nobody today is likely to agree with his concept of absolute monarchy, but it was sincere. It was of course notorious that he had taken bribes (as was charged in the bill of attainder), and much of this bribery could be considered as stealing from the King, as, in the aggregate, vast sums of money went into Cromwell's own pockets that should have been paid into the royal treasury. But this is hardly treason; nor was it true that Paulet said of him just before his fall: "The King has six times as much revenues as any of his noble progenitors ever had, and all is consumed and gone to naught by means of my Lord Privy Seal, who ravens all that he can get." The waste was not due to Cromwell but to the King's utter inability to hold on to what he had. If so large a part of the monastic loot as half was used for public purposes, Cromwell deserves most of the credit. We can see in his famous "Remembrances" the concern he felt about building coastal defenses and repairing roads, bridges, and sea dikes.

This, however, is not to say that Cromwell's condemnation was not justified. Though not a traitor to his prince, he was a traitor to his country, as, for that matter, Henry was too. In spite of the King's grand cant about the way he loved his subjects as a man did his natural children, no King ever loved his subjects less. And in this Cromwell was the man who contrived means for Henry to carry out his will. The whole face of England had been changed by Cromwell from what it had been during the early years of Henry's reign, a time of brilliance and happiness. Instead a pall of gloom had descended; the nobles had been murdered; the poor had been robbed; thousands of helpless monks and nuns had been plundered; the clergy had been browbeaten; and an arbitrary tyranny had been imposed on all classes of society. No man ever deserved his death more than Cromwell did; but if real justice had been done, Henry should have gone with him to the scaffold.

Chapter Sixteen

THE SCAFFOLD

THE FOLLOWING sequence of dates should
be noted: Thomas Cromwell was arrested on June 10; a week later
the act attainting him was read in the House of Lords; yet it was not
until July 28 that he was at last led out to die. In part the delay may
have been due to a consideration of the mode by which he should
suffer—whether by hanging, as a traitor, or by burning, as a heretic,
or by both modes simultaneously, as in the case of John Forest. But
the delay was mainly because he was to be one of the chief witnesses
in the divorce suit Henry had decided to bring against Anne of
Cleves. It was considered only just that, as Cromwell had made this
marriage, he should now unmake it.

One cannot but suspect that a kind of deal was made with him,
such as one suspects Cromwell made with Mark Smeaton in 1536.
Not being a gentleman meant that he should have been hanged,
drawn, and quartered at Tyburn, instead of being beheaded at
Tower Hill. He alone of the five men charged with criminal relations with Anne Boleyn confessed guilt (under torture of course)
and on the scaffold said what might be taken as a reaffimation of his
confession. Cromwell, who had been at once stripped of all his
honors and titles and reduced to being "Thomas Cromwell, Shearman," was well aware that this deprived him of the privilege of the
nobility, the mercy of the ax. He had to do something to earn it;
there may even have been hopes held out to him that, if he performed

this last service to complete satisfaction, his life would be spared.

This at once raises the question whether what he told of the marital relations of Henry and Anne of Cleves was not doctored to suit Henry's requirements. The question remains in spite of Anne's corroboration of the essential facts, for she was in some danger. Reasons for proceeding against her for high treason might have been alleged because of her denial of the suppositive precontract with the son of the Duke of Lorraine. On the other hand, a very handsome reward was held out to her if she would be cooperative: she should rank as the King's sister and be given two manors with commodious houses, and an income of four thousand pounds sterling a year. The only stipulation was that she should not return to Germany. As she had no wish to return, she readily agreed, as she would have had to agree, even had this been against her inclination.

The reason for doubting. Cromwell's words about the marriage is implied in what Professor Pollard writes about Henry: "His case, as stated by himself, was, as usual, a most ingenious mixture of fact and fiction, reason and sophistry." Another professor, R. B. Merriman, says more bluntly, "Cromwell was not the sort of man to whom dying with a lie on his lips would mean very much." Personally I am inclined to believe, after making all due allowances for the circumstances that give rise to suspicion, that the marriage really was null. The only bit of disingenuousness I can discover is Henry's declaration that he had not given full interior assent at the time of the marriage and that he went through with it only because the political situation seemed to demand it. That this motive operated need not be contested, but the King's argument would nullify every marriage of convenience. Without putting it past Cromwell to do some tall lying—especially when by doing so he might hope to escape the barbarities of Tyburn or even to get a reprieve—my opinion is that he told what was substantially true, perhaps even what was absolutely true.

It is likely that, as an expert canon lawyer, Bishop Gardiner instructed those deputed to examine Cromwell in the Tower as to what questions they should put to him, and certainly Gardiner went over the answers given to determine to what extent they might help Henry obtain his divorce. After this Cromwell was obliged to write on June 30 a long letter to the King, embodying what he had said to his examiners, the Duke of Norfolk and the Earl of Southampton.

In this letter, which Cromwell declares was written "before God at the dreadful day of judgement, and also upon the extreme danger and damnation of my soul," again protesting that he is telling "the very truth as God shall save me to the uttermost of my knowledge," he gives an account of the marriage along the lines of what has been recorded in the previous chapter, where many phrases of Cromwell's letter were incorporated. He writes soberly, and to my mind his letter carries all the more conviction from his saying that on certain points he could give no information. Here, had he been lying in this instance, he could have fallen back on invention.

Cromwell's evidence, along with a statement made by the King and another by the Queen, was presented to Convocation early in July. There was no judicial sentence as there had been with Katherine of Aragon and Anne Boleyn. Instead the decision of Convocation—of course in Henry's favor—was presented to Parliament and given statutory effect two days later.

Three main points emerge. The weakest was that, though Henry had in January reluctantly accepted as a fact that Anne had no precontract, he had never been quite convinced that this actually was the case, and the thought had increasingly gnawed at his conscience. Nor was the second point very strong. Cromwell attested that the King had said to him, "If it were not that she had come so far into my realm and the great preparation that my states and people hath made for her, and for fear of making a ruffle in the world, that is to drive her brother in the hands of the Emperor and [the] French King's hands, I would never have married her." But if the third point was valid, that alone would have been quite sufficient to make the marriage null and void: the marriage had never been consummated. Henry said that this was because he had refrained from consummation on account of his conscientious scruples about the precontract, but according to Cromwell's testimony the King's repugnance to his bride was so great that he could never bring himself to consummate the marriage, though he had slept with her frequently.[1] Crom-

---

[1] Merriman remarks in a footnote on p. 298 of his first volume that Henry had accepted the acknowledged fact that Katherine of Aragon and Arthur had slept together, as "sufficient proof" of the consummation of their marriage. Now the fact that he had slept with Anne of Cleves—so he contended—proved nothing. In each case a presumptive proof of consummation must be admitted; in neither case is the proof absolute. And there is this important

well records that the morning after the wedding the King said to him something that does him little credit, as it not only reveals his own coarseness but tends to the gratuitous besmirching of Anne. The King, Cromwell testified, told him, "I have felt her belly and breasts and thereby, as I can judge, she should be no maid, which struck me so to the heart when I felt them that I had neither will nor courage to proceed any further." Just why Henry reached this conclusion is not at all clear—at least not to me; and it might be pointed out that when, only a little later, he married Catherine Howard, he did not discover that his bride was not a virgin. Nevertheless I am prepared to believe that Henry did say, as Cromwell testified, "I have left her as good a maid as I found her, which methought then ye spoke displeasantly," which should be interpreted as a sneering comment to the effect that, so far as Henry was concerned, Anne was left a maid. Cromwell added that, after Candlemas and before Shrovetide, he knew from what the King confided "that ye were in the same case with her as ye were afore and that your heart could never consent to meddle with her carnally." Furthermore, Henry had repeated this to Cromwell at Easter, "and in the Whitsunday week in your Grace's chamber of Greenwich, [you] expect exceedingly lamented your fate, and that your greatest grief was that ye should surely never have any more children for the comfort of this realm if ye should so continue." Finally, Cromwell reminded the King that he had promised, "I would for my part do my uttermost to comfort and deliver your Grace of your affliction." If he had failed to make good this promise, one must suppose that it was in the hope that Henry would eventually overcome his distaste for the person of his wife and so confirm the policy upon which Cromwell had staked everything. Such evidence was invaluable, especially as Cromwell says he is sure that he knows more about these matters than any other man, "your Highness alone except." He adds that the Lord Admiral and divers members of the Council could at least testify that "your Majesty hath not been well pleased with your marriage."

At the end of his letter Cromwell writes, "I am a most woeful prisoner ready to take the death when it shall please God and your Majesty, and yet the frail flesh inciteth me continually to call to

difference: Katherine steadily denied the consummation; Anne of Cleves corroborated Henry that her marriage to him had not been consummated.

your Grace for mercy and pardon for mine offences." If he had let his plea stand with that, one would discover in him no more than a natural hope for a reprieve. But he appends as a postscript, "I cry for mercy, mercy, mercy!" Those who saw that letter were astonished that the merciless Cromwell should be so abject; even those who hated him most had supposed that he was made of sterner stuff.

Earlier the same month, two days after Cromwell had been committed to the Tower, Cromwell wrote Henry a letter whose tone suggests that he believed that the King would accept his explanations, especially as these were coupled with sweeping but rather indefinite apologies for ever having done anything displeasing to the King. "I do acknowledge myself," he wrote at that time, "to have been a most miserable and wretched sinner and that I have not towards God and your Highness behaved myself as I ought and should have done." But having made this general admission, he went on to deny most of the things with which he had been charged at his first examination, even venturing to compare himself to the falsely accused Susanna of the Old Testament. Yet it is not at all clear what all these things were. For instance, he had evidently been charged with something said in a conversation with Sir George Throgmorton and the Chancellor of the Court of Augmentations, Sir Richard Rich, to which he replies that, to the best of his recollection, he had never spoken to them together at the same time. He does acknowledge, however, that he had not kept a secret imparted to him by the Comptroller, Sir William Kingston, the former Constable of the Tower, and also that he had not preserved the King's confidence on some other occasions—in particular that he had discussed the King's marital affairs with the Earl of Southampton. This indiscretion was, however, all to Henry's advantage, as it enabled Southampton to corroborate Cromwell's own testimony. And the mere revealing of a secret (unless it is military information imparted to an enemy power) can hardly be construed as treason. The most serious admission that Cromwell makes is this: "If I have heard of any combinacious conventicles or such as were offenders of your laws I have—though not as I should have done—caused them to be punished." But even here he acknowledges no more than a certain amount of negligence.

Most of his letter of June 12 is given over to reminding the King of his services. "What labors, pains and travails I have taken according to my most bounden duty God also knoweth, for if it were in my power, as it is God's, to make your Majesty live ever young and prosperous, God knoweth I would do it. If it had been in my power to make your Majesty so puissant as all the world should be compelled to you, Christ He knoweth I would." Apparently Cromwell deemed it best not to stress particular services, for almost all of these were contaminated by some piece of ruthlessness or corruption, which would have been promptly seized upon by his enemies. The furthest he goes in this direction is to say, "Sir, as to your commonwealth, I have after my wit, power and knowledge travailed therein, having had no respect to persons (your Majesty alone except, and my duty to the same); but that I have done any injustice or wrong wilfully, I trust God shall be my witness and the world not able to accuse me. And yet I have not done my duty in all things, wherefor I ask mercy." Another admission, made like the others in general terms, is: "I would to Christ I had obeyed your often most gracious grave counsels and advertisements. Then it had not been with me as it is now."

That letter was written on a Saturday and was no doubt at once conveyed to the King. Cromwell's plea fell on deaf ears. The bill of attainder was drawn up and presented to the House of Lords the following week and there, and in the House of Commons, passed with no voice raised in his defense, not one vote in his favor.

This bill, after indicating how much the King had done for his fallen minister, goes on: "Yet nevertheless Thomas Cromwell, now Earl of Essex, your Majesty took and received into your trusty service, the same Thomas being then a man of very base and low degree. And for singular trust and confidence, which your Majesty bore and had in him, did not only erect the said Thomas into the state of an earl and enriched him with many gifts as well as of goods, as of lands and offices," making him "one of your most trusty councillors as well concerning your Grace's supreme jurisdictions ecclesiastical, as your most high secret affairs temporal," in spite of which it had been proved that Cromwell—studiously styled "Thomas," as though he were a lackey—was "a false and corrupt traitor." He had set at liberty those whom he pleased; he had sold "for manifold sums of money" various grants, even to foreigners; and he had appointed commissioners "in many of your great, urgent and weighty causes without the assent or knowledge of your Highness." Furthermore, he had boasted "that he was sure of you"; he had of his own will granted passports; he had allowed a number of heretical books to circulate in England, leading people to disbelief "in the most holy and blessed Sacrament of the Altar and other articles of the Christian religion." No mention was made of his worst offenses in this field—his furthering of the disguised Tyndale-Coverdale translation of the Bible, under the fictitious editorship of Thomas Matthew, or of the later edition of the same made by Richard Taverner. But perhaps these offenses were considered covered by the generalized charge that Cromwell had encouraged heretical works.

A definite accusation of having denied transubstantiation was leveled against Cromwell, but no particulars were given. Nor was it indicated where and when and to whom he had said, "that it was lawful for every Christian man to be a minister of the said sacrament as well as a priest." Though Cromwell had associated with people of these or similar views, there is nothing whatever to show that he held these views himself. But it was perfectly true that as Vicegerent he had "licensed divers persons detected or openly defamed of heresy to preach and teach," and three of them were at that moment in the Tower. But it is not for a moment to be believed that he had said, "that he would fight even against the King to maintain these heresies. . . . And then and there he pulled out his dagger and held it up to high saying these words: 'Or else this dagger thrust me to the heart if I would not die in that quarrel against them all, and I trust if I live a year or two, it shall not lie in the King's power to resist or let it if he would.' " Several of the items in the bill of attainder against Cromwell were as false as the bills of attainder he had drawn against other people. The root of the venomous animosity felt for him is in the words: "Being thus enriched, he had held the nobles in disdain." The nobles now had their revenge—against "Thomas."

Cromwell was attainted by mid-June. Traitors were usually executed within a week of condemnation, on a date set according to the King's pleasure. We have seen why there was delay in his case: he had to give evidence about the royal divorce. But Convocation acted early in July, and by the fourteenth its decision was given statutory effect by Parliament. Nevertheless Cromwell was allowed to live for another two weeks after that. It is just possible that Henry was pondering in his mind whether he should not in decency spare a man who had been so faithful a servant—possible, though from what we know of Henry, not likely. More probably there was some debate as to whether Cromwell should die the ordinary death of traitors at Tyburn or be given a gentleman's death on Tower Hill. It may be that the bloody-minded Norfolk was pressing for the extreme of ignominy and that the milder Gardiner thought beheading would be enough. That there was some discussion about this is revealed by the fact that a compromise was reached in the end: Cromwell was to be mercifully beheaded, but the execution was to be at Tyburn. A further grace was done him in that his son was allowed to retain part of his property and his barony, though not his earldom. This, however, was because the harmless, stupid, indolent Gregory Cromwell was married to a sister of Jane Seymour, the widow of Sir Anthony Ughtred; he was therefore a kind of brother-in-law of the King's.

Francis I, who hated Cromwell, openly rejoiced when he heard of his downfall, though as soon as he was told that Anne of Cleves was going to be divorced, his delight diminished: he recognized that this would mean the end of the Cleves alliance and therefore the removal of pressure on Charles. The Emperor received the news impassively, but he must have been pleased. Henry had already let him know that he was thinking of abrogating the treaty with Cleves; this now occurred automatically. The Duke of Cleves was frigidly polite. He saw that his sister had been well provided for, but he had lost England as an ally. As for the Lutheran princes, they perceived that all chance of bringing Henry over to their side had gone. Cromwell had worked for this for years, and now there was nobody left to strive for such an end. Cranmer, never a strong leader, was for the moment under a cloud. Already it was apparent that a Catholic reaction had set in.

Nevertheless Cromwell's work stood. Though Henry hardened in his orthodoxy, he also tended to harden in his antipapalism. Cromwell had made the King absolute over both Church and State. He probably foresaw that when the young Edward became King the new men would introduce a radical Protestantism, but he was indifferent to this, so long as the royal autocracy, to establish which he had toiled for ten years, remained. Had he lived out his span of years—he was only about fifty-five in 1540—we may be sure that he would have declared himself a Protestant under Edward, a Catholic under Mary, and a Protestant again under Elizabeth. That

273

is, if the Seymours had tolerated him. The kindhearted Mary would in all probability have accepted his assurances that he had been acting only under the compulsion of necessity.

Yet it was mainly with regard to religion that his work had permanence—and with him religion was no more than a means to an end, that end being an absolute monarchy. Here his aims were deflected from their object, for by bringing into being a new landed class, based upon the estates of the monks and nuns, he created what was to prove the most formidable opponent the Crown could have. But this class had a vested interest in the Reformation. By degrees the national liberties were restored, as England was transformed from an autocracy to an oligarchy and from an oligarchy to a democracy. Yet the impression was left that somehow these liberties were bound up with the doctrinal chaos that ensued. Even if this be so, a schism occurred in the very soul of Europe and is the malady from which the modern world suffers. This schism is mainly Cromwell's doing, though there was a moment when (for the sake of political advantage) he was ready to end the breach with Rome.

He died unlamented, except by his son and Cranmer, and he had to wait for Foxe the Martyrologist to celebrate belatedly the "noble acts, the memorable examples, the worthy virtue not drowned by ease of honor in him. . . . Among the which his worthy acts and manifold virtues, in this one chiefly above all the rest riseth his commendation, for his singular zeal and laborious travail in restoring the true Church of Christ, and subverting the Synagogue of Antichrist, the abbeys, I mean, and religious houses of friars and monks."

Standing beside the block he said, "I pray you that be here, to bear me record, I die in the Catholic faith, not doubting in any article of my faith, nor not doubting in any sacrament of the Church. Many have slandered me and reported that I have been a bearer of such as have maintained evil opinions, which is untrue. But I confess that, like as God by His Holy Spirit doth instruct us in the truth, so the Devil is ready to seduce us, and I have been seduced; but bear me witness that I die in the Catholic faith of the holy Church." There is some reason to doubt the literal accuracy of that speech and of the prayer that Foxe reports him saying on the scaffold. If he really affirmed that he had never given support to those who maintained heresy, he lied at the moment of his death; but perhaps he merely meant to say that he had never in his heart embraced heretical opinions,

274

which would have been true. It is charitable to suppose that, when brought face to face with the last reality, some long-suppressed religious sentiments welled up in him and that he died repentant.

The official headsman was at Tower Hill that morning of July 28, where he was cutting off the head of Lord Hungerford. This was why the man who officiated at Tyburn was inexperienced at decapitation. He was according to the chronicler Hall, "a ragged and miserly butcher, who very ungoodly performed his office." A number of strokes had to be given before he hacked off Cromwell's head.

BIBLIOGRAPHY

Allen, J. S., *A History of Political Thought in the Sixteenth Century*, New York, 1928.

Armstrong, E., *The Emperor Charles V*, 2 vols., London, 1902.

Ashley, Sir W. J., *An Introduction to Economic History and Theory*, 4 vols., London, 1888–1892.

Bacon, Sir Francis, *Life of Henry VII*, London, 1622.

Bagwell, Richard, *Ireland under the Tudors*, Vol. I. London, 1885.

Bandello, Matteo, *Novelle*, 9 vols., London, 1791–1793.

Baskerville, G., "The Dispossessed Religious after the Suppression of the Monasteries," in *Essays in History Presented to Richard Lane Poole*, Oxford, 1927.

Belloc, Hilaire, *A History of England*, Vol. IV, London, 1931.

——, *Wolsey*, Philadelphia and London, 1930.

——, *Cranmer*, Philadelphia and London, 1931.

Besant, Sir Walter, *London in the Time of the Tudors*, London, 1904.

Bigham, Clive, *The Chief Minister of England*, London, 1923.

Brewer, J. S., *The Reign of Henry VIII*, 2 vols., London, 1884.

——, *English Studies*, London, 1881.

Bridgett, T. E., C. SS. R., *The Life of Blessed John Fisher*, London, 1888.

——, *The Life of Blessed Thomas More*, London, 1891.

Burnet, Gilbert, *History of the Reformation* (Pocock's edition), 7 vols., Oxford, 1865.

Cambridge Modern History, Vol. II (*The Reformation*), New York and Cambridge, 1894.

Camm, Bede, O.S.B. (editor), *The English Martyrs*, Cambridge and St. Louis, 1929.

———, *Lives of the English Martyrs*, first series, 2 vols., London, 1904.

Campbell, Lord, *Lives of the Lord Chancellors*, fifth edition, London, 1868.

Cavendish, George, *The Life and Death of Cardinal Wolsey*, Temple Classics, London.

Chambers, R. W., *Thomas More*, London, 1935.

Cheney, E. P., *Social Changes in England in the Sixteenth Century*, Boston, 1895.

Child, Gilbert W., *Church and State under the Tudors*, London, 1890.

Constant, G., *The English Schism* (*The Reformation in England*, Vol. I), translated by R. E. Scantlebury, New York, 1934.

Crabites, Pierre, *Clement VII and Henry VIII*, London, 1936.

Creighton, Mandel, *Cardinal Wolsey*, London, 1895.

Demaus, R., *Latimer*, London, 1881.

———, *Tyndale*, London, 1886.

Dictionary of National Biography, Oxford.

Dixon, R. W., *History of the Church of England*, Vols. I and II, London, 1878–1881.

Dixon, William Hepworth, *History of Two Queens*, 4 vols., London, 1873–1874.

Drayton, Michael, *The History of the Life and Death of the Lord Cromwell*, London, 1609.

Dugdale, Sir William, *Monasticon Anglicanum*, 6 vols., London, 1830.

Ellis, Sir Henry, *Original Letters, Illustrative of English History*, 3 vols., London, 1885.

Eyre, Edward (editor), *The Reformation* (*European Civilization*, Vol. IV), Oxford, 1936.

Fanfani, Amitore, *Catholicism, Protestantism, and Capitalism*, London, 1935.

Fisher, H. A. L., *The History of England from the Accession of Henry VII to the Death of Henry VIII* (*The Political History of England*, Vol. V), London and New York, 1906.

Floyer, J. K., *Studies in the History of English Church Endowments*, London, 1917.

Foxe, John, *Acts and Monuments*, edited by J. Pratt, 8 vols., London, 1853–1870.

Friedmann, Paul, *Anne Boleyn*, 2 vols., London, 1884.

Froude, James Anthony, *The Reign of Henry VIII*, 3 vols., Everyman's Edition.

Fuller, Thomas, *The Church History of Britain, from the Birth of Jesus Christ Until the Year MDXLVIII*, edited by J. S. Brewer, 6 vols., Oxford, 1845.

Gairdner, James, *The English Church in the Sixteenth Century, from the Accession of Henry VIII to the Death of Mary*, London, 1904.

——, *Lollardy and the Reformation in England*, 4 vols., London, 1908–1913.

Gardiner, Stephen, *Letters*, edited by J. A. Muller, London, 1933.

Garvin, Katherine (editor), *The Great Tudors*, New York, 1935.

Gasquet, Cardinal, *The Eve of the Reformation*, London, 1913.

——, *Henry VIII and the English Monasteries*, 2 vols., London, 1899.

——, *The Greater Abbeys of England*, London, 1908.

Gee, H. and W. H. Hardy, *Documents Illustrative of English Church History*, London, 1896.

Hackett, Francis, *Henry the Eighth*, New York, 1929.

——, *Francis the First: First Gentleman of France*, New York, 1934.

Haile, Martin, *The Life of Reginald Pole*, New York, 1910.

Hall, Edward, *Chronicle* (the Whibley edition), 2 vols., London and Edinburgh, 1904.

Hallam, Henry, *The Constitutional History of England*, Vol. I, London, 1897.

Harpsfield, Nicholas, *The Life and Death of Sir Thomas More*, edited by Dr. Elsie V. Hitchcock for the Early English Text Society, 1932.

Herbert of Cherbury, Lord, *The Life and Reign of King Henry the Eighth* (reprint from Kennet's folio edition of 1719), London, 1872.

Holinshead, Raphael, *Chronicles*, 6 vols., London, 1807–1808.

Hume, Martin A. S., *The Wives of Henry VIII*, New York, 1905.

Innes, A. D., *England under the Tudors*, revised edition by J. M. Henderson, London, 1932.

Jenkyns, H., *The Remains of Thomas Cranmer*, 4 vols., Oxford, 1833.

Kaulek, J., *Correspondence politique de MM. de Castillon et de Marillac, ambassadeurs de France en Angleterre (1537–1542)*, Paris, 1885.

Letters and Papers, Foreign and Domestic, Henry VIII, Vols. I to XVI, His Majesty's Stationery Office, 1864–1901.

Liljegren, S. B., *The Fall of the Monasteries and the Social Changes in England Leading up to the Great Revolution*, London, 1924.

Lingard, John, *History of England*, Vols. IV and V, Edinburgh, 1902.

Lipson, E., *An Introduction to the Economic History of England*, Vol. I, London, 1915.

Machiavelli, Nicolo, *The Prince*, Everyman's Edition.

Maitland, F. W., *Roman Canon Law in the Church of England*, London, 1898.

———, *The Constitutional History of England*, Cambridge, 1911.

Maitland, S. R., *Essays on Subjects Connected with the Reformation*, London, 1849.

Marti, Oscar, *Economic Causes of the Reformation in England*, London, 1929.

Mattingley, Garret, *Catherine of Aragon*, Boston, 1941.

Maynard, Theodore, *Humanist as Hero: The Life of Sir Thomas More*, New York, 1947.

———, *Henry the Eighth*, Milwaukee, 1949.

Medley, D. J., *English Constitutional History*, Oxford, 1913.

Merriman, Roger Bigelow, *Life and Letters of Thomas Cromwell*, 2 vols., Oxford, 1902.

More, Sir Thomas, *English Works*, edited by William Rastell, London, 1557.

———, *English Works*, edited by W. E. Campbell (to date only the first two volumes have been published), London, 1927, 1931.

———, *Apology*, edited by A. I. Taft, Early English Text Society, 1930.

———, *The Correspondence of Sir Thomas More*, edited by Elizabeth Frances Rogers, Princeton, 1947.

Muller, J. A., *Stephen Gardiner and the Tudor Reaction*, London, 1926.

Murray, R. H., *The Political Consequences of the Reformation:*

Studies in Sixteenth Century Political Thought, London, 1926.

O'Brien, J., *An Essay on the Economic Effects of the Reformation,* London, 1923.

Ogle, Arthur, *The Tragedy of the Lollard's Tower,* Oxford, 1949.

Oppenheim, H. A., *History of the Administration of the Royal Navy and of the Merchant Shipping in Relation to the Navy, 1506–1660,* London, 1897.

Phillips, John, "The Cromwell Family," *Antiquary Magazine,* Vol. II, 1880, pp. 164–168.

———, "The Cromwells of Putney," *Antiquarian Magazine and Bibliographer,* Vol II, 1881, pp. 56–62, 178–186; Vol. IV, 1884, pp. 171–179.

Pickthorn, Kenneth, *Tudor Government,* Vol. II, Cambridge, 1934.

Pocock, N., *Records of the Reformation,* 2 vols., Oxford, 1870.

Pole, Cardinal, *Apologia ad Carolum Quintum Caesarem,* Brescie, 1744.

Pollard, A. F., *Henry VIII,* London, 1913.

———, *Thomas Cranmer,* New York and London, 1906.

———, *Wolsey,* second impression, London and New York, 1929.

Power, Eileen, *Medieval English Nunneries,* Cambridge, 1922.

Prescott, H. F. M., *A Spanish Tudor: The Life of "Bloody Mary,"* New York, 1940.

Read, Conyers, *The Tudors,* New York, 1936.

———, *Bibliography of British History, Tudor Period, 1485–1603,* Oxford, 1933.

Rodgers, J. E. Thorold, *The History of Agriculture and Prices,* Vol. IV, Oxford, 1882.

Roper, William, *Life of Sir Thomas More,* edited by Dr. Elsie V. Hitchcock, Early English Text Society, 1935.

Routh, E. M. A., *Sir Thomas More and His Friends,* Oxford, 1934.

Sanders, Nicholas, *De Origine et Progressu Schismati Anglicani,* Cologne, 1585. (Translated by David Lewis, in English, London, 1896.)

Savine, A., *English Monasteries on the Eve of the Dissolution,* Oxford, 1909.

Smith, A. L., *The Pilgrimage of Grace,* London, 1897.

Smith, H. Maynard, *Henry VIII and the Reformation,* New York, 1949.

Snape, R. H., *English Monastic Finances,* Cambridge, 1926.

Stapleton, Thomas, *The Life and Illustrious Martyrdom of Thomas*

More (translation by Monsignor P. E. Hallett of the life of More in *Tres Thomae*), Cologne, 1612.

State Papers During the Reign of Henry VIII, 11 vols., His Majesty's Stationery Office, 1830–1852.

Stow, John, *Annales*, London, 1615.

——, *A Survey of London*, London, 1603.

Strickland, Agnes, *Lives of the Queens of England*, Vols. II and III, London, 1851.

Strype, John, *Annals of the Reformation*, 4 vols., London, 1709–1731.

——, *Ecclesiastical Memorials Relating Chiefly to Religion and the Reformation of It*, 2 vols., London, 1711–1733.

——, *Memorials of the Most Reverend Father in God, Thomas Cranmer*, 3 vols., London, 1694.

Stubbs, William, *Lectures on Medieval and Modern History*, Oxford, 1886.

Taunton, E. L., *Thomas Wolsey, Legate and Reformer*, London, 1902.

Tawney, R. H., *The Agrarian Problem in the Sixteenth Century*, London and New York, 1912.

——, *Religion and the Rise of Capitalism*, London, 1926.

Thompson, A. Hamilton, *English Monasteries*, second edition, Cambridge, 1922.

——, *The English Clergy and Their Organization in the Later Middle Ages*, Oxford, 1948.

Trevelyan, Sir G. M., *English Social History*, London and New York, 1942.

Tudor Tracts, 1532–1588, with an introduction by A. F. Pollard, Westminster, 1903.

Van Dyke, Paul, *Renascence Portraits*, New York, 1906.

White, Beatrice, *Mary Tudor*, New York, 1935.

Wilding, Peter, *Thomas Cromwell*, London, 1935.

Williams, C. H., *The Making of the Tudor Despotism*, revised edition, London, 1935.

Wordsworth, Christopher, *Ecclesiastical Biography*, Vol. II, London, 1818.

Wright, Thomas, *Three Chapters of Letters Relating to the Suppression of the Monasteries*, Camden Society, 1843.

Wriothesley, Sir Thomas, *Chronicle*, edited by W. D. Hamilton, Camden Society, 1875.

INDEX

283

Cromwell, Thomas (*continued*), 136–137; failure of policy, 138; his venality, 139; his agents, 140; his double-dealing, 141; his acceptance of bribes, 142; occasional acts of kindness, 143; instance of high-handedness, 144; treatment of universities, 144–145; his charity, 146; effort to arrest the enclosure movement, 146; tricking of those who bought exemption, 147; is in danger, 148; appeals of Mary Boleyn to him, 149–150; instructs ambassadors in France, 152; favors alliance with Emperor, 153–154; plot against Anne Boleyn, 154–155; springs trap for Anne Boleyn, 156–157; his part in trial of Anne Boleyn, 158; letter to ambassadors in France about Anne Boleyn, 159; terrifies Cranmer, 159; emerges with enhanced power, 163; threatened by popular rising, 164; regarded as man responsible for the hated policy, 165; his fear at rising, 169; brings Duke of Norfolk out of retirement, 170; demand for his expulsion, 171; as first of English Machiavellians, 171–172; keeps in background, 172; Pilgrims wish to know whether he has been dropped from Council, 173; instigates trouble, 175; at Lord Darcy's trial, 176–177; letter on execution of those in Pilgrimage of Grace, 177; finds pretext for moving against large abbeys, 178; knowledge that monastic suppression, once started, would have to be complete, 179; augments his authority, 180; writes to Wyatt to say that Jane Seymour is quick with child, 180; organizes Council of the North, 181; first contact with Reginald Pole, 184; offers to lend Pole Machiavelli's *Prince*, 185; efforts to abduct or assassinate Pole,

188–190; management of "Exeter Conspiracy," 191; new use of attainder, 191; produces "evidence" against Countess of Salisbury, 192; dogs Pole's footsteps, 193; ability as administrator, 194–195; aim to make monarchy unassailable, 195; attitude toward Scotland, 196; subjugation of Wales, 197–199; repressive Irish policy, 199–203; administration of affairs in Calais, 203–204; religious policy with regard to Calais, 205; guards against Trojan horse attack on Calais, 206; control of Parliament, 206; keeping of possible rivals at a distance, 207; looked upon as glorified "official," 207; in role of revolutionary, 208; assurance to larger abbeys, 209; instances of mildness, 209–210; has arrested Irish monks racked, 210; orders convictions before trial, 211; treatment of friars, 212; execution of John Forest, 213–214; method of forcing "voluntary" monastic surrenders, 215; acceptance of monastic bribes, 216; wish to implicate as many persons as possible in spoliation, 218; attempt to use part of monastic loot for national defense, 219; as connoisseur of literature and art, 219; packing of Parliament, 220–221; his pilfering, 221; seizure of the last great abbeys, 223–225; presidency at Convocation, 227; way of working with Cranmer, 228–229; injunctions to clergy, 230; way of using heretics, 231; secret encouragement of heresy, 232; extortions, 233; concessions for a "consideration," 233; interference with general ecclesiastical affairs, 234; plot to introduce disguised Tyndale Bible, 235–237; efforts to placate Lutheran princes of Germany, 237; rescues Cranmer from charge of heresy, 239; writes to Wyatt about Nicholson case, 240; attempt to woo Smalkaldic League, 243; considers Duchess of Milan as wife for Henry VIII, 244–245; opens Cleves negotiations, 246–248; risks accepted, 249; receives King's confidences about Anne of Cleves, 250; conversation with Wriothesley, 251; attempt to effect marriage between Princess Mary and Philip of Bavaria, 252; created Earl of Essex, 252; quarrel with Gardiner, 253; unpopularity with all classes, 254–255; is despised by King, 256; misjudgment of Henry VIII's character, 256; suppression of Knights of Malta, 256; events seem about to justify his Cleves policy, 257; writes to Emperor abandoning Cleves, 258; Cleves alliance and its effect on his fall, 259; is arrested for high treason, 260–261; is "defended" by Cranmer, 262; charges against him, 263–264; is condemned as both heretic and traitor, 264; guilt of, 265; his fate in the balance, 266; his evidence about King's marriage to Anne of Cleves, 267–269; appeal for mercy, 269–270; defense of himself, 271; bill of attainder against him, 271–272; charges of heresy against him, 272; endurance of his work, 273–274; his execution, 274–275

Cromwell, Walter, father of Thomas, 6, 7

Curwin, Dr. Hugh, Archbishop of Dublin, 97

D

Damplip, Adam, 205
Darcy, Sir Arthur, 217
Darcy, Thomas, Baron Darcy of

Templehurst, 45, 121–122, 169, 171, 172, 176, 177, 193, 254
De Vera Obedientia, by Stephen Gardiner, 85
Defence of the Seven Sacraments, by Henry VIII, 28
Derknall, Robert, 220
Dialogue of Comfort against Tribulation, by Sir Thomas More, 107
Dormer, Lady (later Duchess of Feria), 112
Dudley, Edmund, 148
Dudley, John, later Duke of Northumberland, 80, 148

E

Edward, Prince, later King Edward VI, 82, 85, 251, 256, 273
Elizabeth, the future Queen, 82, 89, 92, 93, 103, 120, 127, 149, 162, 251, 273
Ellerker, Sir Robert, 175
Elstow, Friar, 97, 98
Elyot, Sir Thomas, 75, 122
Empson, Sir Richard, 148
Enclosures, 138n., 146
Erasmus, 7
Evers, Sir Ralph, the younger, 172
Exeter, Marchioness of, 99, 193

F

Featherstone, Richard, 258
Ferdinand, King of Aragon, 2, 3, 29
Ferrara, Duke of, 245
Fineux, Sir John, Chief Justice, 27
Fish, Simon, 60, 61, 79
Fisher, H. A. L., 79
Fisher, John, Bishop of Rochester, 19, 69, 70, 71, 82, 89, 96, 99, 100, 101, 106–110, 115, 118, 129, 133, 145, 208, 254
Fitzgerald, Gerald, Earl of Kildare, 201, 202
Fitzgerald, Thomas ("Silken Thomas"), Earl of Kildare, 201, 202

I

Ilbert, Sir Courtenay, 64
Ingworth, Richard, 140
Innocent VIII, Pope, 29
Isabella, Queen of Castille, 2

J

James V, King of Scotland, 58, 196,
  197, 210, 245
Jordan, Isabel, Abbess of Wilton, 32,
  33, 233n.
Julius II, Pope, 10, 105

K

Katherine of Aragon, Queen of England, 2, 3, 24, 30–32, 37–39, 59, 62,
  70, 73, 75, 81–83, 86–89, 91–93, 97,
  101, 102, 114, 120, 121, 123–126, 128,
  129, 149, 151, 154, 183, 213, 236,
  243, 249, 254, 268
Kingston, Sir William, 53, 54, 110,
  122, 162, 270
Kitchen, Anthony, Bishop of Llandaff, 82
Knight, William, later Bishop of
  Bath, 35
Knolles, Dr. Thomas, 144

L

La Sá, de, Katherine of Aragon's
  physician, 125
Larke, Miss, Cardinal Wolsey's "un-
  canonical wife," 24, 54
Latimer, Hugh, Bishop of Worcester,
  213, 214, 238, 239, 258
Latimer, Lord, 169
Lawrence, Robert, 111, 112
Layton, Dr. Richard, 140, 144, 164
Lee, Edward, Archbishop of York,
  82, 86
Lee, Rowland, Bishop of Lichfield
  and Coventry, 143, 164, 198
Leigh, Dr. Thomas, 140, 164, 168
Leland, John, 219
Leo X, Pope, 18, 28

Levyns, Christopher, 220
Lingard, John, 90
Lollards, the, 25, 80
London, Dr. John, 35, 140, 144
Longland, John, Bishop of Lincoln,
  164, 167n., 210
Lorraine, Duke of, 250, 251, 267
Louis XII, King of France, 2, 38
Louys, Don, Infante of Portugal,
  245
Luke, Walter, 76
Luther, Martin, 4, 28, 69, 73, 79, 81,
  230, 236
Lutheran Princes of Germany, 237,
  243 (*See also* Smalkaldic League)
Lyst, Richard, 98

M

Machiavelli, Nicolo, 8, 29, 185
Mackerel, Dr., Abbot of Barlings,
  166, 177, 178
Madeline, daughter of Francis I, 151
Maitland, F. W., 64
Manners, Thomas, Earl of Rutland,
  122
Mantua, Duke of, 245
Marillac, Charles de, French Ambas-
  sador, 31, 252, 253, 263
Marshall, Thomas, 144
Mary, Princess, later Queen of Eng-
  land, 38, 42n., 80, 85, 92, 93, 97, 123–
  125, 127–130, 151, 166, 184, 224
Mary, sister of Henry VIII, wife of
  Louis XII of France, 2, 15
Mary of Guise, 245, 248
Mathew, David, Archbishop, 255
Matthew, Thomas (pseudonym),
  236, 272
Maximilian, Emperor, 2, 3, 16
Mekins, Richard, 240
Melanchthon, Philipp, 230
Melton, Thomas, 166
Merriman, Professor R. B., 6, 13, 35,
  126, 168, 194, 209, 233n., 267, 268n.
Meyer, Marc, 243, 244
Milan, Duchess of, 244, 247

289

291